Religion and Science in Context

D0222480

How should we think about religion, science and their relationship in modern society? Some religious groups oppose evolution; some atheists claim science is on their side. Others reconcile their religious beliefs with science, or consider science and faith to deal with fundamentally different aspects of human life. What indeed *is* religion: belief or trust in God's existence? How do we distinguish sense from superstition? What does science have to say on such issues?

Willem B. Drees considers contemporary discussions of these issues in Europe and North America, using examples from Christianity and religious naturalism and reflections on Islam and Tibetan Buddhism. He argues that the scientific understanding leaves open certain ultimate questions, and thus allows for belief in a creator, but also for religious naturalism or serious agnosticism. By analysing the place of values in a world of facts, and the quest for meaningful stories in a material world, *Religion and Science in Context* offers an original and self-critical analysis of the field, its assumptions and functions, and ends with a vision of its possible future.

Willem B. Drees is Professor of Philosophy of Religion and Ethics and vice-dean of the Faculty of Humanities, Leiden University, the Netherlands, and the editor of *Zygon: Journal of Religion and Science.*

Religion and Science in Context

A Guide to the Debates

Willem B. Drees

L.C.C.C. LIBRARY

Routledge
Taylor & Francis Group

LONDON AND NEW YORK

First published 2010 by Routledge
2 Park Square, Milton Park, Abingdon, Oxon OX14 4RN

Simultaneously published in the USA and Canada by Routledge
270 Madison Ave., New York, NY 100016

Routledge is an imprint of the Taylor & Francis Group, an informa business

© 2010 Willem B. Drees

Typeset in Sabon by
Taylor & Francis Books
Printed and bound in Great Britain by
CPI Antony Rowe, Chippenham, Wiltshire

All rights reserved. No part of this book may be reprinted or reproduced or
utilised in any form or by any electronic, mechanical, or other means, now
known or hereafter invented, including photocopying and recording, or in any
information storage or retrieval system, without permission in writing from
the publishers.

British Library Cataloguing in Publication Data
A catalogue record for this book is available from the British Library

Library of Congress Cataloging in Publication Data
Drees, Willem B., 1954–
    Religion and science in context : a guide to the debates / Willem B. Drees. –
1st ed.
        p. cm.
    Includes bibliographical references and index.
    1. Religion and science. I. Title.
    BL240.3.D74 2009
    201'.65 – dc22

                                                                    2009012932

ISBN10: 0-415-55616-3 (hbk)
ISBN10: 0-415-55617-1 (pbk)
ISBN10: 0-203-86960-5 (ebk)

ISBN13: 978-0-415-55616-3 (hbk)
ISBN13: 978-0-415-55617-0 (pbk)
ISBN13: 978-0-203-86960-4 (ebk)

Contents

Preface

For over two decades I have been involved in reflections on religion in relation to the natural sciences, as someone originally trained in the natural sciences who was sufficiently fascinated by human cultures and traditions to engage in religious studies – a discipline in which it is much harder to nourish clarity and generate consensus. I served from 2002 until 2008 as president of the European Society for the Study of Science And Theology, ESSSAT. As of 2009 I have served as editor of *Zygon: Journal of Religion and Science*, a scholarly journal with a thousand pages annually, present in more than three thousand academic libraries. Of the many occasions on which I have had the pleasure of presenting and discussing ideas I want to recall here especially the Andreas Idreos Lectures in Oxford in 1998 and the Samuel Ferguson Lectures in Manchester in 1999, hosted so graciously by David Pailin. I have been enriched by all the friends and colleagues that I thus met. This book is written as a whole, but I have liberally recycled ideas, phrases, and paragraphs from earlier publications.

Since September 2001 I have held a chair in Philosophy of Religion and Ethics at Leiden University. As a public university, we engage in religious studies rather than in theology, but as a philosopher it is my duty to combine the outsider perspective typical of historical, social and textual studies with the insider's interest in the reasonability, plausibility or possibility of beliefs held. I thank my academic colleagues in Leiden for all that I have learned from them. I want to express my gratitude to the Netherlands Organisation for Scientific Research (NWO), which funded projects of mine as part of its programmes 'Cultural Renewal and the Foundations of the Humanities' and 'The Future of the Religious Past', and thus made it possible for me to work with the postdocs Tony Watling (Watling 2009) and Taede Smedes and with the graduate student Olga Crapels, and to take the study leave during which this book was written. Rob Hogendoorn and my co-supervisor of his PhD research, Henk Blezer, have made me aware of some of the complexities of the interactions between Tibetan Buddhism and science.

This book was written in 2008–9 while I was the J. Houston Whiterspoon Fellow in Theology and Science at the Center of Theological Inquiry in

Princeton (USA). I want to express my gratitude to the leadership of CTI, William Storrar and Thomas Hastings, and to my fellow fellows at CTI. I am grateful to the Center for the Study of Religion at Princeton University, which accepted me as an affiliate fellow for that period, and thereby provided access to a wide variety of inspiring and informative lectures at the university.

Last but not least, this book would not have been possible without the mental and physical absences graciously allowed by my wife Zwanet Drees-Roeters and our children Johannes, Annelot and Esther. Retreating to write would have been much harder and far less rewarding without their enriching presence in my life.

Chapter 1

'Religion and science' in multiple contexts

Calvin and Hobbes, a boy and his tiger, are walking through a forest. 'Do you believe in evolution?' Calvin asks. 'No,' the tiger replies. 'So you don't believe humans descended from apes?' the boy continues. To which the tiger responds: 'I don't see the difference,' and beats a hasty retreat from the angry boy. The boy asks about the explanation of human origins; the tiger responds with an offence to human dignity. As in this comic strip by Bill Watterson, so too in debates about evolution in the real world: multiple issues are intertwined.

In a lecture at a college in Iowa I presented the grand narrative of modern science, from the Big Bang until Now, and argued for the possibility of a religious appreciation of these insights (Drees 2002a). In the Q&A period a woman asked: 'So, you believe there has been a Second Fall?' At first, I didn't understand the question. She took death to be the consequence of the sin of Adam and Eve, while I had spoken of natural death as arising with the evolution of multi-cellular life, long before there were humans – which for her implied that there had been a Fall before the Fall of the first humans. Whereas the framework of my lecture had been science, her framework was a particular religious one. Miscommunication arises easily in 'religion and science'. Debates are often non-debates, as issues and criteria are framed differently by the various participants.

A good example of the extensive literature on 'religion and science' is *The Oxford Handbook of Religion and Science* (Clayton and Simpson 2006), a thousand pages with fifty-five good chapters on religion and science. Even this extensive survey, including essays by many of the best authors, has some biases. It is mostly Anglo-Saxon with respect to the authors, and also with respect to the treatment of topics. The chapter on sociology and religion ends with remarks about the American constitution. The evolution/creation controversy is discussed in the American context as if issues are the same elsewhere. The authors focus on content, scientific and theological, at the expense of context. Theology, ethics and science have universal ambitions; their truth claims and norms seek to be valid for people of all walks of life and all cultures. While their ambitions are lofty, religion and science are human; contexts and assumptions shape the questions asked, the criteria used, the content proposed.

'Religion and science' speaks of that which we value, that which we hold to be true, and that which we hold to be possible. What is going on in the complex area of debates and non-debates on 'religion and science'? What is to be taken seriously, and what might be dismissed as nonsense? What would be possible venues? What are aims and ambitions of discussions on 'religion and science'? This book is about the ways in which we approach two major dimensions of human existence, the scientific quest for reliable knowledge that surpasses cultural constraints and subjective preferences, and the religious quests for meaning and orientation in our lives, as a major dimension of culture and subjective existence. By considering sources of disagreement and confusion, this guide aspires to assist in developing a better understanding of science, of religion and of the contexts in which these major human endeavours interact.

1966 can be considered the year the modern constructive 'religion and science' discussion started in the United States. The journal *Zygon: Journal of Religion and Science* was founded by Ralph Burhoe, for many years the executive officer of the American Academy of Arts and Sciences, while the physicist and theologian Ian Barbour published his book *Issues in Science and Religion*. Around the same time, on the other side of the Atlantic, a committee of the Dutch Reformed Church concluded that there wasn't much to be discussed, except issues of ethics and ethos, as religion and science each had its own role in human life (Dippel and De Jong 1965). Why did the American 'religion and science' discussion take off at that time, while these Protestants on the European continent weren't interested? Discussions in the United States and on the European continent concern the same science, and they both take place in the context of Western Christianity, broadly understood. Though standing within the same religious traditions, those American and Dutch authors did not have the same view of what religious belief is.

What has been achieved in the decades since 1966? There are books, conferences and lectures on 'religion and science'. Oxford University has established an endowed chair in this area, and so have Princeton Theological Seminary, the Graduate Theological Union in Berkeley and Davidson College (USA). Despite much activity, however, consensus on issues of importance seems far away, the impact on theology and on religious communities is limited and the academic credibility of 'religion and science' remains marginal.

I suspect that the lack of progress has to do with a lack of careful consideration of (a) contexts, (b) purposes, (c) criteria and (d) views of what religion might be. These issues will be addressed in the first four chapters of this book. Thereafter, we will consider three major domains of 'religion and science': (e) mystery in a world made intelligible by the sciences, (f) morality in a world of facts and (g) meaning and identity in a world of matter.

In its structure, this guide isn't organized by scientific discipline, nor is it organized by religion, nor by particular topics such as creation, providence, prayer, sin, evil or the concept of God. A more grandiose project would have to cover all such dimensions and many more. Here we will concentrate on underlying assumptions about purposes and criteria, thereby preparing a canvas upon which substantial views on these issues might be drawn.

Many people are interested in science: engineers who consider applications, patients who hope for cures, business people who look for opportunities, governments that consider what to fund, legislatures that debate ethical restrictions and lay people who are just curious. In this cultural environment surrounding science one aspect may be the formative and normative religious traditions of human societies and the beliefs, values, attitudes, hopes and dreams of individuals.

Religious interest comes in multiple versions as well. There are not only people who believe differently but also agnostics, who argue that we should be modest in our claims as we don't really know. And there are atheists, who think we should not be too modest, as we know that it is not. In as far as they engage science I here consider all such persons as involved in 'religion and science'.

We need not think of scientists and of religious people as if these are distinct groups. A single person may well engage in science and have moral and metaphysical convictions. Thus, I will focus on science and religion as activities, rather than on scientists and believers as persons.

Reflections on 'religion and science' take place in a cultural, social context. Courts have been involved in controversies over the teaching of evolution in American schools. Sponsors donate money for the advocacy of their preferred positions or for their beloved research projects. One never walks alone; contexts and company shape what is going on (Hefner 2008). At least two contexts can be discerned: secularization and the persistence of superstition. As I will argue that location and perspective are important to understand what is going on, I need to be honest on the perspective that informs my writing here. We will come to that later in this chapter.

Secularization as concern

Many participants in contemporary reflections on 'religion and science' are concerned about *secularization,* about religious institutions losing significance and adherence to religious beliefs declining. They value science and have an affinity with religion, and thus seek to understand how both might be significant, meaningful, or even true, rather than being perceived as being in conflict.

In 1633 Galileo Galilei was forced to abjure the idea that the Earth revolves around its own axis and around the Sun. Seen in historical perspective, this decision by the leadership of the Roman Catholic Church was damaging to the church, as the condemnation of Galileo undermined its credibility for centuries. If religion and science are perceived to be in conflict, one has to choose the side of science, on intellectual and moral grounds. The successes of science are intellectual and practical, in developing a deeper and more unified understanding of the world, in making predictions that survive tests, in allowing us to make valuable applications such as modern computers and medicine. Thus, in brief, one might argue that science leads to secularization.

To see the natural sciences as the main cause of secularization in the Western world is naïve; welfare and other social measures have contributed at least as much to the decline of religious institutions. Technology and medicine have moved the boundary between that which is given, whether by God or by fate, and that which is within our reach to do something about. What might have been hubris in previous times has now become a human option, and hence a human responsibility.

Whether it is science or whether it is modernization and secularization in general, religion and science appear to be at odds with each other. Seen thus, 'religion and science' in the Western world can be viewed as a response to secularization, that is a response to the claim that science provides a better understanding of the world and a response to the expectation that the problem-solving attitude of science-based technology and medicine is to be preferred over prayer or other religious responses. If tension between religious affinities and reliance on science provides the incentive for 'religion and science', contributors may look for alternatives to the view that science replaces religion. 'Religion and science' in this context is driven by the perception of conflict.

To counter the idea that science refutes or replaces religion, one might argue that conflict and replacement do not necessarily follow from accepting science. This could be argued in various ways, each with its own assumptions about the nature of religion and the nature of science.

One strategy might be to argue that at heart religion does something not touched upon by the sciences as it addresses values, meaning and ultimate explanations. Religion, thus seen, is complementary to science. Galileo, in defence of his astronomical work, quoted in his 'Letter to Grand Duchess Christina' (1615) Cardinal Baronio who had said that the intention of the Holy Spirit is not to teach us how the heavens go, but how to go to heaven (Finocchiaro 1989: 96). Issues of morality and salvation are distinct from scientific knowledge.

To argue for the peaceful coexistence of religion and science one might also seek to argue that science is mistaken or incomplete, and in need of religious corrections, replacements or supplements, whether an actively intervening God ('intelligent design') or a more 'spiritual' view of reality. Such a strategy deviates from mainstream science, and thus is less effective in countering the idea of conflict, though the replacement is not a replacement of religion by science but of mainstream science by something else, whether considered 'alternative science' or dismissed as 'pseudoscience'.

Another strategy might be to argue that below the surface (or beyond the horizon of current science, or in its history and practice) science depends upon religious notions. If there are laws in nature, should we not also allow for a sovereign Lawgiver, a God who would not have to work against God's own laws of nature, but has set these to bring about God's intentions? Last but not least, an integration of religion and science might be intended, bringing the sciences into a meaningful vision of the way reality is, whether in terms of a theistic metaphysics or in a form of 'religious naturalism'.

Ian Barbour, a major American author on 'religion and science', has proposed to describe the field with the help of four categories: conflict, independence, dialogue and integration (Barbour 1997: 77–105). The preceding paragraphs indicate that one way of reading this scheme is as presenting one problem (conflict), with three possible responses to mitigate the forced choice suggested by the conflict position.

Whether one opts for a friendly separation and division of labour, a modified science, or a more far-reaching integration, the conditions of this development seem to have been set by secularization. Science seems to make religion mistaken or irrelevant. Thus, the interest is primarily in an approach which appeases a potential or real conflict.

For those who see this as the main agenda in 'religion and science', the partners are others with a positive interest in religion and with respect for science, as these are involved in opposing the same opponents. Hence, there is a broad ecumenicity in 'religion and science'. The peer group tends to exclude as allies those who are perceived to be staunch opponents of religion such as Richard Dawkins, Peter Atkins, Edward O. Wilson and Daniel Dennett. And the peer group tends to exclude opponents to science and proponents of odd 'science', whether in the form of 'scientific creationism' or quantum mysticism, as relating to such alternatives would not provide genuine legitimacy for religion in an age of science.

I find this concentration on countering secularization unsatisfactory. The agenda is not positive but negative, even though the negative purpose might be served by a positive case for the independence of religious convictions or by a constructive integration of religion and science in an encompassing vision of reality. Whatever the strategy, the underlying tone, read thus, is defensive: we are judged to be on a slippery slope, on which one has to make a stand against the secularizing impact of science. I think there is at least one other possible agenda for 'religion and science', one that is not driven by concern about secularization but by concern about the persistence of superstition.

The persistence of superstition

One could also engage in 'religion and science' for another reason. The driving concern would not be the future of religion but the persistence of superstition and nonsense, even though we, humans, should know better. Such a context is well expressed in the title of one of the last books by Carl Sagan, astronomer and science popularizer: *The Demon-Haunted World: Science as a Candle in the Dark*. If such darkness is the context and concern, the agenda and partnerships would be different.

Challenging nonsense such as astrology, alien-abduction stories and ineffective but expensive therapies is a most laudable goal, not only intellectually but also socially and morally. Nonsense often goes hand in hand with financial abuse and with raising immoral expectations, as when someone sells nonsensical cures to patients who are fatally ill, or suggests to a bereaved mother the possibility of communication with the dead. If a disease can be healed by 'positive thinking', then the patient who doesn't become well receives the additional burden of failing spiritually. Fighting socially consequential nonsense drives organizations of sceptics, as far as I understand their intentions. 'Religion and science' could have developed more along those lines, but that has not been its prime concern so far.

Challenging superstition would require us in 'religion and science' to address the nonsense in our own field, and thus might upset the ecumenicity that serves us nicely in arguing against secular threats. For those involved in 'religion and science' our primary purpose would then be to challenge nonsense and to pursue truth, rather than to find a place for religion in a world seen through the sciences. This intellectual responsibility would regard critically not only secular challenges, but also the challenges and solutions that we may raise ourselves. Intellectually and morally I consider this a most important aspect of 'religion and science'.

This book

Putting Science in its Place is the title of a book in which the historian and geographer David Livingstone considers the situated character of scientific research. He studies science as situated in laboratories, the outdoors, the museum and hospitals, but also as shaped by particular local, contextual situations. Livingstone (2003: 94) demonstrates how the Galileo affair took place in a regional arrangement of patronage and authority. He describes the reception of Darwinism in Calvinist settings in Scotland, Ireland and the United States. In Belfast Protestants and Catholics used opposition to claims about science replacing religion to criticize each other. In Princeton, the leadership sought to read evolutionary natural history as divine design. In Charleston, in the southern United States, racial sensitivities led to opposition to a single human origin, while in New Zealand the settlers could use evolution to justify their struggle for life at the expense of the Maoris (112–23). Even a single issue like the reception of Darwinian ideas in Protestant circles was very much context-dependent.

Since reflection on religion and its relations to science is a situated business, it seems fair to give readers information on the context of this book and its author, to note my own biases and disputable assumptions. This book is written by a European, a Dutchman, who has been exposed to American conversations.

Even though Europeans and Americans read the same literature, their situations differ. In many parts of Europe there is more indifference about religion, while science is more widely accepted. Thus, in Europe to think about 'religion in an age of science' is to think primarily about religion, with science as the background common to authors, readers and real or fictitious opponents.

In the United States science is distrusted by some as elitist. If there seems to be a conflict between religion and science, it need not be the science that is accepted. Some choose against science when it seems threatening to religious beliefs, and thus opt for 'scientific creationism' or 'intelligent design'. Those who address 'religion and science' in such a context have to do two jobs at the same time, to defend science against religious distrust and to think through the ways religion might need to be adapted in the light of the sciences. In such a context, philosophies of science which limit the pretensions of science may be extra welcome. A climate in which science is distrusted might be served also by popularization of science with a pious gloss at the end, whereas this would hardly count as a contribution to 'religion and science' in a European setting as such publications do not address the relationship between religious convictions and scientific knowledge.

Professional context

The professional setting of my writing is a public university, Leiden University, where I have a chair in Philosophy of Religion and Ethics. As this is a public university, religion may be an object of study, but legitimate methods are those of history, philology and literary studies, anthropology, philosophy and other secular disciplines. We have a bachelor's programme on the world religions, alongside bachelor's programmes on Christianity and Islam, the two largest religious traditions in the Netherlands. For some students, these programs may be the first step in training for ministry, but confessional and practical training is organized separately, complementary to the knowledge and skills provided by the university. This twofold order (*duplex ordo*), with a distinction between 'neutral' and confessional subjects, developed in the nineteenth century as the Dutch version of the separation of Church and State. The institute for religious studies of the public university and the professional Master of Divinity pro-gramme of the Protestant Theological University share a building. We have friendly relations, but serve different masters. Religious studies, rather than 'theology', is the context in which I write, and it is one in which I feel comfortable, though I also have my own religious interests and preferences.

Before becoming a philosopher of religion, with doctorates in theology and in philosophy, I earned a postgraduate degree in theoretical physics at Utrecht University. In 1977 I wrote a thesis on the detectability of Higgs bosons, par-ticles which remain undetected today, but which might perhaps show up in the experiments at CERN, Geneva, when the new Large Hadron Collider is functioning well. I am no longer a physicist, but I hope that love and respect for science, in its results but even more in its persistent raising of further questions, still come through in the following pages.

I am an insider to 'religion and science' discussions. Critical reflections in this book do not only regard others', but also my own work. I have written a book on responses to modern cosmology, *Beyond the Big Bang: Quantum Cosmologies and God* 1990, one on naturalism, *Religion, Science and Naturalism* (1996), and a poetic and narrative interpretation of our cosmic history, *Creation: From Nothing until Now* (2002a). From 2002 until 2008 I served as president of ESSSAT, the European Society for the Study of Science And Theology, the scholarly organization in this field in Europe. As of 2009 I am editor-in-chief of *Zygon: Journal of Religion and Science*, the premier scholarly journal in this area, up to then served by American editors. Thus, my context is also the 'religion and science' field in the Western world. In my own studies I have benefited greatly from two Fulbright scholarships and extended periods of study in Berkeley, Chicago and Princeton. Even though I will be critical of some trends in the field, I feel a strong affinity with the work of many on both sides of the Atlantic. My experience with other regions of the globe is more limited.

Modernity

The family I grew up in was science-loving and politically engaged; it was a secular, social-democratic and religiously liberal environment. A recollection, from the time I was about eleven years old: at the dinner table we discussed what the largest island is. England and Scotland? Madagascar? Greenland? Perhaps Greenland is overestimated because maps are distorted near the poles. Why would Australia not count as an island? And if one accepts Australia, why not the Euro-Asian landmass? Shouldn't we add Africa or does the Suez Canal suffice to consider Africa as separate from Europe-Asia? Things were more complicated than we thought at first. The concept of an 'island' needed to be defined so that continents would be excluded. We had to be suspicious of impressions, as maps might be distorted. Once the question had become more precise, an encyclopaedia would be taken off the shelf, to find the relevant facts. Basic aspects of science have been part of my life from early childhood onwards: a respect for facts, but also a critical consideration of questions, concepts, criteria and first impressions.

My heritage is more than science; the main context is modernity. The *modern* predicament, as I see it, combines *universal ambitions* about knowledge, morality and politics with awareness of *historicity*, of the *contingent* character of social, cultural and biological reality, and with *a critical attitude towards traditional sources of moral and epistemic authority*. The natural sciences and the moral claims embedded in universal human rights have been successful in their global appeal. The dream of a universal language such as Esperanto, that would not be the language of a particular culture, failed, and so have socialist internationalism as well as visions of a world religion and a world government. Perhaps rightly so; some ambitions were too minimalist to live by, while other projects were too Eurocentric to match the modern ambition.

A plurality of particulars might be the contemporary ('postmodern') pre-ference, and there is something to be said in favour of its honesty. There are multiple perspectives, arguments and even criteria across cultures and sub-cultures. However, postmodernism might bring with it a splendid isolation in homely ghettos. The absence of universal criteria or shared foundations, whe-ther qua method or substance, might encourage irrationality and arbitrariness. Postmodernism might generate a pluralism that is inhospitable for an indivi-dual who wants to cross boundaries, leave particular ghettos, and be able to criticize a given culture. In my opinion, there is a great value in the universal ambition of modernity, the quest for truth and knowledge that is not partisan, but then, for the sake of truth, we also need to appreciate the local that is so typical of the richness of bio- and cultural diversity.

We cannot take our traditions and myths as objective truth; what Paul Ricoeur (1967) in the concluding section of his book *The Symbolism of Evil* referred to as a primitive or first naïveté. Rather, we are heading for a different style of believing and belonging; one that is coloured by a particular history but that is also open to alternative voices. At different moments we play different games. We enter a cathedral and may be moved by the light through the stained glass, but we may also observe the cathedral from the outside, seeing the windows but not sharing in the experience of the light coloured by the glass (Yinger 1970: 1). I am at moments an observer, like an anthropologist or a scholar in religious studies, studying what is going on in the tribe of 'religion and sci-ence', while on other occasions I am a theologian or a philosopher, someone who participates in the discussions, and pleads for a particular vision. Insider and outsider perspectives may be distinguished, but they are intertwined.

Preview

The next chapter will analyse some of the interests that drive 'religion and science'; this analysis is mostly in line with the reflections on secularization above. 'Religion and science' will be considered as apologetics for religion but even more as apologetics for science. And what seems to be a dialogue with an external conversation partner, science, is often a fight within the religious community for the proper understanding of faith. Last but not least, 'religion and science' is a way to address the discomfort that may be the consequence of scientific understanding, when we are told that we are driven by selfish genes or that we are nothing but a pack of neurons.

The third chapter is about the understanding of science as a source of insight and about the criteria we might use to distinguish sense from nonsense. Criteria are needed if 'religion and science' seeks to counter superstition, but they are also relevant if one seeks to be plausible in an age of secularization. I will present my criteria in a form inspired by the 'Ten Commandments'.

Disagreements concern not only particular beliefs; they also concern the character of religious faith. We need to reflect carefully on religion, and its intellectual side, theology. The fourth chapter proposes to treat theologies as religious (or non-religious) visions that integrate models *of* the world and models *for* the world, that is worldviews and values.

Given the understanding of science and of theology developed in the previous chapters, the three subsequent chapters will present three major domains in the 'religion and science' discussion. Qua metaphysics, I argue in Chapter 5 that science aligns well with a form of naturalism, but that this does not do away with or limit questions regarding the scientific enterprise. Any science-inspired naturalism has an open end which allows for a theistic, a religious-naturalistic or an agnostic view. Qua morality I stress in Chapter 6 the significance of particular traditions as well-winnowed wisdom, and hence as imperfect human approximations of values that are themselves beyond the actual (just as mathematical truth is the limiting ideal of fallible human knowledge). And in the quest for meaning in a material world, in Chapter 7 I stress the role of creativity, traditions as formative rather than normative, and the role science might play in imagining our place, identity, and responsibility.

In the Epilogue I reconsider the combination of context and content, the emphasis of the earlier chapters and of the later ones, suggesting issues for further research.

From time to time, most extensively in the second chapter, I will refer to titles of books to convey what is going on in this field. Let the reader not be discouraged when these books are not familiar; explicit titles have been picked as illustrations of positions in current debates. Straightforward references are integrated in the text. Full details can be found in the bibliography at the end of the book.

Chapter 2

Worldly interests

Apologetics, authority and comfort

Books, conferences and lectures on 'religion and science' do not always have the same purpose. At least three roles can be discerned: 'religion and science' is apologetics, it is ammunition in the competition for authority within religious traditions and it plays a role in alleviating individual discomfort at the scientific image of the world.

Engaging in apologetics is not a bad thing. I too engage in apologetics, explaining and justifying to relative outsiders what I think and do. I am also involved in intra-religious argument, drawing on science to plead for particular views. And I reflect upon science because I hold that important aspects of human life, such as morality and rationality, need to be understood in the context of a worldview inspired by science. My work is not exempt from the analysis that follows.

Apologetics is the quest to justify a particular belief or practice to others, and more particularly to *outsiders*. We will see that 'religion and science' might serve as apologetics for religion in a secular environment, but even more as apologetics for science among those who consider evolution and other scientific insights threatening to their beliefs and ways of living.

Ideas are presented also to *insiders*, to fellow believers within the same religious tradition. If one's beliefs are in line with modern science they are legitimate, and thus one gains *authority* relative to a colleague, whose views are outdated or superstitious. Arguments in 'religion and science' are not blanket endorsements of religion in general, but rather serve particular religious positions, and thus serve as ammunition in disputes among believers. This has been true of the Galileo case, it is typical of disputes on evolution and design, and it holds for the way the Dalai Lama reaches out to modern science, to mention some of the cases we will return to. 'Religion and science' is in this context 'religion versus religion', one view versus another. Who is to speak for the Church? Who represents the genuine tradition? That is again and again in dispute.

A third function of 'religion and science' might be primarily individual, *to resolve discomfort*. If we are told that we are *nothing but* neurons, or genes, or molecules in motion, it seems that free will, identity, and morality are gone.

A scientific understanding of reality seems to conflict with our common-sense understanding of the world and of ourselves. *Reductionism* seems the bad guy here. However, below I will argue that reductionism is not that problematical. If appropriately understood, reductionism is a form of holism!

Apologetics

In a world where quite a few religious persons think that faith is at odds with the acceptance of evolution, relating religious convictions constructively to scientific knowledge might make science acceptable to religiously minded people. It thus serves as apologetics for science. 'Religion and science' may also serve as apologetics for religion and as apologetics for theology in the modern university, but we will start with 'religion and science' as apologetics for science, a role all too often left implicit. Before coming to this role let us consider the audience, for there is no role if there is no audience.

Public distrust of evolution

In August 2006 the journal *Science* published an article on the public acceptance of evolution in thirty-four countries (Miller *et al*. 2006). At the bottom of the list were Turkey, with more than 50 per cent taking evolution to be false and about 20 per cent not sure, and the United States, with about 40 per cent considering it false and also 20 per cent not sure. For European countries and Japan the acceptance of evolution ranged from 60 per cent to more than 80 per cent.

Details of such findings vary with ways of polling, but these results show that there is a problem with the public acceptance of evolution in societies with a well-educated population and substantial reliance on advanced knowledge and technology. More detailed analysis in the article showed that the rejection of evolution among Americans correlates strongly with belief in substantial divine control and frequent prayer; to a lesser degree this is also a relevant factor among Europeans. As might be obvious from TV and newspapers as well, quite a few hold that acceptance of evolution and substantial Christian faith are at odds with one other.

If one holds that the acceptance of evolution is at odds with religious belief, one faces a choice: accept evolution and give up religious belief, or the reverse, remain in the faith, but reject evolution. Typical examples of evolutionary accounts challenging religious belief are books by Richard Dawkins, *The Blind Watchmaker* (a title challenging classical natural theology) and *The God Delusion*, and by Daniel Dennett, *Darwin's Dangerous Idea* and *Breaking the Spell: Religion as a Natural Phenomenon*. Examples of the other option, rejecting evolution, can be found among advocates of creationism or intelligent design. Some of their titles are explicit too: Henry M. Morris, *The Long War Against God: The History and Impact of the Creation/Evolution Conflict*;

Philip Johnson, *Darwin on Trial*; Michael Denton, *Evolution: A Theory in Crisis* and, to take an example from the Islamic world, Harun Yahya's *The Evolution Deceit*.

Seeking the moderate middle

In this context, typical 'religion and science' literature argues that one does not have to choose. The acceptance of evolution can be combined with religious faith. As examples of such literature, one might consider books by the Roman Catholic authors Kenneth R. Miller, *Finding Darwin's God: A Scientist's Search for Common Ground Between God and Evolution*, and John F. Haught, *God after Darwin: A Theology of Evolution*, and by the Protestant Karl W. Giberson, *Saving Darwin: How to Be a Christian and Believe in Evolution*. Lutheran theologian Ted Peters and Catholic molecular biologist Martinez Hewlett wrote that the identification of Christian faith with the rejection of science would be a tragedy: 'we want our young people to fill the ranks of tomorrow's scientists. We believe both our schools and churches should encourage the idea that science can become a divine vocation' (Peters and Hewlett 2006: vii).

Not only believers argue that science and faith can be combined; some sceptics and non-believers argue the same. Michael Ruse, historian and philosopher of biology, wrote *Can a Darwinian be a Christian?* His conclusion draws heavily on Augustine and other major theologians of the tradition.

> Can a Darwinian be a Christian? Absolutely! Is it always easy for a Darwinian to be a Christian? No, but whoever said that the worthwhile things in life are easy? Is the Darwinian obliged to be a Christian? No, but try to be understanding of those who are.
>
> (Ruse 2001: 217)

And Stephen J. Gould argued in *Rocks of Ages: Science and Religion in the Fullness of Life* that science and religious belief can coexist at peace because they both make important but different contributions to the fullness of life.

Major bodies of scientists who reach out to the wider public have supported such reconciliatory strategies. The National Academy of Sciences in the United States published a booklet on evolution, in its third edition titled *Science, Evolution, and Creationism* (NAS 2008; previously 1984 and 1999). The National Academy presents the case for evolution and for its significance in understanding modern medicine and agriculture, and argues for its inclusion in science curricula of schools. It also addresses the fact that some people 'wonder if it is possible to accept evolution and still adhere to religious beliefs' (NAS 2008: xi).

In response to such concerns, the NAS parades some scientists who are also religiously active, such as George Coyne, a Jesuit priest who directed the

Astronomical Observatory of the Vatican, Francis Collins, an evangelical Christian who headed the Human Genome Project, and Kenneth Miller, the Catholic scientist whose book *Finding Darwin's God* I alluded to above. The NAS also quotes various religious leaders who see no conflict between their faith and science, such as the General Assembly of the Presbyterian Church, the Central Conference of American Rabbis, and the previous Pope, John Paul II. The NAS doesn't venture into the religious discussion itself; their booklet parades some important representatives of religion and of science, underlines the sense of 'awe and wonder at the history of the universe and of life on this planet' (12) and emphasizes methodological differences.

> Science and religion are based on different aspects of human experience. In science, explanations *must* be based on evidence drawn from examining the natural world. Scientifically based observations and experiments that conflict with an explanation eventually *must* lead to modification or even abandonment of that explanation. Religious faith, in contrast, does not depend only on empirical evidence, is not necessarily modified in the light of conflicting evidence, and typically involves supernatural forces or entities. Because they are not part of nature, supernatural entities cannot be investigated by science. In this sense, science and religion are separate and address aspects of human understanding in different ways. Attempts to pit science and religion against each other create controversy where none needs to exist.
>
> (NAS 2008: 12)

Not that the neutrality extends to all beliefs that may be held in a religious context; that would be too much:

> Scientific advances have called some religious beliefs into question, such as the ideas that the Earth was created very recently, that the Sun goes around the Earth, and that mental illness is due to possession by spirits or demons. But many religious beliefs involve entities or ideas that are currently not within the domain of science. Thus, it would be false to assume that *all* religious beliefs can be challenged by scientific findings.
>
> (NAS 2008: 54)

A statement of the InterAcademy Panel, a global network of academies of sciences, both from European and North-American countries and from countries in Africa, Asia, Latin America, and Australia/New Zealand, expressed concern about teaching that would not address evolution properly. To alleviate concerns, the Panel emphasizes the limitation of science:

> Human understandings of value and purpose are outside of natural science's scope. However, a number of components – scientific, social,

philosophical, religious, cultural and political – contribute to it. These different fields owe each other mutual consideration, while being fully aware of their own areas of action and their limitations.

(IAP 2006)

Thus, both 'religion and science' authors and some of the major organizations operating on behalf of the scientific community have sought to appease opposition to evolution – and thereby make science acceptable.

John Paul II

The National Academy of Sciences quoted Pope John Paul II as a religious leader who accepted evolution. When we consider the papal statement in full, there is in an interesting way more ambivalence than the appropriation by the National Academy suggests. The NAS (2008: 13) quotes from a papal message to the Pontifical Academy of Sciences, given on 22 October 1996:

> In his encyclical *Humani Generis* (1950), my predecessor Pius XII has already affirmed that there is no conflict between evolution and the doctrine of the faith regarding man and his vocation, provided that we do not lose sight of certain fixed points. (...) Today, more than a half-century after the appearance of that encyclical, some new findings lead us toward the recognition of evolution as more than an hypothesis. In fact it is remarkable that this theory has progressively greater influence on the spirit of researchers, following a series of discoveries in different scholarly disciplines. The convergence in the results of these independent studies – which was neither planned nor thought – constitutes in itself a significant argument in favor of the theory.

The papal address was in French. The English edition of the Vatican's own newspaper *L'Osservatore Romano* of 30 October 1996 translated the crucial sentence as 'the recognition of more than one hypothesis in the theory of evolution'. However, George Coyne, astronomer, Jesuit priest and former director of the *Specola Vaticana*, the astronomical institute of the Vatican, translated the same remark as 'new knowledge has led us to realize that the theory of evolution is no longer a mere hypothesis' (Coyne 1998: 14; there also the translation from *L'Osservatore*). If the Pope had said that there was more than one hypothesis, he would have played down the theory; if he had said that it was more than a mere hypothesis, he would have accepted evolution. The French original is: 'Aujourd'hui, près d'un demi-siècle après la parution de l'encyclique, de nouvelles connaissances conduisent à reconnaitre dans la théorie de l'évolution plus q'une hypothèse' (John Paul II 1998: 5). This phrasing allows for both translations, but the evolution-accepting version by Coyne (and similarly by the NAS) is convincing given that such a reading makes sense of the reference to the encyclical *Humani Generis*. At the time of the encyclical *Humani Generis* of Pius XII, in 1950, so John Paul II in 1996, there was uncertainty but now evolution is more than a mere hypothesis. Pope John Paul II accepted evolution, without hiding any more behind the provisional, hypothetical character of such a theory.

However, if one reads the papal statement in full the message is more ambivalent. There is a genuine plea for open dialogue on insights from the sciences; John Paul II did so on other occasions during his pontificate as well. He acknowledged that the Church was wrong in regard to Galileo, not only scientifically but, more remarkably, even in regard of Galileo's theological, hermeneutical and exegetical considerations. But further down in his speech on evolution, the Pope argued that

> rather than *the* theory of evolution, we should speak of *several* theories of evolution. On the one hand this plurality has to do with the different mechanisms advanced for the mechanisms of evolution, and on the other hand with the various philosophies on which it is based. Hence, the existence of materialist, reductionist, and spiritualist interpretations.
>
> Pius XII stressed the essential point: if the human body takes its origin from pre-existent living matter, the spiritual soul is immediately created by God. Consequently, theories of evolution which, in accordance with the philosophies inspiring them, consider the mind as emerging from the forces of living matter, or as a mere epiphenomenon of this matter, are incompatible with the truth about man. Nor are they able to ground the dignity of the person.
>
> (John Paul II 1998: 6)

Thus, whereas the NAS and the director of the Astronomical Observatory of the Vatican, George Coyne, have the Pope accepting evolution without pre-conditions, further down a caveat is introduced when it comes to the human soul and mind – a caveat that is implied by the 'fixed points' that Pius XII warned us not to lose sight of. The Church possesses truth that goes against a materialist or reductionist understanding of science.

The Pope acknowledges this tension, but consideration of the scientific method makes it possible to reconcile the caveat with the acceptance of evolution.

> The sciences of observation describe and measure the multiple manifestations of life with increasing precision and correlate them with the time line. The moment of transition to the spiritual cannot be the object of this kind of observation, which nevertheless can discover at the experimental level a series of very valuable signs indicating what is specific to the human being. But the experience of metaphysical knowledge, of self-awareness and self-reflection, of moral conscience, freedom, or again, of

aesthetic and religious experience, falls within the competence of philosophical analysis and reflection, while theology brings out its ultimate meaning according to the Creator's plans.

(John Paul II 1998: 6, 8)

Whatever the nuances relevant for Catholic theology, the initial sentences on the acceptance of evolution suffice for the NAS and quite a few others who are seeking to convince the faithful that evolution is nothing to be afraid of. Counter to such a conciliatory appropriation, one of the leaders of the Intelligent Design movement, the lawyer Philip Johnson, pointed out the papal ambivalence regarding evolution, and thus used the papal statement as an opportunity to stress fundamental differences between an evolutionary and a Christian worldview, as he sees those (Johnson 1997: 84–86).

Contradictory strategies for a common purpose

Quite a few communications presented as 'religion and science', whether on websites or in books, are at heart *science popularization*. To promote the acceptance of science, presenting fascinating scientific insights in a non-threatening way might already be an effective action. Less specific, but already helpful, may be 'awe and wonder' as a response to science, as in the NAS brochure, since such emotional terms bridge some of the distance between scientific analysis and religious appreciation. Elaborate arguments are not needed for most people; the apologetic purpose is served well by popular science with a pious gloss.

Pointing out *parallels* between religious convictions and scientific insights may also be useful. If the parallels are inspiring, science cannot be perceived as a threat to these religious convictions. One may even conclude that the religious tradition was there first, a matter of priority that makes science even less threatening. Arguing for parallels may be found in relation to other religious orientations than Christianity as well. Fritjof Capra's book *The Tao of Physics: An Exploration of the Parallels Between Modern Physics and Eastern Mysticism* (1975) conveyed the message that modern physics presented a view similar to the world view advanced by Eastern traditions. By doing so, Capra contributed substantially to the acceptance of physics among advocates of an alternative lifestyle. Previously, the 'Californian new age' movement had rejected science as technocracy, as marked by the word 'opposition' in Theodore Roszak's *The Making of a Counter Culture: Reflections on the Technocratic Society and Its Youthful Opposition* (1969). One chapter in *The Making of a Counter Culture* deals most explicitly with modern science or 'objective consciousness', which

is an arbitrary construct in which a given society in a given historical situation has invested its sense of meaningfulness and value. (...) In the

case of the counter culture, then, we have a movement which has turned
from objective consciousness as if from a place inhabited by plague.

(Roszak 1969: 215)

Associating science with the plague is at quite a distance from Fritjof Capra's
book, of which the first chapter has the title 'Modern Physics: A Path with a
Heart?' – a question he answers affirmatively. Capra (1975: 17) claims that the
changes in physics in the twentieth century 'all seem to lead in the same
direction, towards a view of the world which is similar to the views held in
Eastern mysticism'. This is not the place to evaluate his claims (see Jones
1986). Roszak and Capra were introduced here to show a change of heart
within this movement, moving to accept fundamental science as it is claimed
to align well with their religious convictions.

In line with the papal acceptance of evolution as a scientific theory (which is
genuine) and the papal caveat (which is genuine too) one might see other
attempts to make evolution palatable by *limiting science's scope and significance*. Thus, we come across arguments against 'scientism' (Midgley 1992;
Stenmark 2001) that seek to make clear that science is important, but not for
all purposes. Accepting science while playing down its significance, it is
attractive to refer to Thomas Kuhn (1962) and other philosophers of science
who have argued that science is tied to paradigms, perspectives and personal
preferences, and hence is not as objective and universal as it seems. We will
come back to such arguments in the next chapter.

Limiting the scope of science further is another strategy that can be useful
for making science acceptable to an audience that considers its religious beliefs
threatened by it. A clear representative is the palaeontologist Stephen Gould,
who argued that we should see science and religion as *non-overlapping magis-
teria* (NOMA; Gould 1999). If they are separate domains, people need not be
afraid of evolutionary ideas, as religious beliefs are not threatened thereby.
Previously we came across Galileo's quote from a cardinal who said that the
Bible does not present to us how the heavens go, but how to go to heaven –
another example of a division of labour. Applied to a more current controversy:
the Bible isn't about the origin of life, but about how to live.

In the opposite direction, towards more integration, reconciliatory goals can
also be served by *ontological arguments*, which argue that there might be
'room for God' in the context of scientific insights, as is the common theme of
a series of conferences on 'scientific perspectives on divine action' organized
jointly by the Vatican Observatory and the Center for Theology and the Natural
Sciences (CTNS; Russell, Stoeger and Ayala 1998).

Various other strategies might also make science more acceptable. One
might point out that there are *major scientists*, of the past and the present,
who are also believers of an appropriate kind. One might also draw on the
history of science to point out the *religious origins of modern science*, for
instance in a reformed emphasis on human work or in a broader conception of

creation as a contingent order (Hooykaas 1972, Torrance 1981; see Drees 1996: 81–86). Such personal examples and historical cases are not much as formal arguments, but they may appease, and thus serve as apologetics for science among those who suspect that their beliefs are under threat.

My point in this section is that a wide range of strategies, among which quite a few are weak as formal arguments, may all be adequate if the purpose is to make science acceptable to a religiously minded audience. The decisive issue is not whether a strategy is logically strong, but whether it is psychologically effective. Promoting science and science-based technology among those who might be reluctant to do so may well be a concern of sponsors rooted in the business community as well as of partners among institutions that serve the scientific community in general, such as academies of science. Thus, my observation is that even though strategies differ, one major role of 'religion and science' in a religious culture is to serve as an apologetics for science.

Responding to atheists: apologetics for religion

'Religion and science' is not only an apologetics for science; it is at the same time an apologetics for religion. This is most obvious when framed as a response to the writings of outspoken atheists such as Richard Dawkins (*The God Delusion*, 2006), Daniel Dennett (*Breaking the Spell: Religion as a Natural Phenomenon*, 2006), Sam Harris (*The End of Faith: Religion, Terror, and the Future of Reason*, 2004) and Christopher Hitchins (*God is Not Great: How Religion Poisons Everything*, 2007). These authors object to religion on moral and political ground as well, but their interpretation of science does play a prominent role in their arguments.

The Catholic theologian John Haught was introduced above as one who tells his religious audience that they need not be afraid of Darwin or of evolution. He fights a battle on two fronts, as he is also the author of *God and the New Atheism: A Critical Response to Dawkins, Harris, and Hitchins*.

Religious groups rejecting evolution and their opponents arguing for the compatibility of religion with modern science are both challenged by the outspoken atheists, though the ways part as soon as they become more specific about that which they advocate. A fairly conservative author titles his book *God is No Delusion: A Refutation of Richard Dawkins* (Crean 2007) whereas another prefers a lighter tone: *Darwin's Angel: A Seraphic Response to 'The God Delusion'* (Cornwell 2007). Are the moderates, advocates of 'mainstream religion' or of a liberal revision, most beleaguered since they are challenged from both sides? Or are anti-evolutionary believers more under pressure, as they have not only to deal with the atheists but also with societies which in principle separate state and church – an arrangement that allows for conservative groups but not so easily for all the views they advocate.

Apologetics for science may be especially relevant to the United States, with its widespread popular sentiment against evolution and against scientific elites, but what about Europe? In the European context a different apologetic agenda may be more significant: not advocacy of science to a religiously minded audience, but advocacy of religion to a science-minded, secular audience. Thus the message for such a purpose might be: Religion is not that impossible, given science.

In such a context, an argument stressing separate spheres (Gould's NOMA) isn't needed to insulate science from pre-existing beliefs. However, such an argument might suggest the relevance of the domain of moral and aesthetic values as complementary to science. Perhaps one might even convey the message that the moral dimension needs a religious framework. It helps religion, at least, if religion is seen as not being against science and as not at odds with socially useful new technologies.

For a few, religion might acquire new legitimacy if it speaks on behalf of the concerned, of those frightened by new technologies – that too implies that it has a meaningful role in our time. About two decades ago there was a book titled *The New Faith-Science Debate*. In the Foreword, Paul Abrecht, an ecumenical leader, writes of a shift in the interaction of science and theology around the middle of the twentieth century, with the discovery of nuclear energy and nuclear weapons. Earlier, there was a clash about belief and scientific knowledge claims, and the churches were on the defensive, he writes. But the situation has changed:

> The contemporary encounter between faith and science is quite different from the earlier one. (...) Today, as a result [of the rapid progress of modern science], science and science-based technology are on the defensive, and religious faith, speaking in the name of troubled and anxious humanity, has begun to ask questions about the consequences of the scientific world view. The enormous power over nature that the contemporary scientific/technological world system provides and the evident misuse of that power encourage the churches, in company with all those concerned about human welfare, to adopt a more critical stance.
>
> (Abrecht 1989: viii)

Religion can claim the moral high ground, so it is suggested. Though moral issues are important, I find the argument problematical. It is not at all clear that the earlier discussion on 'the clash between belief and knowledge' as a challenge to the credibility of belief has been resolved, and is now being replaced by a new one on the consequences. To present oneself as an advocate of a 'troubled humanity' facing the consequences of science and technology would not resolve doubts about intellectual credentials, even if the churches' moral credentials were unproblematic. Exploiting concerns about the problematic consequences of science seems morally dubious.

Apologetics for theology in the Academy

The academic world is another significant context for 'religion and science'. Does theology deserve a place in the modern research university? What are norms for being scientific (or academic)? Can theology live up to those standards? Are standards in the humanities lower than those for the natural sciences? If so, does that help theology? Are the standards for the natural sciences lower than we previously thought? Does that help? In the context of such conversations it may be useful to argue that the structure of theology resembles that of respected scientific disciplines, e.g. by presenting theology in terms drawn from philosophy of science, such as drawing on Imre Lakatos' methodology of scientific research programmes (Murphy 1990).

Alongside such debates on norms in scholarship and the nature of theology is the important question of whether theology should seek to live up to such norms. Thus the question is also what the nature of religious belief is. Is theology explanatory like scientific theories, or is it an existential judgement on meaningfulness? Arguments for a methodological or cognitive similarity don't work the same for different views of what religion is about. We will come back to this in Chapter 4. Controversies are not just about the relations between religion and science; they are as much about the nature of faith.

Something is troubling about academic work in 'religion and science' and that is the avoidance, by and large, of engagement with the history of religions and anthropological and social studies of religions. Such studies of religions are often methodologically agnostic; they focus on functional characteristics of religion. Some of the voices in the secular study of religion are perceived as reductionist and challenging, as they present their views in contrast to the self-understanding of religions. The secular study of religion with its immanent, social and naturalistic vocabulary conflicts with religious interest involved in 'religion and science'. In my opinion, however, the challenge is to be accepted. Avoidance of the social scientific perspective in favour of the natural sciences threatens the credibility of 'religion and science', and thus its relevance.

A functional perspective on religion, or on science for that matter, need not imply that it is merely functional, without truth value. An immanent approach need not exclude a transcendental horizon. To think through the implications of historical and social studies of religion for religious beliefs is a task of the philosophy of religion. This discipline should engage itself with the secular study of religion, while reaching beyond the social-scientific description and understanding to explore what this and other secular knowledge might perhaps imply for the truth or falsity of beliefs (Hubbeling 1987: 3). Philosophy of religion thereby comes in the vicinity of systematic theology, but in its reflections should take into account the outsiders' study of religions.

The two natures of natural theology

Apologetic roles for 'religion and science' are not a new phenomenon. In a study on the interactions of 'religion and science' in the past, titled *Reconstructing Nature*, John Brooke and Geoffrey Cantor have sections on 'Natural Theology and the Promotion of Religion' as well as on 'Natural Theology and the Promotion of Science' (1998: 148, 153). In these sections they highlight two roles of natural theology in the eighteenth and nineteenth century in England: to make religion acceptable, but even more to make science a respectable profession in the eyes of the religiously minded. In the past, natural theology also served to inform people on new scientific insights and to convey to them the message that science is an ally rather than an enemy.

In his inaugural address for the Andreas Idreos Chair of Science and Religion in Oxford, on 14 May 2007, Peter Harrison considered the Royal Society, founded in 1660, and the reception of its work in English society of those days. Different from what one might think from a modern perspective, 'the cultural stocks of experimental science were not particularly high' (Harrison 2008: 256). Science wasn't very useful yet, nor was its pursuit deemed important. Harrison shows that relating science to religion played a major role 'in offering ongoing social sanctions for scientific activity' (259).

Adam naming the creatures, while looking into their natures, was an ideal example. Science was a religious vocation, not only in England, but also, quite some decades earlier, for the astronomer Johannes Kepler (1571–1630), who described the world as a 'temple of God', thus implying that astronomical study was a priestly task, a form of genuine worship and veneration of God (Harrison 2008: 263). Peters and Hewlett, quoted above, were not that far from their predecessors when favouring science as 'a divine vocation'.

While design arguments for the existence of God became at later times apologetically important for religion, their function was different in the seventeenth and much of the eighteenth century:

> Arguments from design were deployed in the first instance to demonstrate the religious usefulness and social utility of a set of otherwise intellectually marginal scientific practices. In other words, it was science that needed religion. The deployment of arguments for God's existence based on the natural sciences was the key strategy of a programme of legitimation, and one that proved remarkably successful in securing social status for the new sciences.
> (Harrison 2008: 264–5)

Harrison also points out that in serving this role, religion became construed as 'a system of ideas' and religions as being 'distinguished primarily by what it is that their adherents believe' (266).

The main intention of relating science to religion was not to reform or serve religion:

Given the current status of science, it is natural to assume that the positive interactions of science and religion during the seventeenth and eighteenth centuries are to be understood primarily as attempts to establish the rational foundations of theistic belief. Arguments from design, thus interpreted, are apologetic exercises intended to support religion. My suggestion is that these are indeed apologetic exercises, but they are apologias for science, not religion, and that their primary function, at least initially, was to provide religious legitimation for the new sciences.

(Harrison 2008: 268–9)

In these pages I have argued that this role as apology for science is not only something of the past. Relating religion and science, whether by demarcation or integration, continues to serve as apologetics for science among religiously minded people who are concerned about threats that science might pose. But it is not just apologetics for science, as science stands for something bigger: modern culture.

More than apologetics: a struggle for the soul of modernity

After the shooting at a high school in Columbine in April 1999, there was on 16 June of the same year a debate in the United States House of Representatives on a law regarding juvenile offenders. Tom DeLay, a leading Republican, read a letter by someone who argued that this shooting was not due to the availability of guns. Juvenile violence was due to broken families, day-care centres, TV and computer games, small families due to sterilization and contraception, abortions, and 'because our school systems teach the children that they are nothing but glorified apes who have evolutionized out of some primordial soup of mud' (DeLay 1999: H4366).

This litany illustrates the fear that with the acceptance of evolution a whole cluster of social values is at stake. The issue is not science but modernity with its social practices and values. Explaining evolutionary insights, providing new data, refuting apparent counter-examples: all this will not really tame the antagonism, as science education does not address the real concerns involved. The basic opposition is one between religious views that reject modernity and religious and secular outlooks that accept and even value modernity. Controversies over evolution are at heart controversies over social issues, reflecting different theological responses to modernity.

Taking stock of the analysis so far: a major role of 'religion and science' in a religious culture is to serve as apologetics for science, a role handled in many ways. But not just for science, as modern culture is at stake. In that light, the issue is not the relationship between religion and science. Rather, the underlying issue is the competition between different religious or ideological views. We can thus consider 'religion and science' as 'religion versus religion', a competition for authority.

Who speaks for the Church?

Religious communities are not homogeneous; there are internal disputes on the proper way to relate the tradition to the modern world. Dissenters, advocates of a minority position, as well as established religious authorities may seek to have the legitimacy provided by science on their side. By arguing for the truth of one's ideas, one also asserts authority. Thus understood, 'religion and science' is a major battleground between revisionists and traditionalists in each tradition. Let me support this thesis with brief reflections on some major cases in 'religion and science'.

The Galileo affair as a struggle for authority

In *The Starry Messenger* (1610) and *The Sun Spot Letters* (1613) Galileo had claimed that his observations with a telescope showed that the Sun had spots and the Moon craters, that there were moons circling Jupiter, while the tides of Venus did not match those that were to be expected on the classical geocentric view. This showed that the Sun was the centre of the planetary system; the Earth was rotating, daily around its own axis and yearly around the Sun.

Opposition came initially from academic colleagues, natural philosophers (scientists) steeped in the Aristotelian scholastic tradition. One of these, Lodovice delle Colombe, introduced in his treatise *Against the Earth's Motion* biblical objections in the scientific dispute. In a battle Joshua had ordered the Sun to stand still, so that the battle could continue until the enemies were totally defeated (Joshua 10). If in this exceptional case the Sun was instructed to halt, the normal case was that the Sun was revolving around the Earth, and not otherwise, so the argument went. Galileo's public 'Letter to Grand Duchess Christina' of 1615 (Finocchiaro 1989) is especially critical of such philosophers and their use of biblical passages in scientific debate. In order to acquire support from his main sponsors and the general public, Galileo apparently felt the need to deal not only with the scientific issues, but also to defuse religious objections.

Once religious issues had been introduced, an academic controversy about astronomical methods and models became a conflict within the religious sphere, between different factions competing for authority, and between different views on Scripture and its interpretation. It became a matter of Church politics, as competing religious orders (Jesuits, Dominicans) and nationalities (Spanish, Italian) took sides. More importantly, the Galileo affair took place in the aftermath of the Protestant Reformation, in the midst of the Thirty Years' War in Europe. The Catholic Counter-Reformation had been shaped by the Council of Trent. There it had been decided in its Fourth Session, on 8 April 1546, that no one should interpret the Holy Scriptures contrary to the sense that the Holy Mother Church has held and holds, or contrary to the consensus of the Fathers, the recognized theologians of the early church. This was directed against the Protestants, who granted lay people the freedom to read and interpret Scripture without priestly, ecclesiastical guidance.

Authority in exegesis became central to the Galileo affair (Pedersen 1983, 1991). Not that Galileo was a Protestant, but in his defence Galileo had addressed the relevance of Scriptural passages. In his 'Letter to Grand Duchess Christina' of 1615 Galileo argued that science might correct our understanding of Scripture in matters physical, though he also argued for the mutual neutrality of Scripture and science in matters essential (McMullin 1967: 33; 1981: 18–25; 2008: 40ff). The condemnation of Galileo in 1633 affirmed the authority of the pope and church officials over lay reading of Scripture.

The condemnation of Galileo was a message about proper behaviour in matters of biblical interpretation, and thus a message against those Catholics who were leaning in other directions. Just as in the initial stages natural philosophers (scientists) were on both sides of the dispute, religiously minded people (and Galileo among them) could be found on both sides of the dispute in its later stages. That is a general characteristic of 'religion versus science' conflicts: religious advocates are also found on both sides at later times, when religion and science had become more clearly distinct entities, such as the late nineteenth century.

A. D. White's 'Warfare of Science with Theology in Christendom'

Andrew White's *History of the Warfare of Science with Theology in Christendom* (1896) is explicit in its title. However, his view is misunderstood if the context that fuelled the polemics is passed over, and the intra-religious dimension is neglected. White was the first president of Cornell University, a non-denominational university in the state of New York, created in 1865 with funds from Ezra Cornell. Cornell University was a Christian university, with compulsory attendance at chapel services (Altschuler 1979: 68, 81). Christian but not tied to a particular denomination. Hence, the founding and development of Cornell was heavily opposed by those in charge of denominational colleges, who objected to Cornell's ecumenical approach, which undermined religious institutions and hence religion as they saw it.

White responded strongly to charges of atheism or infidelity. Earlier in his career, White had not been appointed to a position at Yale since members of the board were not sure enough about his personal religious convictions (Altschuler 1979: 36). By their own standards those board members were probably right. White had refused confirmation in the Episcopal (Anglican) Church because he objected to the minister's view that unbaptized children and members of other churches, including his own grandmother, would be punished eternally (Altschuler 1979: 25). White took religion seriously but quarrelled with sectarianism and theological dogmatism. He envisioned a religion that would be in harmony with science. As he writes in the introduction of his *History of the Warfare of Science with Theology in Christendom*:

Religion, as seen in the recognition of 'a Power in the Universe, not our-selves, which makes for righteousness', and in the love of God and of our neighbour, will steadily grow stronger and stronger.

(White 1896: xii)

As White saw it, there were conflicts between science and dogmatic theology, not between science and religion as he understood it. His *Warfare* may well be understood as a plea for a liberal form of religion, served by a multifaceted argument against narrow-minded orthodoxies.

Similar observations could be made about other incidents that count as conflicts of religion and science, e.g. in the responses to Darwin's ideas. Again and again there was an explicit or implicit religious controversy, which might be summarized roughly as one between liberals and orthodox believers. Science was a minor issue in the controversy, which raged more deeply over the acceptability of a historical understanding of Scripture (Welch 1972, 1985).

That conflicts that appear to be about the relationship between religion and science are often conflicts between adherents of different religious positions within a single tradition is illustrated well by a more recent example, a court case in Arkansas in 1981 on a pro-creation science 'balanced treat-ment law'. Opponents to the creationist position in court were parents and teachers, but also 'the resident Arkansas Bishops of the United Methodist, Episcopal, Roman Catholic and African Methodist Episcopal Churches, the principal official of the Presbyterian Churches in Arkansas, other United Methodist, Southern Baptists and Presbyterian clergy', as well as three Jewish organisations (Overton [1982] 1988:308). These Christians were opposed to the understanding of the Bible and God advanced by their creationist fellow Christians.

Religious attitudes are found on both sides in these conflicts, and thus it would be a mistake to treat such events as clashes between religion and sci-ence. Rather, they show that the attitude relative to science is part of a dispute within a religious community. This applies not only to Christianity, but also to other religions such as Buddhism and Islam.

The Dalai Lama as apologist and as reformer

'Religion and science' is not just an issue within Christianity. An example from another cultural context is the relation between Buddhism and science. Initially, claims about the compatibility or incompatibility of Buddhism with science had their place in polemics related to Christian missionary activities (Lopez 2008: xi). This inter-religious competition has long since subsided, but claims about Buddhism's compatibility with science are alive and well. A major apologetic context is the spread of Buddhism in the Western world, where the message is that unlike the monotheistic traditions, which speak of a transcendent god, Buddhism is at ease with modern science.

Focussing for the moment on Tibetan Buddhism, the fourteenth Dalai Lama is a global ambassador for Buddhism in a positive relation with science. He is the official author of *The Universe in a Single Atom: The Convergence of Science and Spirituality* (Dalai Lama 2005). The emergence of Western Buddhism is also in the background of the Mind and Life conferences, at which the Dalai Lama and some of his entourage meet Western adherents and Western scientists to discuss scientific issues. As argued above, apologetics for religion and apologetics for science often go together. In this case, his engagement with science makes science acceptable to the Tibetan community. The Dalai Lama engages some younger monks in those meetings, and initiated a separate program, 'science for monks'.

If this were all that there is to be said about the engagement of Buddhism and science, it could have been treated in the previous section, as apologetics for religion and apologetics for science. However, discussions on Buddhism and science are also disputes on particular forms of Buddhism. In the nineteenth century, Western scholars became most familiar with the Buddhism of Sri Lanka and South-East Asia (the Pali canon, Theravada Buddhism); among the Western partners, spiritism and theosophy were prominent. After the Second World War, Zen Buddhism became more *en vogue*. 'And since the 1990s, Tibetan Buddhism has displaced Zen to become the chief referent of Buddhism in the Buddhism and Science dialogue, largely through the influence of the Fourteenth Dalai Lama' (Lopez 2008: xii). Thus, the engagement with science is also a competition between Tibetan and other types of Buddhism in their missionary outreach to shape Western Buddhism.

Not only Buddhism comes in multiple varieties; Tibetan Buddhism is not monolithic either. There are four major sects, among them the Gelug to which the Dalai Lama belongs. Indicative of competition within Buddhism is the observation by Donald Lopez that the Dalai Lama in the book mentioned defends in particular teachings of Mahāyāna Buddhism. 'The tenets of the Hīnayāna Abhidarma are also discussed, but often as examples of the Buddhist views that must be dismissed in the light of the discoveries of science' (Lopez 2008: 133). It is far more comfortable to accept science when it can be used against an alternative stream within one's tradition than if it hurts one's own favoured doctrines. Furthermore, in his *Buddhism and Science* Donald Lopez sees the approach of the Dalai Lama and of an earlier twentieth-century Tibetan Buddhist engaged with science, Gendun Chopel, as pleading for a new Buddhism. Which raises the question: 'But what is to become of the old Buddhism?' (Lopez 2008: 152).

Lopez points to many elements not mentioned by the Dalai Lama, elements that are apparently not essential to his version of Tibetan Buddhism. The Dalai Lama, Alan Wallace and other Buddhists who argue for the need to engage with science and for the compatibility of true science and true Buddhism have the ear of the Western world. Less visible, there may well be other Tibetans, including leaders of other sects and abbots of monasteries who are not into this game (see also Lopez 1998). Are they just lagging behind? Perhaps they realize that the flexibility involved in the engagement with science has a price with respect to what they consider authentic Buddhism, a price they are not willing to pay. I would not be surprised if the question of whether to engage with modern science is one which marks the difference for Tibetan Buddhism between reformers and traditionalists, just as much as for Protestant Christianity the struggle over evolution does. As Donald Lopez concludes:

> From either perspective [an insider's one or a historical one], in order to make this 'Buddhism' compatible with 'Science,' Buddhism must be severely restricted, eliminating much of what has been deemed essential, whatever that might be, to the exalted monks and ordinary lay people who have gone for refuge to the Buddha over the course of more than two thousand years.
>
> (Lopez 2008: xiii)

In the Dalai Lama's quest to understand modern Western knowledge, we also have a contest for the authority to set the course for future Buddhism. The engagement is not only with science for science's sake. Science is an instrument in a struggle over the reform of Tibetan Buddhism. One might argue that at the same time the Western appropriation of Buddhism has been to the service of reform agendas in the West, to defend theosophical claims about esoteric truth or to defend a non-metaphysical emphasis on the moral examples of Jesus and of Gautama.

Islam and Islamism

The world of Islam provides additional examples. Even though the popular understanding, especially since 11 September 2001, is that Islamist groups oppose Western culture, their main opponents are not Westerners. The fundamental issue is a struggle for authority within the Islamic world. Who speaks for the true faith?

As is to be expected in this context, Islamic literature on religion and science is quite diverse (Edis 2007; Guessom 2008). There are quite a few contributions on 'religion and science' by Islamic authors who seek to affirm traditional readings of the Qur'an. There are those that reject the sciences, as important issues are to be resolved in reference to Qur'an and Hadith; others claim that there are strong parallels, as the exact sciences confirm insights already present in the Qur'an (and thus confirm its miraculous, divine origin). Here too there is an alternative attitude towards the interpretation of the Qur'an, acknowledging the role of hermeneutical processes and human interpretation, concentrating the significance in a moral or metaphysical core (e.g. Taji-Farouki 2004).

The physicist Pervez Hoodbhoy was, in his book *Islam and Science: Religious Orthodoxy and the Battle for Rationality*, highly critical of the appalling state of science in Islamic countries and the role of religious orthodoxy and fundamentalism, which presents itself as advocating 'Islamic science', e.g. at the Scientific Miracles Conference in October 1987 in Islamabad. 'Instead of the orthodox programme, what is needed is a framework for thought and action, based upon science and reason, but in harmony with the inherited cultures of the Muslim peoples' (Hoodbhoy 1991: 135).

Mohammed Iqbal (2002a, 2002b) is far more part of an Islamic revival that seeks to integrate science into an Islamic view; according to such an approach, there is no autonomous sphere addressed by science, nor can science have primacy over religious matters. However, unlike some others who find modern insights in Qur'anic texts, Iqbal holds: 'Thus, instead of finding the Big Bang in the Qur'an, a deeper reflection would focus on the relationship between the fundamental assumptions of modern cosmology and the Qur'anic cosmos, its metaphysical roots, and its ontological structure' (Iqbal 2002b: 36).

'Islam and science' cannot but be a part of the wider struggle as to which Islamic voices will have the upper hand, between a traditional and mainly antimodern interpretation and a more liberal one. Controversies in Christianity in the nineteenth century, over Scripture, science and historical knowledge, have close parallels in current controversies among Muslims.

Who speaks for *the* Church? Who speaks for *the* Muslims, for *the* Hindus, for *the* Jews, or for *the* Buddhists? The definite articles hide a plurality of voices and opinions, traditional and modern, orthodox and reformist. When one aspires to claim to represent the true understanding of the true faith, allies and arguments are welcome. Having science on one's side can be valuable. That is not just a matter for liberals and modernizers; quite a few of the orthodox prefer to have science on their side as well. In the controversies over evolution the advocates of creationist understanding do not just give up on science; they rather argue that science is misunderstood and dominated by a particular ideology, and that they represent the more genuine scientific spirit, which in the long run will turn out to be on their side.

I started this chapter with a consideration of the role of 'religion and science' as apologetics, for science and for religion, to relative outsiders. In this section, I argued that the discussions are driven as well by competition within religious traditions. In the final section of this chapter, I will focus on tension within the individual, the tension between our self-image and images presented in the name of science.

'Nothing but ... ': How to live with the scientific image?

The Astonishing Hypothesis is that 'You', your joys and your sorrows, your memories and your ambitions, your sense of personal identity and free will, are in fact no more than the behavior of a vast assembly of nerve cells and their associated molecules. As Lewis Carroll's Alice might have phrased it: 'You are nothing but a pack of neurons.'

Thus the opening lines of *The Astonishing Hypothesis: The Scientific Search for the* Soul, by Francis Crick (1994). Crick was involved in the discovery of the double helix structure of DNA in 1953, but here he is after something even more grandiose: the understanding of human consciousness and the human sense of being a self. Each of us is 'nothing but a pack of neurons'.

The expression refers to *Alice in Wonderland*. At what turns out to be the end of her wandering in Wonderland the little girl Alice is about to be beheaded by order of the Queen and King of Hearts. At that point, Alice retorts against them and their court: 'you are nothing but a pack of cards' – and then awakes in the presence of her older sister. The cards are not even cards; they are leaves scattered in the wind.

Crick's statement may be heard as one more example of the onslaught of science on our self-image. If we are *nothing but* neurons, or selfish genes, or molecules in motion, or atoms, what about important notions such as free will, identity, rationality and morality? The 'scientific image' of reality seems to conflict with our common-sense understanding of the world and of ourselves, our 'manifest image' (Sellars 1963: 5). Given this threat, a function of 'religion and science' might be *to resolve discomfort about the scientific image of ourselves*.

The sense of being under threat may be due in part to an all too grand self-image, to hubris. We like to think of ourselves as more perfect (rational, moral and humane) than we are. In a weekly cartoon by Peter de Wit, in *De Volkskrant*, a Dutch newspaper, the main character is a psychiatrist, aptly named Sigmund. Some years ago, we saw his client walk into his office speaking of computers which will soon become like humans: 'They seem to be *listening*.' Upon which the shrink responded: 'They *seem* to be listening. Indeed, that makes them remarkably human.'

Even if we avoid overstatements about human nature, something seems to be lost when we accept the scientific image. For many, *reductionism* is the bad guy. Thus in 'religion and science' some argue for an alternative to reductionism. Perhaps the understanding promoted by physics is incomplete; we need a view of fundamental reality that is richer than the scientific image provides. Or else, out of the world of atoms a world of complexity and richness emerges. In contrast to such pleas for a different science, I suggest that we can bite the bullet and accept reductionist science as correct, while arguing that nonetheless we can sing, love, argue and do whatever else seems to be important to humanity, as realistic forms of sentience, morality, free will, love and rationality are really there in this world described by the sciences. If appropriately understood, reductionism might be a form of holism! We will consider some examples of each of these three approaches in 'religion and science'.

Arguing for a richer reality

Some contributions to 'religion and science' argue for a richer view of reality than the one provided by the currently accepted 'reductionist' sciences.

They seek to stay clear from 'reductionism', 'determinism', 'materialism' and 'mechanistic views', to mention just a few of the labels used pejoratively, and treat value, meaning and consciousness as fundamental aspects of reality. Not only would this account for our inner life, but at the same time this seems to be religiously satisfactory in finding meaning and value in reality, without appealing to any particular experiences or revelations in history. Some of this comes with a quest for a different science, a 'postmodern science', or, as the process theologian David Griffin titled a book, for *The Reenchantment of Science* (Griffin 1988).

The philosopher Frederick Ferré wrote:

> If the image of the Garden, in which humanity and nature interact with balance and mutual benefit, becomes a fundamental image for our world, it will of course be easier to see how the Machine can fit – as an inorganic simplification and servant of the organic – than it is now to understand how a Garden could come to grow in the cosmic Machine.
>
> (Ferré 1993: 95)

To what extent has science abandoned 'the mechanistic world view' and accepted an 'organic' view of reality? I am not convinced by the analysis of science offered by Ferré in which references to quantum physics and ecology have a prominent place.

As I see it, quantum physics introduces into our understanding of reality uncertainty and correlations between events far apart, but does not thereby introduce into our picture of the world holism in a sense related to subjectivity or values. The same holds for ecology. Scientists have uncovered many subtle relations between various species in a single environment. If science were exclusively defined in terms of analysis of constituent particles, it might miss such relations. However, this view of science is a straw man, easily dismissed because it is too simplistic a caricature. Relations between systems and their environments, and of various systems with each other, are within the domain of the natural sciences as they have developed over the last few centuries. There is no need to mark such issues as signalling a shift from a world without values, subjects and colours to an organic world.

That it would be easier to understand how the Machine fits in the Garden than vice versa betrays resistance against mainstream theories of evolution, which see more complex entities as products rather than as initial states. Claims about a transition from modern to postmodern science seem to me to underestimate the success and the potential for further development of modern science in the way it has progressed over the last few centuries. There are interesting changes in science which have triggered various debates in the philosophy of physics and elsewhere. Ideas on space and time, substance and determinism have acquired new shapes. However, neither these changes in science nor these philosophical discussions warrant the claim that there has been a 'reintegration of understanding with valuational intuition' (Ferré 1993: 95).

A radical alternative would be one which would in some way reject the overall order of the sciences, from physics via chemistry towards biology, and from there on to psychology and the behavioural sciences. In discussions on the relationship between science and religion the most prominent example of such an alternative is process philosophy, which draws on the categoreal scheme developed by Alfred N. Whitehead in his *Process and Reality* (1929). On this view, 'values' and 'choices' are relevant at the most fundamental level of reality. Physics is adequate for uninteresting entities such as electrons or stones, which have a rather limited spectrum of choices. However, features of reality which show up most clearly in human relations are characteristic of the most fundamental structure of reality; 'the Garden' has priority over 'the Machine'.

The attempt to develop such an alternative view of the fundamental structure is legitimate. It would be a remarkable change in the history of ideas if such an alternative organization of scientific knowledge replaced the consensus view, but it is not to be rejected *a priori*. However, such proposals will have to be able to offer alternative accounts of well-confirmed phenomena, experiments and observations. Such accounts should have detail and precision comparable to those of the currently dominant view. With respect to process philosophy, the proposal mentioned above, I am not convinced that the categoreal scheme which gives a metaphysically basic role to values and choices can be developed in sufficient quantitative detail, nor do I expect it to be true or useful. However, such approaches are among the intellectually sophisticated proposals in 'religion and science'.

Better chances for defending a richer view of reality might be found, in my opinion, not in the substances of science, say in quantum physics or chaos and non-linear thermodynamics, but in a reflection on the practice of science. For instance, when one argues for a purely mechanistic and determinist view of reality on the basis of a particular experimental set up, one still *argues*, and thus assumes that reasons are relevant, and the experimental set up may require a particular form of *freedom*, not so much on the side of the observed system as on the side of the scientists who design the experiments and intentionally test various alternatives.

Consistency seems to bring with it that if there is a freedom of choice among alternatives for the experimenter, the results cannot be used to deny the reality of subjectivity with such freedom. Philosophically, one school that might be introduced here is Scottish Realism, with as a central figure Thomas Reid (1710–96); a modern-day advocate is Nicholas Wolterstorff (2001). Another author who shifts the focus from the understanding of scientific theories to the position of the observer and researcher is Thomas Nagel, in a book titled *The View from Nowhere* (1986), a title that reminds us that when we report our observations of the external world we do so from our particular vantage point, with all the bias and selectivity this involves. In Chapter 6 I will return to a view of the human person in the context of the scientific image.

The emergence of emergence

Rather than writing value and meaning into the basic constituents of reality, some argue that such important aspects belong to organisms that have emerged out of more simple constituents.

> Reductionism has led to very powerful science. One has only to think of Einstein's general relativity and the current standard model in quantum physics, the twin pillars of twentieth century physics. Molecular biology is a product of reductionism, as is the Human Genome Project. But Laplace's particles in motion allow only *happenings*. There are no meanings, no values, no doings. (...)
>
> Life, and with it agency, came naturally to exist in the universe. With agency came values, meaning, and doing, all of which are as real in the universe as particles in motion. 'Real' here has a particular meaning: while life, agency, value, and doing presumably have physical explanations in any specific organism, *the evolutionary emergence of these cannot be derived from or reduced to physics alone.* (...) More, all this came to exist without need to call upon a Creator God.
>
> (Kauffman 2008: x)

'Emergence' has become a popular term in 'religion and science' discussions (e.g. Clayton 2004; Clayton and Davies 2006; Clayton and Peacocke 2004; Goodenough 1998; Gregersen 2003, 2006; Morowitz 2002; Murphy & Stoeger 2007; Silberstein 2006). The rhetoric is that of anti-reductionism, although like the reductionists the emergentists object to any additional ingredients (that would amount to dualism or vitalism) and object to an additional organizing actor – Kauffman's reference to the absence of a need for a 'Creator God'.

'Higher' entities or phenomena come about by the organized interplay of 'lower' entities. Thus, even though the analysis of the behaviour of higher entities may need a vocabulary of its own, their existence is understood to be material in kind. An often used example: 'paying someone money' is always a physical process – material objects (coins, paper) change places or the state of the computer at the bank is modified – but the economics of paying is not intelligible when described in such physicalist terms. A more simple example: wetness is a property of drops of water, but it isn't a property of individual molecules of H_2O.

As I understand it, 'emergence' is a useful notion within science, as it is useful to correct an unwarranted extrapolation from fairly simple connections between theories at different levels of description (e.g. the reduction of thermodynamics to statistical mechanics) to all cases. 'Emergence' is a word that indicates that 'higher' level phenomena are fruits of 'material processes' even though our description of the 'higher' level phenomena cannot be reduced in a straightforward way to a description of the underlying processes.

It is hard to see how that which emerges could be more fundamental in an ultimate sense. One might even argue the contrary, as that which emerges is to some extent secondary, a consequence of conditions and components. In his *Theology for a Scientific Age*, Arthur Peacocke wrote that God, as the source of the personal, has to be at least personal (1993: 106–12). If one takes evolution and emergence seriously, as Peacocke does, then his argument is misguided, as evolution and emergence imply that something may come to be that relative to its source has genuinely new properties. Thus such an argument for the personal characteristics of God as the source of personal being seems to fail. When I challenged him on this point, Peacocke agreed that his consideration was more like an argument of the eleventh-century theologian Anselmus than it was causal. That is, God as the being worthy of worship has to have the highest perfections available, and we consider personal characteristics to be perfections not found in, say, stones. That may be a fine argument, but it raises the question of whether the emphasis on emergence does the theological or valuational work it is assumed to do.

What is 'emergence' to deliver as a vision of nature? One expectation seems to be that emergence provides a way to go beyond the domain of the sciences. Samuel Alexander, in his *Space, Time, and Deity* (1920), suggested that the deity was always 'the next level up', a level that would be immanent (as fruit of the processes at lower levels) while at the same time transcendent, as 'more' than evident in those processes by themselves. Such a usage of 'emergence' brings with it the value judgement that higher in the sense of emergence would imply being of greater value. The scientist Stuart Kauffman titled his book on emergence *Reinventing the Sacred: A New View of Science, Reason and Religion* (2008). Ursula Goodenough and Terrence Deacon gave their contribution to the *Oxford Handbook of Religion and Science* the title 'The Sacred Emergence of Nature' (2006).

Emergence stands for a vision that appreciates nature as a creative process and seems to accept the scientific understanding of this process as well. As a vision it is opposed to 'reductionism' or 'materialism'. Upon closer inspection it is hard to see the difference between materialism and emergence, since emergence tells us how complex behaviour arises in and through material structures. The main difference with 'reductionist' visions seems to be that 'emergence' serves as label for a view that values 'higher' over 'lower' structures, 'complexity' over 'simplicity' and often 'culture' over 'nature'.

Reduction, elimination and simplification

Advocates of a richer view of reality, including many advocates of emergence, are worried by reductionist explanations since they fear that successful reduction eliminates or unfairly simplifies the phenomena considered. Let us first consider the concern of simplification.

Assume we attend a concert. Is the music the same as if we were to listen to a CD at home? Sound waves bring the music to us. My ears don't care whether the music is made by a cello or by speakers – as long as it is the same mix of oscillations. To have exactly the same mix of tones and overtones one needs the same acoustics, and thus the concert hall. If one considers the issue in sufficient detail, a perfect copy is extremely demanding. In one of the novels of Lewis Carroll, *Silvie and Bruno Concluded*, there is a discussion on the making of maps. One person claims they have extremely good maps, with many details. The other trumps his claim: they have made a map that matches the original in all detail, on a scale of a mile to a mile! However, this map has not been used: 'the farmers objected: they said it would cover the whole country, and shut out the sunlight. So we now use the country itself, as its own map, and I assure you, it does nearly as well' (Carroll 1939: 617).

With the concert it might be the same: the best way to make a perfect copy is to bring inspired violinists, cellists, oboists and others onto the podium of the Concert Hall. A concert may be nothing but sound waves, but that does not imply that the same result can be created more easily. Furthermore, there is more that generates the experience, such as the warm red colours in the Hall, the names of great composers on the walls, the view of the conductor and musicians. That is all 'nothing but light', one could say in a reductionist fashion, and that would be true. But to engineer the same experience while listening to a CD one would have to evoke the same visual input. And there is more: the comfortable chairs, the fact that we have freed ourselves to go to the concert, my companion. All these things make it a special occasion, and all are mediated by material processes and senses sensitive to sound, light and touch.

Reductionism need not imply that the same result can be achieved more easily. There may well be processes which we cannot predict – in the sense of having a way to calculate ahead of the process what the outcome will be – since the fastest way to find out may be to go through the process. Simplification is often useful (as are maps that are not 1:1 copies of the landscape), but in the philosophical reflection we need not mistake the simplification for the genuine process. Reductionism or materialism that aligns itself with simplification is easily refutable, but then the mistake is in the simplified vision of reality, and not in the materialism itself.

Let us now consider the other concern, reductionism as resulting in the elimination of the phenomenon under consideration. This is mistaken. Discerning the physiological basis for a trait affirms its reality. Genes are not less real for being understood as strands of DNA, and pain is not less real if understood physiologically. Rather the opposite: if the doctor can locate the bodily process underlying my pain, my friends will take my complaints more seriously. Any scientific description of a table – even when understood as mostly empty space with a few electrons and nuclei – will have to incorporate the fact that I cannot put my hand through the table, unless with considerable force and with major consequences for the table and for my hand. We may have to give up some philosophical notions attached to substance, but we do not eliminate common-sense solidity.

Tables and trees, humans and bees – we all consist of atoms: hydrogen, carbon, oxygen and the like. If one takes anything apart, one will not find additional substances. This has brought some to a negative statement of human worth. If we were to buy in the cheapest way the ingredients necessary for a human being, we would not need to spend much: we need water, some rusty nails (for the iron in our blood), some matches for the phosphorus, some charcoal for the carbon, et cetera. A human does not add up to much. That may seem to be a message from the sciences.

However, if one continues this assessment of the economic worth of humans, there is something else – the costs of labour to put it all together in the right way. Labour has been invested in us, by our parents, partners, friends and teachers and by ourselves, from embryological development to reading dull books. There has also been labour invested in the construction of humans during our whole cultural and evolutionary history. That too is part of the 'value' of a human being, and if one stays with the economic analysis that drives up the price enormously. One could reconstitute out of the constituent parts a simple chemical substance quite easily (e.g. water out of hydrogen and oxygen), but to reconstitute a human from matter is way beyond what is, or will become, feasible.

So what is the concern about reduction? As far as the entities involved, reductionism seems our best scientific understanding of the world: everything is composed of substances studied by physics. What these substances are is known in many ways – atoms and molecules, photons, quarks, etc. – but deep down we do not have the ultimate foundation, as we develop physics from our range of experiences and delve deeper and deeper. This unfinished quest within physics brings us to an issue I will address in Chapter 5, that of limit questions. Here, however, I do not focus on those limit questions but on the relation between 'higher levels' of reality and descriptions given by physics. Claims that conflate reductionism with simplification or elimination should be dismissed, but that does not deny that our view of reality in its ontology has become reductionist; the ingredients, deep down, are those studied by physics. At the same time, the concepts and explanations we use are often not those of physics. Higher levels have their own descriptions. In that descriptive and epistemic sense, of explanations and understanding, our view of reality should be non-reductionist.

Let us return to the example of paying someone some money. Every time you pay someone, there is a change in the physical world: coins or paper money changes place, or bytes in a computer are set differently. But it would be useless to describe the monetary transaction in terms of the physical change – as it is not just some atoms of copper, some pieces of paper or some magnetic states that have changed. The categories that are fruitful in understanding our world are different for economy than they are for physics. There is an even stronger form of non-reductionism. In many cases the original entities do not exist anymore. When two atoms of hydrogen form one hydrogen molecule, there is a genuine new entity with new properties. It is not a bag with two balls in it. Rarely will one find someone who argues that current entities are not real as they came forth out of earlier ones; children are not less real than their parents. Why would one then deny the reality of higher-level entities if they have emerged out of more elementary systems?

In a nutshell, the scientific image is that everything is 'nothing but the stuff studied by physics', atoms and the like, but also that more complex entities, including us as human beings, are not adequately described by physics; we need other concepts and explanations to do justice to the rich possibilities of nature. In these reflections on reductionism I have combined two moves. There is a good case to be made against all-too-pretentious forms of reductionism. Higher levels are real, and they do need their own concepts in order to be described adequately. At the same time, some forms of reductionism seem to hold true; more complex entities are made out of more simple ones. There are underlying processes. So what! Pain does not become less real or less painful when its physiological basis is unravelled. Such a form of reduction is not elimination; rather, it is integration of these phenomena into our picture of the world. Such a reductionism might even be renamed as a form of holism!

Roles of 'religion and science'

In the previous sections we considered what the engagement with 'religion and science' might do, rather than engage with the ideas themselves. 'Religion and science' is about the truth of ideas, but it is as much about authority within religious traditions, about a place for theology in the academy, about the acceptance of religion in a science-minded culture and about the acceptance of science in a religiously minded culture. Not addressed in any detail here, but equally real, are the social and moral issues that relate to science and technology; issues that also engage the values that people have, and the religious articulations and authorities involved.

Most significant of these and least recognized, it seems to me, is the role of 'religion and science' in intra-religious disagreements. Even if people have the same beliefs, they need not mean the same by 'believing'. Within traditions there are multiple views. What is most important to some seems totally uninteresting to others. Some focus on a tradition which provides a worldview. Others emphasize tradition too, but more as a source of identity, or as the framework that provides normative orientation for actions. When it comes to worldviews, bookshops do not present us only with philosophically abstract ones such as theism, panentheism, pantheism and naturalism. Books and TV deal also with witches and vampires, while for many the most important issue is life after death rather than God. Thus, what are we after when we advocate religion: myth, mystery, metaphysics, morality, magic? Different answers as to what religion is give a different shape to the 'religion and science' discussion, as we will consider in more detail in the fourth chapter.

A self-reflective consideration of interests served by 'religion and science' may not be appreciated by all participants, just as many scientists don't like science studies of a sociological kind. However, I think we ought to think through, clarify and appreciate outsider perspectives on religion and thus uncover the situated character of 'religion and science' dialogues. 'Religion and science' has multiple roles, depending on the audience and context, in faith communities, universities and society at large. There are substantial differences between, for instance, European and American situations, and these have their consequences in the intellectual debate. This self-reflective task should not be, however, the only approach, as we also need to go ahead in our role as people who argue about ideas, about their truth or plausibility. Which raises the question of what the criteria are by which we can judge different positions. What is a sensible approach, and when may ideas be dismissed as superstitious? The next chapter is an attempt to reflect upon criteria that might be relevant in making such judgements.

Chapter 3

Science, sense and superstition
Criteria

A student submitted a paper in a course on 'religion and science'. She was convinced that at the Resurrection, when Jesus became Jesus Christ, something of cosmic significance had happened. She had an idea what that might have been: physics' most famous formula, $E = mc^2$, only then became true to reality; before then, it would have been $E = mc$. Why? Well, Jesus became Jesus Christ – you see the extra c, of cosmic proportions? I rejected the paper. The student felt I had rejected her religious beliefs; I had not been sufficiently tolerant of religious and cultural differences, but rather followed my own prejudices.

In popular culture there is the persistence of magic in popular TV programmes and elsewhere, as well as the emergence of fundamentalist versions of religious traditions. These are not just private aberrations as they may have social consequences. Alternative medicine is a public issue since public money is involved in health care. I am also concerned about false hope, paid for with real money. Pseudo-religion and pseudo-science reveal real desires and fears of people, in problematical forms.

In the first chapter I spoke of two different contexts for 'religion and science': secularization and the struggle against superstition. The apologetic agenda was prominent in the second chapter. This chapter will be more about the quest for quality. How to promote quality in reflections on 'religion and science'? How to avoid the multiplication of nonsense, especially in an area loaded with personal preferences? Both in the academic and in the public domain we need to distinguish genuine spirituality from superstition. In my opinion, every sincere author on 'religion and science' should feel sympathy for the organized sceptics and secular humanists, since their criticisms are often made for the sake of rationality, integrity and prudence. We need to attempt as good as we can to differentiate between genuine spirituality and superstition.

Are there any sensible criteria when we have to do with the reception of science and the future of religious thought? What can be appreciated as genuine spirituality in an age of science and what should be dismissed as superstition? Universally accepted criteria for quality do not exist nor can they exist, just as a simple, univocal and context-free demarcation between science, bad science and pseudo-science is impossible. Particular convictions about the nature of science and the character of theology are always involved.

In articulating criteria I express my affinity with sceptical thinking, my positive appreciation of the Enlightenment and of the modern habit of questioning claims. Science is not merely a collection of facts (knowledge), but it is also an attitude of testing knowledge claims. In this chapter, we will first consider the nature of science, and thus the standing as well as the provisionality of scientific insights. Thereafter, I will offer ten criteria, drawing on the Ten Commandments. Not that the criteria are of a similar significance, but this provided me with an inspiring framework.

A critical attitude towards authority and speculation is, in my opinion, an issue of intellectual, moral and spiritual sincerity. In this spirit, the criteria that will be proposed are open to criticism as well. Learning what someone else takes as professional norms in reflection on 'religion and science', and where it differs from another person's view, may contribute to clarity on the issues themselves. A risk is that we humans easily apply double standards, so that the standards by which we judge others we do not apply to ourselves. In order to be sincere, we need to apply the same criteria to our own convictions as to the X-files. Or, to appropriate a biblical phrase, there is no greater command than: 'You shall criticize yourself as your neighbour' or, even more appropriate, 'For with the judgement you pronounce you will be judged, and the measure you give will be the measure you get' (after Matthew 22: 39).

The nature of science

In evaluating proposals in 'religion and science', scientific credibility is a major issue. Before listing particular criteria, we will consider the nature of science. What is this human effort called 'science', and why would it deserve such standing?

'Science' refers to a variety of disciplines. Physics concentrates on underlying laws, entities and processes, whereas biology faces the variety of organisms. Chemistry is done in the laboratory, whereas geology is primarily done in the field. When one is interested in causal explanations the focus often will be on physics. When the prime interest is in analyzing human experience there will be a greater interest in psychology and neurology, and thus in issues of reductionism. When it is about human responsibility, transformative disciplines such as chemistry and various branches of engineering take precedence over sciences such as geology or astronomy that are more descriptive and explanatory in kind.

Not only are there multiple disciplines. Within each discipline there are theories of different standing. In principle, all scientific ideas are provisional and revisable. However, in the last few centuries the natural sciences have become a cumulative enterprise in which major segments of knowledge have been consolidated. The information embodied in the periodic table of elements – an overview of the chemical elements, starting with hydrogen, helium and lithium – is as secure as anything could be. It is integrated in the web of our knowledge and of our actions in many ways. It embodies knowledge produced by scientists from different countries and cultures, such as the Englishman John Dalton, the Frenchman Antoine Lavoisier and the Russian Dmitri Mendeléev, and has since been tested and used across the globe.

Aside from such well-established knowledge there are ideas that are corroborated only partially, as well as more speculative ideas and wild guesses. Many of these may disappear, but some such ideas might become part of consolidated knowledge. Theological reflection is often interested in areas where speculative ideas abound, such as ideas about 'the beginning' of our universe, the nature of substance 'deep down' and ideas about causality and indeterminacy. Those are issues where science may be most relevant for metaphysical reflection, but precisely those areas of science are also those where the interpretation of findings and ideas is least certain.

A very brief introduction to philosophy of science

The methodological core of modern science is found in a persistent interaction between rational and empirical approaches; it is from this that it draws its strength. The interplay of empirical and rational factors, and the human factor that comes into this mix, isn't an easy issue.

Science aspires to be about the world, and hence we need to observe the world. We do more than merely observe, since the world is confusingly complex. We do experiments. By creating small known differences in conditions and observing carefully the variation in outcomes we get a sense of what factors might be relevant. To find out whether a pharmaceutical drug has therapeutic value we give the drug to some and not to others and compare the two groups. We try to get rid of irrelevant differences, such as differences by age or gender. And, to exclude psychological influences, we give the others an alternative pill without revealing who gets what. We also want to exclude influence by the one who hands out the drugs and thus don't tell that person who gets what; such an arrangement is called 'double blind'.

Science is not only about observations and experiments, but also about analysis. Theories are formulated, often in mathematical terms. Maths itself is not a natural science, as it is not about the world. Rather, mathematics is a tool which allows us to describe possible ways the world might be. With the help of mathematics we generate explanatory models of causal processes that might have created observed phenomena. For instance, when studying relations between the pressure, volume and temperature of a gas, a regularity was found, as a generalization from observations: $p.V/T$ is constant, the law of Boyle–Gay Lussac. In the nineteenth century, scientists invented a model which describes a gas as consisting of many minute balls moving in all directions, balls which have a certain velocity (related to temperature) and thus have a certain impact on the walls (generating pressure). This model allowed them to derive the regularity found. In such a way, scientists might come to develop a model that aspires to describe underlying causal processes. Is the model the truth? No. It may be quite adequate, but atoms and molecules are not really balls. A model gives insight, but has its limitations as well.

Science has an observational and experimental side and a theoretical one. The ideal is the combination and confrontation of these two. One view of science has been *inductive*, bottom-up: from observations we conclude to a general regularity, a law of nature. Thus experiments with gases may be summarized in the law of Boyle–Gay Lussac mentioned above.

We do not observe gravity; we observe objects that fall and hit the ground. Underlying mechanisms that involve forces or other theoretical notions cannot be found by induction from the phenomena. In developing scientific models there is a role for imagination. And if one proposes a theory or hypothesis, one may formulate 'what if' questions: 'If this were true, what would follow that would be observable?' That is, a hypothesis is followed by the deduction of consequences, the formulation of predictions. These predictions can be put to the test. If experiments and theory agree, the theory might be right, though it remains a hypothesis, a guess about nature. If experiments and theory disagree, the theory has to be discarded as wrong; it has been falsified. Such a view of science is called *hypothetical-deductive*.

This understanding of science, as creative ideas which can be falsified, has been articulated by the philosopher Karl Popper (1902–94), who made falsifiability (the possibility of being shown false) the prime criterion for deciding what ideas are to be considered as scientific. If someone presents ideas which are immune to falsification, due to vagueness or due to the inclusion of a conspiracy theory which would see any counter-example as forgery by an enemy, such ideas are not science. For Popper an example of such an ideology masquerading as science was the communist view of historical development. If we cannot say what would refute a theory, the theory might well be meaningless. Unfalsifiable approaches that masquerade as science are, in Popper's view, pseudo-scientific.

Understanding science in terms of falsifiability is not fully realistic with respect to science as practised. Imagine a researcher who has invested intellectual effort in a particular theory which has been successful in many cases. Assume the scientist is confronted with one lone observation that would falsify the theory. Will he immediately dump the theory as falsified and start again from scratch? This is unlikely. Rather, the scientist will question whether the experiment has been done well. Maybe the equipment did not function properly, or did not measure what we thought it measured. Or there may have been a dubious assumption in the calculations, or we just made a mistake. Falsification means that the world says 'No', but it is not univocally clear whether it is a 'No' to the theory, to the derivation of predictions or to the equipment used. This insight is named after Pierre Duhem (1861–1916) and

Willard Van Orman Quine (1908–2000) as the Duhem–Quine thesis: ideas are never tested in isolation but in larger wholes of assumptions in models and experimental set ups, and thus one can never be sure precisely what aspect of the larger package has been falsified. How apparent counter-examples are handled may thus vary from person to person.

The idea that science has an impersonal rationality and objectivity has also been challenged by studies of the history of the sciences. A classic example has been the shift from a geocentric to a heliocentric view of the Solar System, as it occurred with the work of Copernicus (1473–1543), Galileo (1564–1642) and others. Observations were involved, but the clash between the two views was also one about the criteria by which to judge theories and observations. Thus it was argued by Thomas Kuhn in *The Structure of Scientific Revolutions* (1962) that the development of science takes place within a larger framework of ideas, a 'paradigm'. Alongside normal, piecemeal development in science there are occasional 'scientific revolutions' during which a 'paradigm shift' takes place. The ideas of adherents of the old and the new views are 'incommensurable' as there is no neutral position from which to evaluate the merits of one paradigm relative to those of the other. Since Kuhn, historians and sociologists have shown extensively the human character of science, its individual and social dimensions, not only for 'the context of discovery' (where the human, constructive and creative character always had its place) but for the practice as a whole.

A merely inductive approach (generalizing from data) and a purely hypothetical-deductive approach (inventing theories, discarding those that fail tests) are too simplistic to set the standards for science. Other ways of understanding the development of science have arisen. Some authors emphasize that ideas are never tested in isolation, and even that words do not have meaning in isolation (a view inspired by the later writings of Ludwig Wittgenstein). Thus, Quine suggested that all knowledge should be seen as 'webs of belief', confronted with reality at its edges (Quine and Ullian 1978). He claimed that any particular belief may be held true as long as one is willing to make sufficient adaptations elsewhere in one's web of beliefs so as to maintain coherence. *Coherentism* may have attractive possibilities for theologians, as one might present religious ideas as part of a large 'web of beliefs', while denying the possibility of any immediate test of the claim that God exists. It would be the coherence of the system of ideas and beliefs as a whole that makes it more or less reasonable.

Another approach has emphasized *competition* between hypotheses or theories. We opt for the more plausible explanation (among those thought of so far), though even for the preferred one there may be apparent counter-examples which have not yet been successfully handled. According to Imre Lakatos's understanding of scientific research programmes, scientists working in a certain field may pursue a research programme in the context of which certain ideas are taken to be right, a core of theories and methodological beliefs, which are supplemented in their daily work is with additional hypotheses regarding the situation, the ways it might be modelled, the ways calculations can be simplified, additional factors dismissed as irrelevant, and so on. This combination of a hard core and a variety of additional, auxiliary hypotheses results in predictions. If predictions do not fit newly acquired data, researchers will modify some of their auxiliary hypotheses, while sticking to the core of their approach. Thus, a research programme is flexible but also resilient regarding the hard core of beliefs involved. It has to prove itself in a world with competing research programmes. In this competition, it may turn out that one programme has more difficulty in responding to novel data than another, making more arbitrary, *ad hoc* moves to protect its core. Such a programme is to be abandoned in favour of its competitor.

Imperfect, human and significant

Though there is no generally accepted single understanding of the rationality of science, extreme relativism does not seem justified. The demise of the idea that science delivers undisputable truth in an impersonal and ahistorical way saves us from seeing science in all too lofty, almost miraculous terms. However, once we have avoided overstatement, we run the risk of understatement, as if science's human character could deny its significance as a human approach to reality that provides increasingly adequate knowledge.

A helpful analogy is the development of precision tools. Can one understand that one can make a precision tool for measuring lengths in microns (a micron is a thousandth of a millimetre) if one has to start with a shed which contains only large and imprecise tools? The answer is: Yes. We can trace the history of technology, and thus come to see how new instruments have been made by means of a preceding generation of instruments. One could not construct a precision instrument at the level of microns with Stone-Age axes. Our current generation of tools is the fruit of a long chain of technological improvements. Rather than a jump from the bottom to the present level, the history of technology resembles an ascending spiral.

Piecemeal improvements of techniques, methodological norms, theories and questions characterize the development of science as well. Some scientists proposed new instruments, others proposed a modification of accepted procedures, others posed new questions, and thus new challenges. Science is the interplay of theories, concepts, criteria of credibility, instruments, sets of questions considered significant. As analysed by Philip Kitcher in *The Advancement of Science* (1993), a temporary consensus on criteria, methods, questions and theories frames the work of individuals, who at the same time may propose some changes, thereby shaping a new consensus.

Among the criteria that have come to be accepted are some that surpass the criteria that humans are naturally inclined to use. Logical and mathematical analysis, criteria such as universality and coherence and the variety of ways of experimenting and testing claims, for instance by doing experiments 'double blind', are important for the credibility of science, precisely because they surpass and correct the conclusions of ordinary psychological mechanisms.

Science is a human project, the work of individual scientists and the social interactions by which these individuals modify the consensus about claims, questions, procedures, criteria, instruments, assessments of authority and the like. Such a view of science is realistic and modest, but then we have to make clear why this human practice deserves pre-eminence over other practices such as astrology, sport, politics or art.

The first step in any argument for the importance of science should be to note the limited character of the claim. Health is improved by physical exercises rather than by exercises in physics. The arts have goals that are different from those of the sciences, and thus the arts are governed by different notions of excellence. Science is not the sole practice in which we pursue a form of excellence. Rather, science deserves to be appreciated as our major *cognitive* enterprise, claiming to generate factual and theoretical knowledge.

There are other human practices which aspire to make cognitive claims. An astrologer, for example, might claim to inform us about a person's character or about next week's opportunities with respect to finances or intimate relations. In the last century our experience with the natural sciences has shown that its claims are effective in handling reality and contributing to a coherent account of reality. The astrologer's cognitive claims do not show similar practical and intellectual fruits, and thus seem less worthy of our interest and appreciation.

Whether one considers the study of extraordinary and scientifically marginal claims worthwhile will depend on one's assessment of the utility of pursuing such a project, given what others have been doing so far, what other projects one might engage in and one's expectations about the feasibility and fruitfulness of such research. There is in principle no external constraint on the projects to be explored.

Such a liberal attitude in no way entails that all projects deserve equal funding or equal status in curricula. Many would-be scientific ideas conflict with experiences and experiments, are inconsistent or imprecise, stand in splendid isolation from other knowledge or introduce *ad hoc* elements which seem artificial or superfluous. Some cognitive projects which aspire to be recognized as scientific fail not so much due to beliefs they advance but due to their lack of proper development in relation to new discoveries. For instance, creationists advance positions which were part of the scientific consensus in geology and palaeontology about two hundred years ago. In those times, they might have been considered scientific, but they haven't integrated subsequent discoveries well. Repeating previously held positions without accommodating more recent observations is not likely to promote epistemic goals. There is no global criterion which delineates the proper sciences and excludes all other practices which compete for cognitive credibility, but consistency, precision, fertility, avoidance of *ad hoc* elements and coherence with other knowledge are among the general criteria which we use to evaluate cognitive practices (McMullin 1992, 1994).

Valuing science is sometimes dismissed as *scientism*. Scientism is a critical term to indicate that science is used inappropriately as an authority (Stenmark 2001). It is indeed important to realize that science is not able to answer all our questions. Some questions of everyday life are not scientific though they are factual, for instance the simple question: 'What is your name?' Other questions address aesthetic or moral issues; we will come back to the distinction in the next chapter. My claim here is that for the kind of questions science is adequate for, science is more adequate than any human alternative, whether relying on intuition, consulting tarot cards, a horoscope or a religious authority.

Provisionality and continuity

There is also a question as to what kind of knowledge science delivers. It does not deliver the certainty that in Antiquity and the Middle Ages was considered the hallmark of *scientia*. All knowledge is in principle provisional, though many insights will not be abandoned. And even some theories that have been shown false, such as Newton's theory of gravity, continue to be put to use. Its replacement by Einstein's theory of general relativity resulted in a different ontology, a different understanding of the inventory of the world. Rather than gravity as a force, we came to consider it as a manifestation of the curved nature of space-time. Continuity is not necessarily to be found at the level of specific ideas about the ultimate nature of material entities and their interactions. But then we still speak of the Sun rising, even though it would be better to say that the Earth is turning around its axis. With science we have to accept that there may be descriptions that are adequate in a particular context, at a particular scale, even if when we zoom in or out they are not adequate any more.

In that sense there are good grounds to be careful about 'realism'. Science is about reality; it is the world out there that decides which of our ideas continue to be taken seriously. But our theories are not straightforward depictions of reality; one cannot move easily from scientific theories to metaphysical conclusions. If one links scientific realism with the attempt to develop 'a world-picture, something that purports to be the "One True Story of the World"' (Van Fraassen 1994) it becomes vulnerable.

In debates among philosophers of science, realists and empiricists to a large extent come to take a similar stance with respect to the extremes. They agree on the presence of regularities in empirical reality and on the instrumental success of science. The claims of most scientific realists are moderate. Even though theories may change, the instrumental success of theories and related practices justifies committing ourselves provisionally to the existence of the entities described in those theories or assumed to be used in those practices. A strong claim, a metaphysical realism that assumes that science offers access to the one true, unchangeable view is avoided by the defenders of realism as much as it is objected to by empiricists rejecting realism.

For example, both Ernan McMullin, a defender of scientific realism, and Bas van Fraassen, an empiricist, agree on the inappropriateness of metaphysical extensions of scientific conclusions. McMullin rejects the link between scientific realism and metaphysical realism; scientific realism 'is not immediately undermined by the rejection of metaphysical realism' (McMullin 1984: 25). Current theories need not be true or approximately true and theoretical explanations are open-ended, allowing for metaphorical extensions (ibid.: 36). Explanatory success allows us, 'in favorable cases, to make a truth claim *of a limited sort* for the theory' (McMullin 1987: 52; emphasis added). And Van Fraassen (1980: 69) is interested in knowledge about the world, but concerned about claiming too much. He identifies the following question as one that he and realists might have in common: 'How could the world *possibly* be the way physical theory says it is?' (Van Fraassen 1984: 171). This is not the place to sort out the disagreements among philosophers of science on realism and criteria for the evaluation of theories. However, by and large, both realists and empiricists give us good grounds to be cautious in moving from actual science to metaphysical claims.

If science is provisional and marred by diversity, what should the philosopher or theologian do when engaging with contemporary science? Should one refer to those scientists who defend views close to one's own preferences, or should one rather consider the challenges that come from other views? There seem to be at least three different options in this respect.

Eclecticism: one takes whatever fits best. This attitude is present in much religious abuse of speculative scientific statements. Such a way of drawing upon science may contribute to the intelligibility of one's view, as the scientific notions may serve as a model for the religious ideas, but its engagement with science makes no additional contribution to credibility.

Wait and see what becomes the consensus might seem a wise strategy in areas where the science has not led towards consensus yet. There is, I agree, no strict need for consistency between theological ideas and current scientific insights as the science is provisional, though the sciences seem to be stronger with regard to ideas they exclude than in theories they affirm.

Reverse eclecticism, taking science 'where it "hurts" most' (Eaves 1989: 203), where it seems most at odds with one's metaphysical or religious convictions. This would be most rewarding. The worst possible cases provide the best opportunity for gaining credibility.

Ten Commandments for 'religion and science'

Science is a human project, which delivers something remarkable: knowledge that approximates quite well to the ideal of knowledge independent of cultural and personal bias. If one accepts this view of science, how to deal with it in 'religion and science'? We will attempt to deal with that question by articulating ten criteria for serious work in 'religion and science'.

No other gods: freedom and restraint

Science is always provisional; theories may be abandoned for better ones. Academic freedom implies that there should be no premature restraints. However, science is also highly selective, testing and discarding ideas day by day. We don't believe in a flat Earth, nor do we consider it plausible that the Moon is made of green cheese. How to balance openness and selectivity? How to navigate between the best available knowledge and marginal proposals that may bring us further, but may also lead us astray? Arguing that before the resurrection of Christ relativity theory was different seems to stretch academic freedom too far. In my opinion the worst sin in 'science and religion' can be expressed with a paraphrase of the first of the Ten Commandments:

1.   You shall have no other sciences before me.

We need to relate to science as it is, as the cumulative result of the work of many scientists, rather than invent our own science. Do It Yourself science, of which the replacement of $E = mc^2$ by a pre-Christ $E = mc$ is an example, is of no help at all in that enterprise. It makes a caricature of 'religion and science'. It is dishonest to one's audience and to the work of many others.

If a spiritual thinker or theologian has a bright idea to change a scientific theory, the idea may in principle be a contribution worth considering. But for such a revision of science the proper and decisive *audience* is the relevant scientific community. If my student had aspired to make a case for the formula $E = mc$ as a formula deserving genuine consideration, she should have made her case to specialists in relativity theory and other branches of physics, geology and cosmology. If they could be convinced that her alternative was a serious option, it would become an idea worth pursuing in religious reflection, but only then.

Is this too strict? There are ideas that are not generally accepted within the scientific community but still deserve to be taken seriously. It can be a very valid intellectual exercise to think through, for instance, the implications of the ideas of the physicist David Bohm for our conception of time and timelessness, even though those ideas are marginal in the scientific community. However, in presenting such explorations one should be honest about the standing of these ideas within science, and thus underline the hypothetical character of the extrapolations.

Regarding consolidated science I see two ways to preserve our sanity while reflecting on religious issues in relation to the sciences. One is to draw upon widely accepted textbooks, which do reflect the current view of the relevant scientific community. Furthermore, it may be valuable to have a scientist working in the field 'looking over your shoulder', not necessarily one who agrees on the philosophical or spiritual views presented, but as someone who sees to it that the scientific discipline is dealt with in a way that respects its work and that this is recognizable to significant peers.

When speaking of the scientific consensus, above, I referred to the periodic table of elements, which may seem an unproblematic example, but homeopathy and other forms of alternative medicine as well as some spiritual worldviews are at odds with it. More alive in the present is the question of whether to accept the current scientific consensus on biological evolution. Would it be appropriate to allow 'Intelligent Design Theory' a place at the table in science (and in science education)? Should it be treated as a competing scientific theory? Is it fair to present this as an issue of academic freedom and respect for the openness of scientific research? Given the significance of those debates, let us consider in somewhat more detail the discussion on 'intelligent design'.

An aside on ID

In Autumn of 2004, a school board in Dover, Pennsylvania, adopted a statement to be read to children in secondary school at the beginning of biology courses on evolution (Jones 2005: 1f):

> The Pennsylvania Academic Standards require students to learn about Darwin's Theory of Evolution and eventually to take a standardized test of which evolution is a part.
>
> Because Darwin's Theory is a theory, it continues to be tested as new evidence is discovered. The Theory is not a fact. Gaps in the Theory exist for which there is no evidence. A theory is defined as a well-tested explanation that unifies a broad range of observations.
>
> Intelligent Design is an explanation of the origin of life that differs from Darwin's view. The reference book, *Of Pandas and People*, is available for students who might be interested in gaining an understanding of what Intelligent Design actually involves.
>
> With respect to any theory, students are encouraged to keep an open mind. The school leaves discussion of the Origins of Life to individual students and their families. As a Standards-driven district, class instruction focuses upon preparing students to achieve proficiency on Standards-based assessments.

This statement seems fairly innocent. There is an occasional unhappy formulation ('Gaps ... for which there is no evidence'), but what could be against continuous testing of theories, considering an alternative point of view and keeping an open mind? What is wrong with the statement of then president George W. Bush on 1 August 2005 that 'both sides ought to be properly taught

(…) so people can understand what the debate is about'? (See www.time.com/time/nation/article/0,8599,1089733,00.html, accessed 3 March 2009.)

'Teach the Controversy' is a phrase used in the USA in arguments for the inclusion of 'intelligent design' in the biology curriculum. It is an expression that may confuse liberals who have no sympathy towards the anti-evolution movement but who do believe strongly in academic freedom and freedom of expression. Is academic freedom genuine if the dominant understanding of such freedom excludes those who propose alternative understandings of reality? It is my hypothesis that this ambivalence of liberal-minded persons who accept science but also value freedom of expression explains some of the discrepancy between the percentage of those who don't accept evolution and the, significantly higher, number of those who hold that alternative points of view ought to be taught (Miller 2006).

Advocates of ID don't plead for openness for its own sake; they call for openness in the expectation that a particular result will follow. If only the dogmatism of the evolutionists could be replaced by genuine openness, the truth (as the faithful see it) would come out victoriously. As a leader of the ID movement, Philip Johnson, wrote: 'If we get an unbiased scientific process started, we can have confidence that it will bring us closer to the truth.' Evolutionary naturalism is like a great battleship, 'armored with philosophical and legal barriers to criticism and its decks are stacked with 16-inch rhetorical guns to intimidate would-be attackers' (Johnson 1998: 453). Johnson charges that the evolutionists resort to legal defences.

The phrase 'teach the controversy' may already be beyond its high point, as the Dover ruling described 'teach the controversy' as part of a particular set of religious tactics (Jones 2005). A more indirect strategy has since been presented: '*critical analysis of evolution*', with adherents of ID advocating that arguments against evolutionary explanations be taught (without invoking 'intelligent design' as an alternative view). The Discovery Institute has a one-page document on its website titled 'Is Critical Analysis of Evolution the Same as Teaching Intelligent Design?' (www.discovery.org/scripts/viewDB/filesDB-download.php?command=download&id=875, accessed 22 October 2008.) They answer their own rhetorical question in the negative.

Not all advocates, however, keep 'critical analysis' and ID fully apart. Joel Borofsky, former assistant to William Dembski, a major author in the Intelligent Design movement, comforted a disappointed Kansas citizen who took it that 'critical analysis' had nothing to do with ID: 'It is really ID in disguise' (wikipedia, s.v. 'Critical analysis of evolution', accessed 3 March 2009). And according to a newspaper in Charleston on 2 November 2006, Karen Floyd, the Republican candidate in South Carolina for the position of State Superintendent for Education, also connected 'intelligent design' and critical analysis of evolution, and reached even further back to Young Earth Creationism: 'Students are smart,' she said, 'and they connect the dots: Some will wonder: "How many dinosaurs boarded Noah's Ark?"' Mrs Floyd was defeated by a margin of a few hundred votes in a state-wide election on 7 November 2006.

In the court case on the Dover school board and the statement to be read there was extensive evidence that school-board members intended to promote creationism (Humes 2007). Furthermore, at the trial it was shown that in the book *Of Pandas and People* 'intelligent design' had been substituted for 'creationism' after earlier court decisions had ruled out teaching of creationism in public schools. In this context, the judge took 'intelligent design' to refer to a particular religious position.

Back to the general issue of this section, when to admit on the podium views that aspire to be treated as scientific in nature though they aren't in line with the scientific consensus. Can ID be compared to scientific theories that at one point were marginal, but in the long run came to be accepted? A positive answer to this question would not suffice in a plea for inclusion of ID in the curriculum at the level of secondary schools; there was no reason to teach drifting continents before a modified form of this idea was accepted by the scientific community. But if we concentrate for the time being on the scientific standing of ID and pleas for more opportunities in the scientific sphere, the analogy between ID and scientific ideas that once were marginal might provide some insight.

To evaluate the analogy of ID with theories once marginal, Matthew J. Brauer, Barbara Forrest and Steven G. Gey have analyzed some controversies. They consider as a scientific theory 'endosymbiosis', the idea advocated first by Lynn Margulis that mitochondria and other organelles in eukaryotic cells have not evolved within the cell, but rather go back to independent cells that have been incorporated into the eukaryotic cell. This theory does not fit the earlier neo-Darwinian model of shifting frequencies in the gene pool. The idea was rejected for many years. 'However, initial scepticism was overcome by several strongly suggestive observations. (…) In the light of such evidence, all of her former critics have been won over. Her hypothesis was not a vague statement of the inadequacy of current evolutionary science to explain certain patterns (though this would in some sense have been true). Rather, it was a robust statement, entailing a definite outcome, that could be and was tested' (Brauer *et al.* 2005: 78).

The idea that AIDS is caused by a virus, HIV, has also been controversial, but this debate had a quite different development. Peter Duesberg published a paper in 1987 that considered HIV a benign 'passenger virus'. At that point this was still an option, but soon after the evidence for a causal link between HIV and AIDS had become convincing to almost all in the scientific community. By 1988 the controversy had escaped the boundaries of the scientific community and Duesberg was using the popular press to attack his research colleagues as part of the 'AIDS establishment'. Duesberg and others who challenged the understanding of HIV were not successful among their scientific colleagues, but had a substantial public podium. 'Duesberg's HIV scepticism has not been a significant *scientific* controversy', and his ideas 'are clearly not significant enough to be part of a biology course' (Brauer *et al.* 2005: 79–80).

The authors compare the impact of these two controversies to the impact of the ID literature, concentrating on one of the most well-known scientists pleading for intelligent design, Michael Behe. If one checks whether colleagues engage in substantial discussion, and thus refer to the work, remarkable differences in citations may be found. Margulis's work was referred to quite often, well before it was accepted; Duesberg's far less. Behe's work on apparently irreducible structures was referred to even less than Duesberg's. Besides, Behe is cited mainly 'in the context of the philosophical and cultural controversy' (Brauer *et al.* 2005: 81). Searching for typical ID-specific terms such as 'irreducible complexity' unearthed only a few publications in the scientific literature.

Such differences in the reception by the scientific community do not show that the ID position is wrong. What they do indicate, however, is that there is currently no genuine scientific controversy over ID, but rather a cultural and political one. The non-scientific nature of the controversy undermines significantly the legal demand for attention in science curricula.

Rather than aligning themselves with Duesberg (though there are some direct links) pleas for 'teaching the controversy' have referred to controversies on global warming, stem cell research and cloning (Brauer *et al.* 2005: 79; Philip E. Johnson and Jonathan C. Wells of the Discovery Institute have supported the AIDS reappraisal movement; see www.virusmyth.net, s.v. 'The Group', accessed 3 March 3 2009). However, the controversies over cloning and the use of stem cells have a moral and political rather than a scientific nature. 'Global warming' seems closer to the mark, but there too dissident views over global warming are to a large extent driven by dissident policy views. This is hardly a scientific controversy, though there are uncertainties in modelling and measuring changes which allow policy makers to play down the unwelcome message (Petersen 2006).

'Teach the controversy in science classes' is the demand, if spelled out in more detail, but what if the controversy is not a scientific one but rather a cultural, political or religious one? And if one wants to be generous and consider ID immature science, why then give it a podium in secondary schools?

Academic freedom, freedom of speech and freedom of religion are important, but they do not require that a podium of such a kind is provided. As long as the professional community in biology does not consider it a scientifically interesting theory, it seems inappropriate for outsiders to treat it as one. If we seek to be serious and credible in reflecting on religion in relation to scientific knowledge, inventing alternative sciences seems not a promising strategy.

No graven images: against the adoration of simple solutions

In 'religion and science' some authors construct their own images of how things hang together. How seriously should these be taken? The message of this commandment is: seriously, but not too seriously, because a particular proposal may do some things well at the expense of other aspects not considered. Avoiding ambiguity or indeterminacy of expressions is desirable, but resolving ambiguities by throwing out nuances and meanings is not helpful in exploring reality.

One-track papers assume homogeneity or transparency, taking the meanings of central terms or the character of science or of religion to be clear and uni-vocal, whereas in reality multiple meanings are present. In this context, one might pay special attention to simple words such as 'the'. The use of the defi-nite article suggests that there is a singular and definite issue, e.g. 'the believer', whereas in fact there are many believers, who do not only believe different things but also differ on what believing is.

2. You shall not bow to a model or system as if it has caught univocally all aspects of reality, nor shall you abuse the current limitations of models as gaps for God.

Do not use the name in vain: against easy consonance

Science-and-religion discussions run the risk of using God's name in vain. This may have to do with knowledge and language. Sometimes arguments are pur-sued without restraint, as if we have knowledge of the unknowable. We should be alert to where and when to bring our arguments to a close. There is also the risk that we use our language as if it were fully transparent. The need for interpretation when appropriating texts from a few thousand years ago is not always taken into account, for instance in claiming that there are parallels between the creation story of Genesis 1 and the Big Bang theory. Not only the temporal distance between us and the text, but also considerations of genre should give us reason to tread carefully rather than rush in: Is Genesis 1 explanatory narrative, historical description or expressive poetry?

The subject of 'religion and science' can also be chosen too narrowly, as if 'religion and science' is only about 'creation'. More careful consideration shows that every aspect of theology is at stake. How to think about God when there is no heaven 'up there'? How to think of divine action in the light of the lawfulness of natural processes? How to think about death in the light of evolution? How about sin if altruism and deception developed out of enlightened self-interest? What about the significance of Jesus of Nazareth in a universe which may well have planets with other sentient beings?

When it comes to unwarranted pretensions there is one theological issue which troubles me most. The ambition of many in 'theology and science' is to show coherence or consonance between scientific and theological ideas, to dis-cern how our world fits into a cosmic order. Sometimes this takes the form of natural theology, arguments from natural reality as to the plausibility of a Divine design. Sometimes this takes the form of a theology of nature, an attempt to think about natural reality in the context of religious convictions. Whatever the conception of theology, as long as the aim is to show harmony between religious and scientific insights the emphasis seems to me one-sided if not even misguided. Religion is not only a reflection of positive experiences but also a protest against experiences of injustice or human disorder. Science and religion have different relations to reality; the one describes and explains, whereas the other looks primarily for transformation towards justice and perfection.

This is a modern version of the problem that led Marcion to the first major heresy in the history of Christianity. Marcion did not see how the Creator of this ambivalent world could be the loving Father of Jesus Christ. He came to believe that they were two different gods: the Creator with a sense of justice that was fairness ('an eye for an eye') was not the same as the God of forgiveness, of loving beyond what is deserved.

This challenge is still with us in contrasts such as between facts and values, between reality as it is and as it should be. The issue is not the origin and explanation of evil, but its acceptance. Mixed feelings about the world have emerged quite explicitly in the modern period. The French philosopher Voltaire gave his poem on the Lisbon earthquake of 1755, 'Poème sur le désastre de Lisbonne' (1756), the subtitle 'or an examination of the axiom "All is well"'. Another illustration can be taken from Dostoyevsky's *The Brothers Karamazov* (Book 5, Chapter 4). One of the brothers, Ivan, argues that the suffering in this world is not justified by heavenly meaning. 'And if the suffering of children is required to make up the total suffering necessary to attain the truth, then I say here and now that no truth is worth such a price. And above all, I don't want the mother to embrace the torturer whose dogs tore her son apart! She has no right to forgive him!' Even the promise of heaven up there does not really solve the problem. It is especially this – broadly indicated – issue of the tragic and evil aspects of reality that should make everyone hesitant about too close an integration of scientific and theological ideas.

Any theological proposal which speaks only of consonance or harmony between religious beliefs and scientific insights is fundamentally incomplete. Any interesting theological reflection should pay attention to dissonance, to the evil and tragic aspects in lives. Morally, the religious quest cannot be only a quest for ultimate understanding, completed when we know 'the mind of God', but should also be a quest for change, if not redemption.

This desire creates a great difficulty in assessing quality. Intellectually one might equate quality with seeking as much harmony with the scientific description of our world as possible, whereas morally and spiritually there ought to be a clear sense of disharmony. Of the Ten Commandments this is captured well in the third one, about not using the name of God in vain, for it seems to me to be in vain if God is invoked as an ultimate explanation, if knowledge of the unknowable is claimed or the eyes are closed to dissonance.

3. You shall not take the name of the Lord God in vain, since human limitations and the tragic aspects of reality preclude any easy consonance of science and faith.

Observe the Sabbath day and other religious practices

Scholars involved in reflection on science and theology often treat science and religion as partners in a cognitive enterprise that seeks to understand the world. However, religious practices and beliefs are phenomena in the world and thus also objects of scientific study. The study of human religions is primarily the business of anthropologists, sociologists, linguists and historians though there have been ventures from sociobiology into the study of religion as well.

In their studies, religions are by and large understood as functional phenomena in social contexts. Rituals allocate to individuals various roles and enhance the sense of community. Such a functional understanding of religions makes me hesitate about studies in 'religion and science' which focus exclusively on ideas, as if the ideas can be abstracted from the ways they function. There is a legitimate place for metaphysical speculation, e.g. about the nature of time and the ground of existence, but such metaphysical reflections only become *religiously* relevant when integrated into a web of beliefs and practices which shapes human lives. Thus, in the study of religions we should keep the following commandment:

4. Observe the Sabbath day and other religious practices, for they are as essential as the more metaphysical aspects of religions.

Honour your father and your mother

Engagement in historical studies clearly befits the fifth commandment, to honour one's parents. The study of the history of science and religion is valuable, in my opinion, but not so much as an ally for any particular position, whether the idea that there have been conflicts again and again or the idea that religion provided the matrix in which science could develop. Rather historical studies show how complex the interactions have been, and how far from obvious may be distinctions which we do not bother to think about. As John H. Brooke (1991: 4f) wrote,

> it is almost always assumed that there are lessons to be learned from history. The object of this book is not to deny that assumption but to show that the lessons are far from simple. (...) The real lesson turns out to be the complexity.

Contemporary historians have made clear that counter-examples to any stereotype can always be found. Streamlining the historical account of science in its relation to religion is a temptation which should be avoided. Furthermore, historians have made clear that our current distinctions between 'science' and 'religion' are not useful when seeking to understand authors such as Newton who did not live by such modern distinctions. History includes many shifts in meaning of the terms 'science' and 'religion', and of the boundaries between the domains thus referred to. Taking science and religion as clearly defined entities involves the danger of neglecting the variety of activities covered by these terms and isolating both religion and science from their cultural and social context. As the concepts 'science' and 'religion' are subject to change, the scholars Lindberg and Numbers (1986: 354) conclude that

> we must not ask 'Who was the aggressor?' but 'How were Christianity and science affected by their encounter?'

Not only do meanings change over time, but they are also diverse and used eclectically at any moment, since the style and strategy pursued by an individual often reflect rhetorical needs of the moment in relation to the audience.

From the historians studying such interactions we can learn that positions of various contemporary authors may be understood better when attention is given to their understanding of religion and of science and to the audiences to which they are addressing themselves. This would be a contextual and non-religionist approach, which avoids simple conflict-interpretations as well as apologetic attempts to claim support from the history of science for traditional beliefs.

Though a thorough historical tour is fascinating, studies of particular historical cases cannot be transposed to our time since each episode is embedded in its own wider context. This is especially true of studies which focus on a few heroic individuals, for instance on the faith of a major scientist. We should explore the avenues that are open to us in an intellectually honest way, given the resources of our own time. Hence we have to move on from historical studies to reflections on contemporary science. A 'flight to history' is inadequate. Thus history, but with respect of differences:

5.   Honour your father and your mother, but treat them as history.

You shall not kill

Scholars, editors, teachers and students shouldn't kill, nor be killed. We have to accept those from whom we differ. But neither should everything pass; critical consideration of ideas, arguments and data is an intellectual and moral responsibility. Luckily we can shoot down ideas without shooting down people. We can discuss ideas critically while respecting those who express them.

The merciful editor might do more than shoot down ideas. He or she could also take time to care for a paper and a person, and to see whether the engagement that lies behind the paper can find more fruitful articulation. Even if a student or colleague is not articulating a position with which one sympathizes, one still may engage in critical reflection and attempt to see the other's position from that perspective, seeing whether the presentation and defence of the ideas involved can be improved. Whether ideas are improved or abandoned,

6. You shall not kill people but ideas.

Do not commit adultery

More respectful than inventing one's own science (see above, 1) but still very problematic is selective use of science, of those theories that fit one's own programme, without paying fair attention to insights that appear to be more challenging.

Let me give an example from an exchange at a conference some years ago. The theologian Wolfhart Pannenberg had discussed life in relation to insights into non-linear thermodynamics followed by a cultural understanding of humanity, with no serious attention given to intermediate biological layers, what might be referred to as sociobiology, evolutionary psychology or the behavioural/genetic paradigm. The geneticist and theologian Lindon Eaves was offended and asked about Pannenberg's anthropology: 'Does it address scientific anthropology where it "hurts" most or is it merely an eclectic aggregation of those anthropological ideas which are most convenient for theology?' (Eaves 1997b: 341; see also 1997a: 327). Selective and eclectic use of science might make the task of a theologian easier, but at the expense of credibility. A better alternative would be to engage science where it 'hurts most'; to engage in reverse eclecticism (see above and Drees 1990: 186f). The basis for such resistance against a selective use of science is the coherence of the sciences.

Science does not consist merely of isolated theories of which some can be accepted and others disregarded, according to one's own preferences. Disciplines have integrity by themselves, but they are also connected in multiple ways. In the nineteenth century, physics and biology were at odds – biologists spoke of hundreds of millions if not billions of years of evolution whereas physicists gave a mere twenty million years as the best estimate for the age of the Solar System. With the discovery of nuclear fusion as a source of energy the coherence between biology and physics was restored. In the long run coherence between the various sciences has proved to be a very reliable guide.

This coherence of the sciences, even more than any particular statistical proof, makes scientists extremely sceptical of astrology and homeopathy as purported knowledge which stands apart from well-established science. Astrology does not fit with our understanding of the way forces at astronomical distances work. And homeopathy is at odds with the basics of chemistry. There may well be wisdom in folk medicine but to accept the efficacy of dilutions which reduce concentrations to less than a single molecule per portion is not a minor addition to the whole of knowledge but rather would throw out the basics of chemistry and physics.

One cannot choose only bits and pieces of scientific insights into our world. It is just as in a personal relationship such as marriage: one has to engage with the whole person, warts and all – which may be more demanding than dealing only with the easy pieces but will be more rewarding in the long run. In this light, the seventh of the Ten Commandments is very appropriate.

7. Neither shall you commit adultery by selectively using those aspects of science that accord to your preferences, but rather engage science where it hurts most.

For it is like adultery to walk away from the challenge of a deep relationship with the whole enterprise when one goes for more partial, eclectic and hence superficial relationships.

Neither shall you steal

There are virtues that are typical of academic writing in general. One is the quest for conceptual clarity. Papers which use their central terms in a vague and ambiguous way often fail to make a case for anything. However, demanding definitions can also be demanding too much too early; it is impossible to define all terms in a discussion and still get started. As J. L. Mackie (1967: 178) wrote, 'a demand for definition can be a sophistic device for preventing the discussion of substantive issues'. Concepts come into sharper focus when one discusses their adequacy or truth, or their implications. This is certainly the case when it comes to theological terms such as 'God'. An initial definition may be useful, but ideas about the meaning of 'God' should be open to development in the course of subsequent arguments.

Conceptual clarity may be bound to a domain. When one comes across words such as energy and complementarity in a religious context, or grace and sin in a treatise on 'religion and science', there is a question as to whether these words have the same meaning in the hybrid exercise as they had in their domain of origin. A shift from one domain to another involves continuities and discontinuities in meaning.

A second aspect of academic writing is the use of sound arguments. Arguments come in several varieties, from the verbal and imaginative to the formal. Especially tricky is the reliance on analogies and metaphors. Stories and thought experiments are risky as they may well involve hidden assumptions about the nature of the world. In science the basic hidden assumption is that the world of the thought experiment is like our world (*ceteris paribus*) except for the specific elements modified in the thought experiment. However, in philosophy and even more in theological reflection such hidden assumptions may be far less clear, while nonetheless doing most of the work. This point is very well made by K. V. Wilkes in the first chapter of *Real People: Personal Identity without Thought Experiments* (1988). As another example, stories supporting arguments about the 'anthropic' character of our universe deserve very careful reading. This has been done well for Leslie's 'Doomsday argument' by Dennis Dieks (1992), in a paper missing from Leslie's bibliography in his *The End of the World* (1996).

One would also hope that well-known fallacies are avoided. One of them is the genetic fallacy, assuming that the truth of a belief follows from its origin. Another is the naturalistic fallacy, moving unwarrantedly from 'is' statements to 'ought' statements. Quite often one also finds the fallacies of division and of composition, assuming that what is said of the whole can be said of each individual, and vice versa. For instance, since a house is made of stones and stones do not provide shelter, a house cannot provide shelter. If humans were only made of atoms and atoms don't think, humans would not be able to think – and hence there must be something else. We also suffer in our business from a fallacy of misplaced concreteness, assuming that where there is a word there must be an entity to which the term applies, rather than, for instance, a relation or a property.

Last but not least in this category, clarity about sources is an obvious thing to require. It allows others the opportunity to scrutinize the point of departure. An argument will not be better than warranted by the material put into it. Fair attribution and fair descriptions of ideas and positions of others, quoting them fairly, is an intellectual, moral and spiritual obligation. Alas, some observers have found that 'for the creationists, misleading quotation has become a way of life' (Kitcher 1982: 181). Anyhow, 'religion and science' should aspire to exemplify academic virtues.

8. Neither shall you steal ideas, confuse concepts or present fallacious arguments.

Do not bear false witness against your neighbour

In academic courses on 'religion and science' the philosophy of science text that is most often required reading is Thomas Kuhn's *The Structure of Scientific Revolutions*, according to a statistic compiled by CTNS (Berkeley) on the basis of courses that won prizes in a Templeton Foundation programme supporting such courses. Kuhn's book is very significant, but its popularity in the context of science-and-spirituality might be cause for concern as it has become an icon for a social view of science. This alleged message of Kuhn's book has attracted authors on 'religion and science' who were keen to suggest that since science is more subjective and tied to 'paradigms' than previously thought, the social and subjective aspects of religion should be no reason for concern either.

My concern is that genuine reflections on the nature and history of science are abused in such a *tu quoque* argument, suggesting that a loss of credibility for science would be a gain for theology. I consider this a mistake for various reasons.

Such arguments too often use, or rather interpret, the conclusions without paying sufficient attention to the careful analysis that grandmasters in philosophy and history of science such as Thomas Kuhn have offered (see Horwich 1992). This is like summarizing evolutionary biology, quantum physics or the history of religion-and-science interactions in a few slogans. The polemics then focus on the grand scheme as summarized in this way, whereas the power of these research programmes is in the rich details.

Through the research of Kuhn and others, certain legends about science have rightly been exposed as illusions, but that does not mean that there cannot be a more nuanced view of science as a social enterprise which delivers genuine knowledge in a cumulative way. As Philip Kitcher says in *The Advancement of Science* (1993: 390), which in my opinion offers just such a more nuanced view:

> Flawed people, working in complex environments, moved by all kinds of interests, have collectively achieved a vision of parts of nature that is broadly progressive and that rests on arguments meeting standards that have been refined and improved over centuries. Legend does not require burial but metamorphosis.

There is also a moral concern regarding downplaying science. It is morally preferable to use one's knowledge rather than to wilfully close one's eyes. Some authors in 'religion and science' seek to play down the epistemic significance of science, arguing that it is as much about dogmatic frameworks and prejudices as is religion (as if such a *tu quoque* argument would help religion).

In one (in my opinion horrific) example, Canadian authors treated the theory that HIV was the cause of AIDS as just a theory that fitted the interests of the pharmaceutical industry and served discrimination (Stahl *et al.* 2002: 110). In their rejection of consolidated science, the authors were explicitly voicing support for the South African leader Thabo Mbeki, who by his denial of the viral background of AIDS deprived millions of effective treatment.

There is a major moral risk in playing down established science. This is related to 'the ethics of belief', though the demands articulated by William K. Clifford in his original contribution (1879) were unrealistic. Playing down established science, even if for morally lofty purposes, may have immoral consequences. Working with the best knowledge available, rather than playing down such knowledge, may well be morally required.

Downplaying the cognitive claims of science makes life for religious believers too easy. It suggests that one need not pay attention to the challenges posed by scientific insights regarding reality and human nature. To say it once more with one of the Ten Commandments:

9. Neither shall you bear false witness against the credibility of science so as to keep substantial insights or challenges at bay.

Do not covet anything that is your neighbour's

Religious utterances can be seen as cognitive propositions ('God exists'), as expressions of emotions and attitudes ('He is my brother' – I will treat him thus) and as stories and rituals shaping a culture. Thus, aside from the cognitive dimension there are moral and aesthetic aspects to religions (Lindbeck 1984; Drees 1996: 24–49). 'Religion and science' tends to concentrate on the understanding of religious discourse as claims about reality. However, those other aspects of religion have to be taken into account as well. Science is not irrelevant to those aspects. For example, neuroscience and evolutionary biology touch upon human emotions and human culture.

Reflection on the diversity of aspects of religion is not merely relevant for understanding organized religion; it is also necessary for understanding 'spirituality' in our culture. Sometimes spirituality is associated with a particular set of metaphysical beliefs, say about the presence of a spiritual dimension independent from material reality, whereas spirituality may also be understood as referring to a certain way of life. The self-understanding of Christianity in mainstream Protestant thought in Europe seems to be swinging back from a life-oriented approach which was more prominent in exegesis and systematic theology in the period after World War II to an emphasis on tradition, on angels and other forms of supernaturalism which becomes indistinguishable from magical thinking.

An ahistorical discussion of particular religious views, say on divine action or on time and eternity, may be an interesting exercise in religion and metaphysics. However, a more complete account of 'religion and science' needs to take into account the social dimensions of religion as well, and with those dimensions the social context in which religious ideas have their origins and functions. We cannot assume a culture-free culture and generalize as if our Western intellectual and social arrangement is global and timeless, with universal concerns and questions.

Science, mathematics and ethics too have their social histories, but the way this affects their credibility may well be different as these various human practices are developed by humans in different ways. Thus it is not sufficient to claim credibility for the cognitive and metaphysical claims of the religious enterprise by analogy with the cognitive credibility of the scientific enterprise. Rather the case has to be made separately for each enterprise, such as science, ethics and religion. This was already explicit in the tenth commandment, which can be rephrased as follows:

10. Neither shall you claim your neighbour's credibility, or that of his laboratories, his fieldwork, his calculations, his instruments or anything that is your neighbour's.

Respecting science and respecting differences

It is not irrelevant what views we will defend. Quality is important. In this chapter we have considered some aspects of the quest for quality in religious reflections on science. Basically, the criteria proposed here are about respecting science and about respecting differences between science and other important human endeavours, thus appreciating the best available insights in various domains, without claiming that epistemic support transfers easily from one domain to another one.

1. You shall have no other sciences before me.
2. You shall not bow to a model or system as if it has caught univocally all aspects of reality, nor shall you abuse the current limitations of models as gaps for God.
3. You shall not take the name of the Lord God in vain, since human limitations and the tragic aspects of reality preclude any easy consonance of science and faith.
4. Observe the Sabbath day and other religious practices, for they are as essential as the more metaphysical aspects of religions.
5. Honour your father and your mother, but treat them as history.
6. You shall not kill people but ideas.
7. Neither shall you commit adultery by selectively using those aspects of science that accord to your preferences, but rather engage science where it hurts most.
8. Neither shall you steal ideas, confuse concepts or present fallacious arguments.
9. Neither shall you bear false witness against the credibility of science so as to keep substantial insights or challenges at bay.
10. Neither shall you claim your neighbour's credibility, or that of his laboratories, his fieldwork, his calculations, his instruments or anything that is your neighbour's.

Chapter 4

Hunting a Snark?

Religion in 'religion and science'

'The seven world religions' were displayed prominently on the cover of the popular magazine *Le Point* in France on 21 July 2005. The issue had contributions on Hinduism, Buddhism, Judaism and Islam, and on Roman Catholicism, Protestantism and Eastern Orthodox Christianity. What many consider differences *within* Christianity the editors took to be of such importance as to make these into three separate religions. Classifications are interesting.

Not only are there multiple religions; there are also multiple aspects of religion. Is religion about belief in God's existence, or should a particular attitude of trust be considered primary? Or is it about communal practices, such as rituals and rules on food, marriage and much more? Must there be holy books and priests? Is it a matter of church attendance and group identity or rather 'the feelings, acts, and experiences of individual men in their solitude, so far as they apprehend themselves to stand in relation to whatever they may consider the divine', as William James wrote in his *Varieties of Religious Experience* (1902: 31f)? Defining religion is notoriously difficult, if not impossible (De Vries 2008; McCutcheon 2007; Platvoet and Molendijk 1999; Smith 1998; for a history of the category 'religion' see Harrison 1990).

Despite the difficulties, it might be useful to have some idea of what 'religion' in 'religion and science' might mean. Otherwise, one might end up with a situation not unlike the one described by Lewis Carroll in 'The Hunting of the Snark' (1939: 767):

> 'The rest of my speech' (he explained to his men)
> 'You shall hear when I've leisure to speak it.
> But the Snark is at hand, let me tell you again!
> 'Tis our glorious duty to seek it
>
> To seek it with thimbles, to seek it with care;
> To pursue it with forks and with hope;
> To threaten its life with a railway-share;
>
> To charm it with smiles and soap!
> For the Snark's a peculiar creature, that won't

Be caught in a commonplace way.
Do all that you know, and try all that you don't:
Not a chance must be wasted to-day!'

The hunting party is frantically searching, without success. Perhaps the Snark is difficult to catch; they may not have the right weapons. Perhaps the beast doesn't exist. Or is the problem in our words? The hunters do not agree among themselves as to what they are after. A sobering thought, when considering the continuing quest for God.

This chapter considers the meanings of religion and theology, in an attempt to clarify to some extent the aims and structure of 'religion and science'. The *multiple meanings of religion* are the topic of the first section. Given that there are multiple meanings, it is a matter of religious and social importance to have the authority to define what genuine religion is – and thus it is relevant to ask *who is to define what religion is?* – a question that will be addressed in the second section. One recurrent issue is also whether one needs to be religious to understand religion. Are atheistic critics of religion misguided, because they cannot know what they are talking about? We'll consider the *insider-outsider problem* in the context of religion and science in the third section.

Within 'religion and science', beliefs and theologies are of particular interest. In the fourth section I will offer *a proposal for understanding integrated religious and non-religious views*, what one might also call 'theologies', by offering a scheme that relates them to metaphysical and to moral ideas; this scheme seeks to clarify various possible roles of the sciences relative to such theological proposals. Those roles of science will be the subject of the three subsequent chapters.

What might 'religion' be?

There are a multitude of religions in this world, just as there are many languages, cultures and subcultures. Furthermore, there are manifold practices and beliefs that are more or less religious. Bookshops have major sections on mind and spirit; we have seen the popularity of *The Celestine Prophecies* and *A Course in Miracles*, and there will be new contenders again and again. TV had *The X-Files* and *Charmed* mixing the supernatural with science fiction and magic. Magazines need an astrology column to sell. In addition to mainstream healthcare we find a wide variety of healers and therapists, many of whom have a religious or 'spiritual' approach on our wellbeing. The distinction between what is genuine faith or spirituality and what is superstition is not a scholarly distinction but a partisan one. Before becoming involved in such judgements, scholars of religion (and I assume that one who reflects on religion and science thereby to some extent aspires to be scholarly about religion) should seek to understand the nature of the bewildering variety of religious beliefs and practices.

Each religion and each understanding of religion has its own discussions on 'religion and science'. Some religions have a strong emphasis on God as the

Supreme Being who takes an active interest in processes in this world, whereas other traditions such as Buddhism may do without such a concept. Some understandings of religion give prominence to extraordinary experiences, whereas others may locate the religious dimension in ordinary life with its moral choices, existential burdens and ritual practices. Whereas evolution/ creation is a major issue for some Christians, it is not so for Buddhists, for whom the understanding of mind and perception is more significant. For someone whose Christianity is primarily moral, inspired by the Sermon on the Mount, the atheist who rejects miracles is tilting at windmills; he is not an opponent but besides the point. There is no essence or single archetype of 'religion', no univocal definition; there are a variety of religions and there is variety within each religion.

Multiple modalities of religion

The discussion is not only shaped by the particular religion one has in mind, but also by the particular aspects of religion considered. Many classifications are possible. Eric Sharpe distinguished between four functional modalities of religion, not so much as phenomena (like ritual and myth) but rather as emphases (within religion) and hence as categories of analysis when considering religious life. Sharpe (1983: 95) gives the following summary:

(1) Existential: *Faith* in the sense of *fiducia*, 'trust'
(2) Intellectual: *Beliefs* in the sense of those statements to which one gives conscious assent (*assensus*)
(3) Institutional: *Organisations* within which (1) and (2) are held and maintained, and by which they are transmitted.
(4) Ethical: *Conduct* vis-à-vis the members of (3) and others.

The *existential mode* is the most individualistic one. At the heart of such belief is acceptance of a transcendent order, a sense of dependence upon that order and an attitude of trust. A Dutch songwriter, André Hazes, had in one of his popular songs the line 'She believes in me.' 'Belief' in such a love song does not refer to knowledge: she believes that I exist. My existence is assumed, but the important meaning of 'she believes in me' is relational and fiduciary: she has confidence in me, in my behaviour and in my future with her. Using religious terms one might say that the Devil believes that God exists, but the Devil does not trust God or commit himself to God. The Devil is not a believer in the existential sense of believing. Well, maybe the Devil is afraid of God – and in that sense there is engagement. Existential belief need not be accompanied by positive emotions alone; fear and trembling could be involved in the relationship as well.

If personal experience is of major importance, as it is with this emphasis in religion, doctrinal articulation may well be deemed secondary. Mystics across traditions may recognize each other, and contemporary spiritual seekers often engage in extensive bricolage, drawing on many sources and traditions. There can also be orientation based on the experience of certain inspiring leaders; in such cases believers have become followers. In the 'religion and science' field, some of the interest in this area has recently taken the form of work concerning research on human experience, and especially on the functioning of the brain. This is also a focal point in research on Buddhism and altered states of consciousness.

In the *intellectual* mode, convictions or beliefs would be more significant aspects of religion than experiences. Belief involves ideas about God or the gods, the Absolute, ultimate Nothingness and ideas about the human condition with its sins and delusions. Here we enter the area of doctrinal disputes, in which the one who disagrees might be deemed a heretic, a term that would not be applicable if the experiential aspect was central. The emphasis on the cognitive content of religious beliefs is especially prominent in an apologetic context (communicating with outsiders), during internal disputes and in teaching the next generation (catechism). In the field of 'religion and science' this mode most often takes centre stage, in discussions on creation and evolution, in arguments for the existence of God, in reflections upon human nature, and so on. Though the other modes are as important when studying religions, we will return to this aspect of religion, beliefs, whether metaphysical or moral in kind, when we come to speak of 'theologies' below.

The *institutional mode* emphasizes religious organizations into which one is born, such as the state, tribe, caste or family, and organizations to which one belongs by choice. Emphasis on individual choice is relatively recent, and predominantly European and American. Even there, someone might self-describe as Catholic 'by birth', thus indicating that that is part of their heritage and identity, without necessarily believing Roman Catholic doctrine. Religious communities are significant as communities, as forms of extended family, as social support in times of need. In this light, secularization in Europe may well be driven more by the loss of social function of religious communities, as the state took on responsibility for social welfare, than by loss of intellectual belief. In socially challenging environments religious communities tend to be more prominent, as witnessed by the role of churches formed by migrants. The social sciences have a professional interest in this institutional dimension. In relation to the natural sciences, this institutional mode is less prominent. An exception is the sociobiological study of David S. Wilson, *Darwin's Cathedral* (2002).

In the *ethical* mode, duties and moral obligations are primary. This gives structure to the relations between leaders and people, between men and women, between generations and between insiders and outsiders. Often much more is allowed relative to outsiders than within the group. Religion has often served to create and consolidate social order by ascribing authority to religious and secular leaders ('God save the Queen'). It also strengthens social roles, e.g.

in marriage rituals and other rites of passage, such as those of a soldier who commits himself or a monk who vows celibacy, poverty and obedience. In 'religion and science', this side has received some attention, e.g. in studies regarding the biological and cultural basis of morality, especially the possibility or impossibility of altruism and self-sacrifice.

Deciding which of these modes has priority is a chicken and egg problem; the different modes evoke each other. The distinctions may serve to clarify, but they need not be taken as absolute distinctions. Perhaps various modes developed separately, each for good reasons, while their integration gave rise to the modern sense of religion (Söling 2002). The main role of the map here is to alert us to the fact that religion has multiple facets, and that a full consideration of religion in the light of the sciences should be fair to all these dimensions.

We tend to think that doctrine is more important than myth, and that myth gave rise to practice. However, as early as 1889 William Robertson Smith warned in his *Lectures on the Religion of the Semites* that it might well be the other way round (Segal 1998). Think of the following analogy. When putting their children to bed, parents have come to tell a narrative explaining why the seal is to the right of the bear and why the little rabbit is blue. Did the story precede the practice? It may well have been that there was this daily moment of intimacy, with the stuffed animals that had come to the child more or less haphazardly, and the mythic narrative encapsulates this moment but is not itself its core, and certainly not its origin. In thinking about religions, we tend to look for a creed and for sacred books, as did those who collected *The Sacred Books of the East* in the nineteenth century, but that assumes that there is a common intellectual and institutional structure to various religions – a creed, a sacred book, priests, and so on. This may well be a mistake made by scholars who themselves are too much shaped by Western examples, and by their academic bias towards the intellectual and literate.

In discussing religion in 'religion and science' we need to be alert not only to the diversity of religions, as large-scale traditions, and to the diversity within traditions, but also to the variety of aspects involved. At any one moment, one may limit oneself to one facet, but then we should not be too surprised if a conversation partner misunderstands us at first, as they were thinking of something else and thus posing different questions and having other concerns. In the next section I continue this exploration of diversity with special atten- tion to the question 'who defines?', and hence for what purposes a particular understanding of religion is advocated.

Who defines?

Who is to say what religion is? That is, who defines what is to be considered as fitting the concept 'religion'? And, furthermore, who is to decide what *genuine* faith is? Or more practically speaking: what purposes are served by using the concept in a particular way? These are the questions to which we will turn now. Is the question 'What is religion?' an academic one? Or is it one that is to be understood in its social context? One important example of this will be the understanding of 'religion' in public debates, where advocates of secularism and of 'strong religion' (Almond *et al.* 2003) serve each other well to the exclusion of moderate religious and secular voices. Both opposites understand theology primarily in terms of truth claims and the pious attitude as deference to the authority of the tradition and its scriptures, read in a more or less literalist way. Those reflecting on religion in relation to science often find themselves caught in the middle, seeking to articulate forms of religion that respect the tradition but give substantial weight to modern insights.

'What is religion?' as an academic question

Is the question 'What is religion?' an academic question? Is posing this question just like asking 'What is a black hole?' in astrophysics? If so, to answer the question is a job for those who study religions, or, more broadly, for those who study human societies. They would have to make proposals as to what distinctions best serve to clarify the phenomena.

The best definitions don't come at the beginning of research, but rather at the end of our exploring. They embody insights gathered so far. If one begins to distinguish mammals from fish by having mammals live on the land and fish in water, the whale is classified as a fish. After studying whales one may come to an improved understanding which finds expression in new definitions of fish and of mammals.

When we come to religion we already have a whole history of research, both theological and anthropological in kind. One anthropologist studying religion is Clifford Geertz. He observed that

> sacred symbols function to synthesize a people's ethos – the tone, character, and quality of their life, its moral and aesthetic style and mood – and their world view – the picture they have of the way things in sheer actuality are, their most comprehensive ideas of order.
>
> (Geertz 1966: 3; 1973: 89)

This insight regarding the role of symbols in synthesizing ethos and worldview brought him to an oft-quoted definition:

> a religion is (1) a system of symbols which acts to (2) establish powerful, pervasive, and long-lasting moods and motivations in men by (3) formulating conceptions of a general order of existence and (4) clothing these conceptions with such an aura of facticity that (5) the moods and motivations seem uniquely realistic.
>
> (Geertz 1966: 4; 1973: 90)

As a definition of the empirical phenomena of religiosity this is not perfect. There is too much emphasis on the cognitive role of symbols as contributing to conceptions of the order of existence, thus bypassing ritual, social and other non-cognitive roles of religious symbols. The definition can also be challenged as inadequate with respect to philosophical complexities of representation and truth (Frankenberry and Penner 1999). Besides, the definition suggests a causal arrow from symbols via conceptions to moods and motivations, whereas the symbols may also *express* moods and motivations rather than establish them. The observation about synthesizing ethos and worldview quoted above has less of this causal suggestion in it. Nonetheless, as a definition that involves the cognitive side of a religion, what could be called 'a theology' or 'a religious vision' (or non-religious equivalent), Geertz's definition highlights the observation that in religious thought conceptions of the order of existence are intertwined with the appreciation of reality and norms for our behaviour. To speak of the world as God's creation has both a descriptive and a prescriptive aspect to it. We will return to this in the final section of this chapter, when considering the nature of religious visions.

A definition to some extent has a *pragmatic* role. Physics is able to deal well with concepts such as energy and gravity, but the question 'What is energy?' makes physicists uneasy. Most of them would consider this a question that is not within their domain, or one that is not even properly posed. In his *Lectures on Physics*, Richard Feynman has a section titled 'What is energy?' He speaks of conservation of energy as the 'strange fact that we can calculate some number and when we finish watching nature go through her tricks and calculate the number again, it is the same'. And at the end of the section: 'It is important to realize that in physics today, we have no knowledge of what energy *is*' (Feynman *et al.* 1963: 4–1, 4–2). A metaphysical claim as to what energy is might be beyond our reach.

Furthermore, the boundaries of a concept may be vague, and sometimes necessarily so. If one is to develop a theory about the way multiple biological species may radiate from an earlier species, one needs a concept of species that allows for such a transition, where in the era of the transition it is not clear whether organisms belong to the earlier or to the later species. That the boundary is not sharp need not count against the usefulness of a concept, just as the gradual transition from day to night does not make the concepts 'day' and 'night' meaningless.

Even though definitions are never perfect, one needs a provisional grasp of the area to be explored and analyzed. In that context, one may prefer to begin with a few *examples* of what is considered religious, and suggest studying other phenomena sufficiently similar. However, this strategy of operating on the basis of a few examples has certain risks as well, as peculiarities of the exemplars chosen may skew the analysis.

In the history of the concept 'religion', Western Christianity has been the prominent model, and this has brought with it certain expectations. A 'Holy

Book' seemed characteristic of Christianity, and also of Islam and Judaism, as the alternatives best known to scholars of religions. When exploring Asia in the colonial period Max Müller and his colleagues thus collected various writings in the series *Sacred Books of the East* (nineteenth century), assuming that the canonical authority of holy books is central in each religion. Furthermore, as this was typical for Christianity, it was expected that a believer adheres to a single religion at most. However, this may not do justice to countries such as Japan where ritual practices from different religious traditions such as Buddhism and Shinto are often part of the life of a single individual operating in various social spheres.

The nature of rituals, religious officials, narratives, myths and hymns may be vastly different from one tradition to another. Whereas for a Protestant reading the Bible is central, and the intention is to understand the moral or intellectual meaning of the text, Muslims in Indonesia may recite the Qur'an in Arabic without even understanding the language; the recitation itself is religiously significant. If we begin with a single exemplary tradition, or at best a few, we may skew our understanding with assumptions adequate for the first example but not for other traditions.

'What is religion?' as an academic question engages us in a project that is open ended, always inviting further study, given the diversity of human practices and beliefs. But, as we will come to consider now, it is often not just an academic question.

'What is religion?' as a political question

Asking 'What is a human?' or 'When does life begin?' in a conversation about human embryos may seem a scientific question, but it is not. It is a political question. If the nature of the question 'What is religion?' is of such a kind, clarification and explanation is not the primary purpose. Rather, the purpose of the question may be to ascribe a certain status to the phenomenon thus classified. Or the purpose may be to dismiss certain challenges as irrelevant, as when Galileo stated that the Bible does not intend to teach us how the heavens go, but how to go to heaven. By offering a particular understanding of what genuine religion is, certain challenges can be dismissed as applying only to superstition but not to genuine religion. Such labelling is socially useful but academically problematic: academic definitions of superstition as distinct from genuine religion are hard to come by; the point of the label 'superstition' is dismissive.

That understandings of religion have political significance is typical of the debates over evolution. Though the dispute seems to be about science, the struggle is to a large extent about the nature of religion. Whether one sees evolution as a challenge or as irrelevant to faith reflects different understandings of the nature of faith, and this shows up in legal disputes. For instance, in 1981 the legislature of the State of Arkansas passed a law that described its purpose as 'to require *balanced treatment* of creation-science and evolution-science in public schools; to protect academic freedom by providing student choice; (...) to bar discrimination on the basis of creationist or evolutionist belief'. As I have already mentioned in Chapter 2, this law was challenged in court by parents and teachers, as well as by bishops of the United Methodist, Episcopal, Roman Catholic and African Methodist Episcopal Churches, the principal representative of the Presbyterian Churches in America, United Methodist, Southern Baptist and Presbyterian clergy and three types of Jewish organizations. Thus the case was not just one of 'science versus religion' but at least as much a case of 'religion versus religion'. The judge, William R. Overton, concurred as he deemed 'creation-science' a religious rather than a scientific position. Thus the law favoured one particular religious position over and against other religious views, which was against the separation of Church and State. Therefore he declared the law unconstitutional (Act 590; Overton [1982] 1988).

The offence that creationist or intelligent-design presentations give to mainstream believers is not just that they disagree on a particular detail of faith, but that the creationists claim to represent genuine faith, and thus claim to represent religion as it really should be, thereby relegating other believers to a secondary status if not dismissing them as almost atheists. And vice versa; adherents of mainline churches (to use this label for simplicity's sake) may well dismiss others as not grasping what religion is really about, and thus as clinging to the wrong issues.

One recurrent pattern in defining religion for tactical reasons can be found when we consider the understandings of religion in public conversations in secular democracies. In this setting, the extremes seem to provide a useful service to each other, by sharing the answer to the question 'What is religion?', even though advocating different policies. We will turn to this now.

'Religion' and secular politics

There are authors who prefer to exclude religion from public debate. They consider religion to be private and hence unable to provide generally acceptable premises. Religious expressions and arguments need to be reformulated in terms acceptable to all. It may even be inappropriate to refer to one's religious preferences, as religion serves as a 'conversation stopper', as the philosopher Richard Rorty (1994) called it. This is a position which Rorty (2003) later retracted, partly in response to criticisms by Nicholas Wolterstorff (1997) and Jeffrey Stout (2004).

In opposition to the secular exclusion of religion from the public sphere, some advocates of religious positions such as John Milbank, Stanley Hauerwas and Alisdair McIntyre have rejected secular liberalism, suggesting that secular views fall short in providing substantial values that are essential to a flourishing human society (Stout 2004). By objecting to the secular character of society, they agree with their opponents that religion and secular democracy are incompatible.

Is the definition of religion shared by secular voices and religious traditionalists, which results in an understanding of the situation as characterized by a choice between these two positions, adequate? Empirical results seem to suggest that the exclusion of the middle excludes a very major segment of the population from being heard in what they consider important. In the Netherlands, a poll (Drayer 2004) showed that adherents of the outspoken theistic and the outspoken secular position together formed just about one third of the people questioned (twenty per cent claimed to believe in a personal God; thirteen per cent defined themselves as atheists), whereas the largest groups said they believed in 'something' (⅓) or considered themselves agnostic (⅓). According to a more recent Dutch survey (Kronjee and Lampert 2006: 176), slightly over a quarter of the population can be considered, qua lifestyle, members of a church and another quarter as more or less humanist or atheist. Another quarter consider themselves religious or 'spiritual' without affiliation. It is especially members of this latter group, as well as quite a few of the religious humanists and of the mainstream church members, who are not well served by the strong definition of religion shared by religious traditionalists and advocates of secularism. Religious positions that are less explicit by the standards of traditional religion are present in substantial numbers in other European countries as well.

In response to theocratic and atheistic exclusionary ways of defining religion in relation to democracy, Stout (2004) argues that in the United States there is an 'Emersonian piety' alongside an 'Augustinian' one. 'Emersonian piety' refers to the poet Ralph Waldo Emerson, but his name is used by Stout as a label for a religious attitude; about a century earlier, William James (1902: 33) also spoke of 'Emersonian religion'. 'Emersonian piety' is not deference to higher powers, to theological truth as a given, or reverence for authority, but rather it is characterized by self-reliance, by taking responsibility for one's own thinking. This need not be self-reliance as if our achievements are ours in isolation from a tradition shaped by earlier generations. Rather we can be grateful to earlier generations and to the whole of nature, the sources of our existence, without moving from gratitude to passivity. Respecting previous generations does not take the form of fixation of their traditions; their lives and contributions are honoured by moving on from where they brought us, by engaging in further explorations (Stout 2004: 38).

Stout argues a systematic thesis, namely that the polarization between the secular exclusion of religious voices and the religious sentiment against secular culture rests upon a shared assumption regarding the nature of religion and the nature of secular culture. Whereas a highly absolutist, authoritarian understanding of religion makes it hard to incorporate religious voices in a democratic process (thus justifying the secular exclusion, as well as the fear that religious voices are excluded), a more tentative attitude in religious life is not at all in conflict with democracy, understood as a process of conversation, of exchange of reasons for one's values and concerns when challenged, rather than as the exclusion of all religious voices.

The empirical observations regarding the Dutch religious landscape and the systematic position defended by Stout suggest a similar conclusion. There are strong forms of religion and outspoken opinions on democracy and Enlightenment values that exclude each other, but these do so on the basis of a shared understanding of the concept of religion. Those who are moderate may be more comfortable with Stout's characterizations of religion and of democracy than with the more exclusionary ones. The controversy is to some extent a controversy over the meaning of 'genuine religion'.

By way of summary, I want to emphasize three theses. First, a choice as to what really counts as religion is a major component of controversies, in society and in 'religion and science' debates. Second, strong forms of secularism and strong forms of religion serve each other well to the exclusion of moderate religious and secular voices by sharing an understanding of religion in which theological truth claims and piety as deference to authority are important central characteristics. Third, such definitions are scholarly inadequate as they exclude various other options. Rather than serving academic analysis, their understanding of religion serves advocates of strong religion and advocates of strong secularism by focussing the debate on their own position and on their preferred opponent, to the exclusion of moderate alternatives.

Let me add one self-reflective worry. Above, I challenged advocates of the secularization thesis and adherents of strong religion who deplore secularization but agree with the others on the understanding of religion. But are such criticisms not serving particular interests as well? Indeed, the more moderate view is partisan as well. It serves church leaders who need a market and those believers who want their church to be a community open to all who earnestly seek, whether they seek God or their deepest self. And observations on the persistence of religion in multiple forms are also useful to scholars of religion, who thereby justify the continuing relevance of their academic disciplines in a way that would not be possible in the context of the polarized understanding of developments in terms of strong religion or secularization.

In the next section, we will consider the study of religion – and especially the question of whether one has to be religious to understand it. If that were the case, one could conclude that atheists do not just disagree with believers; they do not understand what it is to be a believer.

Insider-outsider problems in the study of religion

Can someone who is tone deaf understand music? In his study on *Das Heilige* (1917; trans. 1950: 8) Rudolf Otto wrote at the beginning of the third chapter:

The reader is invited to direct his mind to a moment of deeply-felt religious experience, as little as possible qualified by other forms of consciousness. Whoever cannot do this, whoever knows no such moments in
his experience, is requested to read no farther (...). We do not blame
such an one, when he tries for himself to advance as far as he can
with the help of such principles of explanation as he knows, interpreting
'aesthetics' in terms of sensuous pleasure, and 'religion' as a function of
the gregarious instinct and social standards, or as something more primitive still. But the artist, who for his part has an intimate personal knowledge of the distinctive element in the aesthetic experience, will decline his
theories with thanks, and the religious man will reject them even more
uncompromisingly.

According to Otto personal experience is necessary to gain access to the real
meaning of religion. Unlike Otto, I make no claim for the priority of the par-
ticipant over the observer, as if the one has real knowledge and the other
merely an incomplete and distorted understanding. However, I think it is
heuristically useful to pay attention to differences in their approaches. Speaking very generally, an *insider* participates in practices considered meaningful,
true or right. An *outsider* might concentrate on the discourses of insiders, on
the contexts and interests involved and consider the way these practices may
be useful to insiders. The insider might speak religiously of revealed knowledge with universal and timeless significance, whereas the outsider sees texts
that have been made by humans for humans in particular historical contexts
(McCutcheon 1999).

An insider has some problems that the outsider need not have. When considering implausible, immoral or horrible stories from the Bible, an outsider
might treat such passages as throwing light on what people once believed; they
do not imply any particular challenges to the outsider's own attitudes. A
believer for whom the Biblical text is normatively significant has a problem:
can one read those texts as relevant for us, and as appropriate to the story of
God, without endorsing their unwelcome aspects? This problem is as old as
religion; allegorical interpretation and other distinctions between the literal or
superficial meaning and the deeper meaning have been made again and again.

Similarly, though suffering may be an existential issue for all humans, the
question of how to acknowledge the reality of evil in combination with
belief in a good and almighty God is only a problem for a believer. Religious
discourse on God's reasons for allowing suffering might be interpreted by an
outsider in psychological terms, as involving cognitive dissonance (McCutcheon
2007: 54–56).

From an external perspective it may be argued that belief in the truth of
religion plays an important functional role. In the definition by Clifford Geertz
quoted earlier in this chapter one element is that a worldview is clothed 'with
such an aura of facticity that the moods and motivations seem uniquely

realistic'. The beliefs need not be true, but they need to be believed as truth. Geertz's definition is typically an outsider's definition which depicts religious symbols as useful (moods and motivations). However, his 'aura of facticity' implies that for the believer cognitive aspects are involved.

Insider-outsider problems are not exclusive to the study of religion. The human sciences have to face them all the time: humans speak of their ideas, ideals and feelings where the psychologist or sociologist might see interests and group pressure. And there are the neurologists and other physiologically minded observers who speak of brain processes and hormones when a subject claims to be in love, enchanted by a smile and personality.

With the problem of understanding reasons (an insider concept, related to mind) in a world of causes (brain processes) comes the question of what the relationship is between the explanation of behaviour and its justification. Similarly, there is the issue of values humans aspire to in a world apparently driven by interests: what is the legitimacy of moral discourse used by naturally evolved beings? Even science, the study of nature, may be considered in a dual perspective, as a quest for truth, driven by rational considerations, and as an all too human enterprise, driven by a drive for power and reward.

Philosophy might serve as mediator between the two perspectives, by dispelling false oppositions such as the one between brain and mind or the one between evolved and moral. The philosophy of mind typically addresses the question of how neural processes can be bearers of meaningful discourse. Meta-ethics and philosophy of biology concern the multiple ways in which 'selfish genes' might give rise to moral individuals (e.g. Midgley 1994). The philosophy of science is addressing the question of how fallible human practices can deliver more or less objective, culture-independent knowledge (e.g. Kitcher 1993).

Let us return to religion. My teacher in philosophy of religion, H. G. Hubbeling, defined the task of philosophy of religion in relation to religious studies as follows:

> Science of religion does not ask for the truth or falsity of religious institutions or statements, it just describes and explains them. Philosophy of religion, then, may be characterized as follows: *Philosophy of religion = science of religion + the investigation of truth or falsity*.
>
> (Hubbeling 1987: 3)

Philosophy of religion stands between the insider and the outsider perspective and thus comes close to systematic theology, the intellectual concern of the insider.

However, there is also a relevant distinction between the philosopher of religion and the systematic theologian: 'in a philosophical statement a reference to revelation is not permitted, whereas in theology one may refer to revelation as an argument' (Hubbeling 1987: 1).

Hence in philosophy of religion we do not have the insider perspective based on particular religious creeds, revelations or experiences but we do have the attempt to think through the truth and value *of* religion with the best available truth *about* religions. That is the spirit in which I think we ought to engage in religious reflection with a perspective that is external to religion, namely science. Thus 'religion and science' has to be philosophical, not in a strong disciplinary sense but in the sense that it deals with the outsider perspective on religion, human nature and the world while considering at the same time its possible meaningfulness, truth and value. In the next three chapters I will offer some explorations that move within this arena, approaching insider issues, about the place of mystery and ultimacy in a scientifically intelligible world, the place of values in a world of facts and the quest for meaning in a material world, but addressing those while operating from an outsider's perspective, engaging scientific knowledge and attitudes.

Theologies as packages

We already came across the remark by the anthropologist Clifford Geertz that 'sacred symbols function to synthesize a people's ethos – the tone, character, and quality of their life, its moral and aesthetic style and mood – and their world view – the picture they have of the way things in sheer actuality are, their most comprehensive ideas of order'. This led to the definition of religions as systems of symbols. Here I want to use his definition as a stepping stone towards an understanding of the cognitive side of a religion, what could be called 'a theology' or, to be more inclusive, an integrated religious or non-religious vision of life. In this approach conceptions of the order of existence are intertwined with the appreciation of reality and norms for our behaviour. To speak of the world as God's creation has a descriptive and a prescriptive aspect to it. In the same article, Geertz also speaks of models *of* the world and models *for* the world, that is of models that seem to be descriptive and models that articulate a normative orientation and transformative ambition. In order to acknowledge the concentration on cognitive and normative dimensions I will speak here not of 'a religion', as Geertz does, but of 'a theology' or of 'a religious or non-religious vision'.

Theologies as 'cosmology and axiology'

Typical of theologies and non-religious visions, as systematic positions, seems to be that they offer a particular view of the way the world is *and* of the way the world should be, of the True and the Good, of the real and the ideal. Each theology is a particular relationship between a cosmology – as a view of the way reality fundamentally is (what one might also call a metaphysics or an ontology) – and a view of the values that should be realized, an axiology, that is a philosophically reflected articulation of our moral intuitions. A typical example: God created this world (a cosmological claim) and hence we need to be good stewards (a normative claim). Note that 'cosmology' here does not refer to a branch of astrophysics but to a more encompassing philosophical discipline.

Hence as a heuristic to clarify and explore a complex area of discussion I suggest the following 'formula' for understanding the nature of 'theologies', religious or non-religious visions of life:

a theology = a cosmology *and* an axiology.

The *and* is not a mere addition, but the crucial issue: how the two are brought together; we will return to that below. 'Axiology' is a grandiose term for a theory of values, that is a philosophically reflected articulation of our moral intuitions. I speak of theologies in the plural, and hence of 'a theology', to indicate that we are not referring to a single discipline, nor to a single view. Rather this heuristic formula seeks to give an opportunity to understand each of the manifold theologies that people have as views of God, humanity and the world in which moral and factual aspects are interwoven.

To insiders in science-and-religion discussions this may seem to resemble the scheme proposed by Nancey Murphy and George Ellis (1996). However, my formula is a heuristic thesis for exploring the field, whereas Murphy and Ellis present a substantial thesis about the proper relationship between theology, ethics and the sciences. I do not want to make a statement on 'the moral nature of the universe'; the formula and scheme that follows also allows us to describe and analyse positions which consider the universe to be amoral, whether indifferent, meaningless or evil. Unlike Murphy and Ellis, for whom each level of understanding requires a higher one until it finally includes a doctrine of God, I do not consider an atheist to be deficient in understanding; rather, he or she holds a different existential position. Furthermore, I do not line up ethics with the social sciences as they did, as if ethics fits among the sciences, as I am convinced of the categorical difference between moral values and any factual analysis, including one by the social sciences.

Theologies can relate and prioritize cosmological and axiological aspects in many different ways; the 'and' can have many different meanings. The definition allows one to concentrate on *existential* issues which become prominent when our reality is not in accord with what we think ought to be, thus stressing the tension that might be involved in the 'and' in the formula. But it may also be about *supernatural* or *magical* elements, as particular claims regarding the cosmological order.

Within the Christian tradition, there are, upon this definition, various theologies. When the emphasis is on God's saving activity, the tension between the way the world is and the way it should be and will be is prominent, whereas in creation-oriented views (whether ecologically inspired or as natural theologies) cosmology and axiology stand less in contrast; a prophet emphasizes the tension, whereas a mystic stresses the way we belong to reality. Whiteheadian process thought is one particular articulation of the interplay of axiological and causal elements. This way of integrating regulative ideals into cosmology has required particular, and in my opinion problematic, choices in cosmology, choices regarding pan-experientialism and regarding the place of physics in the order of the sciences. However, it is an interesting and relevant attempt to integrate valuational and causal elements in a single categoreal scheme.

William James spoke of the connection of a worldview ('the universe') with values and attitudes ('manner of acceptance') in his *Varieties of Religious Experience* (1902: 41) as follows:

> At bottom the whole concern of both morality and religion is with the manner of our acceptance of the universe. Do we accept it only in part and grudgingly, or heartily and altogether? Shall our protests against certain things in it be radical and unforgiving, or shall we think that, even with evil, there are ways of living that must lead to good? (…) It makes a tremendous emotional and practical difference to one whether one accepts the universe in the drab discolored way of stoic resignation to necessity, or with the passionate happiness of Christian saints.

In my opinion, the attempt to combine 'is' and 'ought' statements is what makes theology valuable *and* problematical.

The difficulty of the combination finds expression again and again in the problem of evil, which typically concerns the relationship or tension between the two main components. The formula also hints at a major difference between theology and philosophy. In philosophy, mixing 'is' and 'ought' statements is considered fallacious. One cannot get from the factual claim that a substance is natural to the recommendation that it is good – a herb may well be poisonous. To move from factual claims to normative ones would be to make 'the naturalistic fallacy'. Despite such categorical distinctions made by philosophers, religious belief lives on the combination. In beliefs about creation we find interwoven with each other ideas about ultimate origins and about appropriate behaviour. Even believers who do not argue from facts to value judgements (which would clearly be fallacious reasoning) tend to hold facts and values together in a single normative vision of the way things are and should be.

'Religion and science' plays a problematic role precisely at this interface. It often appears to be an attempt to use cosmological discourses to resolve value issues. This move does not work; whether certain phenomena can be understood in reductionist terms or in terms of emergence, or both, does not determine their significance and value. In engaging in 'religion and science' it is necessary to analyze the cosmological aspects, the contribution science makes to our worldview, but it is also of major importance, as a matter of intellectual and theological honesty, to acknowledge explicitly where other judgements come into play, judgements that are not based on science but on moral, aesthetic or religious preferences. Those evaluations are not forced upon us by science, but independent relative to scientific information. Science has been so successful in a culture-transcending way, precisely by abstaining from value judgements. By introducing such evaluations, we shift from knowledge to belief, and thus engage in religious reflection (theology) rather than in philosophy or science.

A scheme

So far, I have described theological convictions as combining cosmological and axiological ones. Each of these is related to underlying disciplines, such as ethics and the natural sciences, while these in turn are related to observations, experiments and moral intuitions. Deep down, of course, both of these sequences of human analysis relate to the world in which we live and the experiences we have. Thus there are two levels at which integration occurs, the theoretical level of theologies (or, to use a more neutral term, religious and non-religious visions) and practice, in lives as lived.

A cosmology, a view of the way things ultimately are, is related to the sciences. However, the relationship is not straightforward. One may distinguish between science and any interpretation of science as a view of reality, that is any worldview, cosmology, metaphysics or philosophy of nature. A cosmology, in this sense, is a view of what the world might be like, given what we know and also what we know not to be the case; science may well be stronger in what it excludes than in what it includes. Any such metaphysics is an interpretation of scientific knowledge, constrained by the sciences but also underdetermined by them.

It may be useful to distinguish further between various aspects of the sciences: theories, taxonomies and empirical generalizations and observations and experiments. At the 'high' end there are theories that describe vast domains of realities. That is where the integration provided by the sciences is most clearly in sight. Among these are Newton's understanding of forces and motion; the atomic theory of matter with the periodic system; electromagnetism; evolutionary theory; quantum physics; Einstein's improved understanding of motion, space and time. At the 'low end' there are the manifold observations and experiments that connect scientific ideas to the world.

Relationships between the high end and the low end are various. Some of these are inductive in kind, generalization towards general rules or statistical expectations. Major relations are, however, hypothetical-deductive, where the creative researcher postulates entities, forces or causal factors that may explain the observed phenomena. Certainty is always limited. Inductive generalization may be of limited validity beyond the phenomena that formed the basis for the generalization as conditions not yet taken into account may be essential.

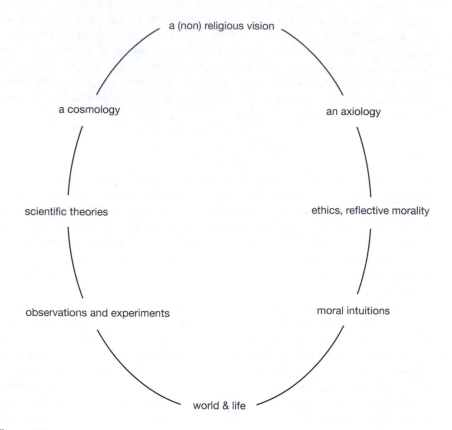

a (non) religious vision

a cosmology

an axiology

scientific theories

ethics, reflective morality

observations and experiments

moral intuitions

world & life

Figure 4.1

Hypothetical-deductive approaches acknowledge openly the creative and provisional nature of the hypothesis, which may be refuted if deduced consequences do not match observations. However, even such refutations are not final, since it may be that one does not consider the theory itself refuted, but rather one of the additional hypotheses involved, such as hypotheses regarding the measuring equipment or the initial conditions, an insight regarding the underdetermination of refutations and theories that has come to be known in philosophy as the Duhem–Quine thesis.

Given a particular theory, any metaphysical or cosmological inferences drawn from it may be speculative and disputable. Does quantum mechanics force upon us an indeterministic metaphysics? Not necessarily, as witnessed by the continuing debates over the interpretation of quantum mechanics. Does the Special Theory of Relativity that describes space-time as four-dimensional force upon us the idea that time is spatial and the future is just as much 'already there' as the past is? Again, interpretations diverge. Precisely where the cosmologically most interesting issues are, such as the nature of time and causality, science and its interpretation is most speculative. Chemists work with the periodic table, and atoms consist of protons, neutrons and electrons, and the first two are made up of quarks and gluons, and these ... : what is the end of the line? The Big Bang theory is a very successful theory describing the evolution of the universe, but precisely when we get to the very beginning, beyond the Planck horizon, the theory becomes unreliable as we need a quantum theory of space and time, an area of quantum cosmology where approaches are as much guided by pre-conceived philosophical ideas and preferences in mathematics as by observations. In a review article Jeremy Butterfield and Christopher Isham (2001: 38) wrote about theory construction in this field of quantum gravity and quantum cosmology:

> In this predicament, theory-construction inevitably becomes much more strongly influenced by broad theoretical considerations, than in mainstream areas of physics. More precisely, it tends to be based on various *prima facie* views about what the theory *should* look like – these being grounded partly on the philosophical prejudices of the researcher concerned, and partly on the existence of mathematical techniques that have been successful in what are deemed (perhaps erroneously) to be closely related areas of theoretical physics (...).
>
> The situation (...) tends to produce schemes based on a wide range of philosophical motivations, which (since they are rarely articulated) might be presumed to be unconscious projections of the chtonic psyche of the individual researcher – and might be dismissed as such! Indeed, practitioners of a given research programme frequently have difficulty in understanding, or ascribing validity to, what members of a rival programme are trying to do. This is one reason why it is important to uncover as many as possible of the assumptions that lie behind each approach: one person's 'deep' problem may seem irrelevant to another, simply because the starting positions are so different.

Underdetermination is a genuine issue, especially so when one comes to metaphysical or cosmological conclusions regarding the nature of nature. However, underdetermination need not be understood as 'anything goes' since lower levels and requirements of consistency considerably constrain the options.

Two levels of integration

The scheme presented has two levels where different strands come together (cf. Hübner 1990). One level arises due to intellectual effort to think through facts and values, the issues of what is and what should be; that is the level of theology or non-religious visions. However, whether intellectually articulate or not, values and facts are intertwined also in daily life, when people perceive their environment and make choices as to how to act. Regarding religion, there may be the level of theological reflection and speculation, but there is also religious and human life, communities that come together for worship, individuals who pray or just light a candle, one who experiences the beauty of a forest in the Autumn or that of the Sun setting over the North Sea, someone touched by music or moved by a poem, attention given by a friend, the joy of a communal meal, and much more.

'Life as lived' may feed into the intellectual reflection, as it is the point of departure of observations about the world, and hence of science, as well as the sphere of human intentions and actions which incites moral reflection. It may also be affected by the intellectual reflection, whether at the highest level indicated or at some lower level; human life should be where the reflections land again. People may be changed by the engagement with a theological vision, whether for better or for worse. Two levels, 'reality itself' and 'reflection about reality', are distinguished, but the reflections shape the ways people live, and thus become reality. That they become a reality for those who live within that framework of understanding does not determine the truth of the theological integration. Like the symbols Geertz spoke of, our speculative thoughts may have an aura of facticity, and thus function well, without being adequate depictions of the way things are. This question will return in the next chapter, when we study the scientific understanding of reality and questions of ultimate explanation.

The next three chapters deal with different vertical lines in the scheme presented. First, we will consider the left-hand side, the scientific–cosmological column. How much do we know about reality? What does that imply for a religious understanding of reality? To what extent can science deliver certitude, or are we limited to 'an aura' of facticity, as in the definition of religion given by Geertz? The sixth chapter will deal with the right-hand side – morality and values. Could one not subsume these under the scientific side, as evolved strategies that promoted survival? The final chapter addresses the central axis of the scheme – what can we say about the intellectual integration in relation to lives as lived? A central term will be 'meaning', not in the sense that a dictionary gives the meaning of terms, but in the sense that humans find their lives more or less meaningful. Such judgements engage our imagination in integrating our legacies and new knowledge creatively.

But is this really religion?

Does it do justice to religious faith to present theologies as efforts to integrate factual and moral concerns? Above we quoted Rudolf Otto, who suggested that the one who lacks personal religious experience should not speak of religion; in his view religion is a category of its own and not to be conflated with something else. Here I will regard some remarks by Friedrich Schleiermacher, a German theologian who in the period following the main writings of the philosopher Immanuel Kant suggested that religion should be granted a domain of its own, alongside theoretical reason (science) and practical reason (ethics). In the second of his speeches on religion 'to its cultured despisers', in 1799, he said on these three domains the following.

> If you put yourselves on the highest standpoint of metaphysics and morals, you will find that both have the same object as religion, namely, the universe and the relationship of humanity to it. This similarity has long since been a basis of manifold aberrations; metaphysics and morals have therefore invaded religion on many occasions, and much that belongs to religion has concealed itself in metaphysics or morals under an unseemly form. But shall you, for this reason, believe that it is identical with one of these? I know that your instinct tells you the contrary, and it also follows from your opinions; for you never admit that religion walks the firm step of which metaphysics is capable, and you do not forget to observe diligently that there are quite a few ugly immoral blemishes on its history. If religion is thus to be differentiated, then it must be set off from those in some manner, regardless of the common subject matter.

Schleiermacher ([1799] 1996: 19) thus acknowledges that all three have the same subject matter, namely the universe and the relationship of humanity to it. In that sense, his remarks may well be taken as support for the scheme presented above. However, Schleiermacher (*ibid*.: 20) is very critical of carrying over notions from one side to the other.

> You take the idea of the good and carry it into metaphysics as the natural law of an unlimited and plenteous being, and you take the idea of a primal being from metaphysics and carry it into morality so that this great work should not remain anonymous, but so that the picture of the lawgiver might be engraved at the front of so splendid a code. But mix and stir as you will, these never go together; you play an empty game with materials that are not suited to each other. You always retain only metaphysics and morals. This mixture of opinions about the highest being or the world and of precepts for a human life (or even for two) you call religion! (...) But how then do you come to regard a mere compilation, an anthology for beginners, as an integral work, as an individual with its own origin and power?

Thus, in the terms used here, the 'and' of the scheme, the attempt at integration, is the sticky point. For Schleiermacher (*ibid*.: 22f), the resolution has been to take leave from any engagement with metaphysics and morals.

In order to take possession of its own domain, religion renounces herewith all claims to whatever belongs to those others and gives back everything that has been forced upon it. It does not wish to determine and explain the universe according to its nature as does metaphysics; it does not desire to continue the universe's development and perfect it by the power of freedom and the divine free choice of a human being as does morals. Religion's essence is neither thinking nor acting, but intuition and feeling. It wishes to intuit the universe, wishes devoutly to overhear the universe's own manifestations and actions, longs to be grasped by and filled with the universe's immediate influences in childlike passivity. Thus, religion is opposed to these two in everything that makes up its essence and in everything that characterizes its effects.

The approach presented here respects that the theological integration is not itself part of either metaphysics or morals; in that sense I concur with Schleiermacher. Furthermore, my scheme differentiates between the intellectual integration and life as lived; religion as feeling, as a creaturely sense of dependence upon all, is not to be found in the intellectual integration but in the fullness of life as lived.

While granting such characteristics, I cannot take the theological reflection to be totally independent from modern knowledge and moral discourse. Not that the theological vision arises out of the cosmological information, as in natural theology, or just recapitulates values. Not that either science and its philosophical interpretation nor morality and its more reflective articulation need religion or theology; they can do well without the integrative project. However, religion cannot exist without engaging our ideas about the way the world is and the way the world should be. In this sense the scheme proposed is more in line with the anthropological definition of Geertz than with Schleiermacher's claim for independence. But in the integration itself, the religious heart of the matter, there may well be something that does not come from either side, but from religious life, whether ascribed to upbringing or to a personal sense of being grasped by something deeper, by a moral and aesthetic sense of harmony and beauty or disgust and anger, by awareness of our ultimate dependence.

Chapter 5

Mystery in an intelligible world

In theologies humans integrate their ideas about the way things are (world-views) with their convictions as to how they should be (values); this was the understanding of religious and non-religious visions I proposed in the previous chapter. In this chapter I will consider in more detail the impact of modern science on our ideas of the way things are. In the light of the sciences I will consider possible interpretations of current insights about the nature of nature.

In brief, I will argue the following. Science shows us that reality has integrity and coherence. All phenomena in the world are intelligible as natural phenomena. Thus *naturalism* as a view of reality seems a plausible interpretation of the world understood scientifically. The integrity and coherence of reality gives some urgency to the question of in what sense one might speak of divine involvement in the course of nature. If one accepts the naturalistic thrust of science, the idea is that everything in nature is in principle intelligible, I will argue that there are nonetheless limit questions with respect to the world studied scientifically, and that these limit questions might be interpreted theistically by seeing the universe as creation. Modern science and cosmology thus allow for a form of theism that respects the naturalistic tenor of science, a *naturalistic theism*. However, appreciation of the integrity, coherence and creativity of reality might also be articulated as *religious naturalism*, ascribing religious significance to the natural. Given the intellectual and religious respectability of both naturalistic theism and religious naturalism, a third option is to appreciate scientific insights while acknowledging our intrinsic limitations regarding the ultimate nature of reality, and thus to be a *serious agnostic*.

The nature of nature

The universe, nature, in its development turns out to behave according to regularities, laws of nature, perhaps incorporating within their operation some elements of indeterminacy or chance. Some centuries ago, the role of natural laws seemed quite different. Newton's theory of gravity, published in 1687, explained the orbits of the planets in our solar system. However, small deviations from the regular orbits seemed to accumulate, needing from time to time a special act from the creator to keep the planets on course. When 'Nature' was compared to a clock, the analogy referred not only to its regularity but also to the need for maintenance from time to time.

The French mathematician Pierre Simon Laplace (1749–1827) showed that deviations did not accumulate disastrously. This is captured well in an anecdote of which the historical veracity may be doubtful. When Laplace presented a copy of his book on the movements of the planets to Napoleon, so the story goes, the latter is said to have remarked that Newton in his treatise referred to God, whereas Laplace didn't do so. Upon which Laplace replied: 'Your Majesty, I did not need that hypothesis.' Indeed, contemporary cosmology and physics can do without a 'God of the gaps'.

With the development of modern science our perception of nature's integrity and coherence has grown. Isaac Newton unified heavenly and earthly dynamics. James Clerk Maxwell and others in the nineteenth century developed a unified understanding of electricity and magnetism. Albert Einstein's Special Theory of Relativity resolved an inconsistency between electromagnetism and dynamics; his General Theory integrated gravity into the picture. In the latter half of the twentieth century, theories of elementary particles have been developed that have integrated to an ever increasing extent the fundamental forces and entities (e.g. 't Hooft 1997).

Not only has our understanding of natural processes developed towards greater coherence, but so too has our understanding of natural history. Astrophysics, geology and evolutionary biology provide us with a grand narrative that traces our present state back to a particular beginning about fourteen billion years ago ('the Big Bang'). Current evidence and well-tested theories have allowed us to reconstruct past developments in increasingly substantial detail.

In the course of that natural history there has been an accumulation of skills for effective living, passed on as information embodied in DNA. Such a cumulative history has marked the transition from a world of cause and effect to one of functionality, from a world of physics and chemistry to a world that also needs history to be understood. Evolutionary history brought forth organs and organisms that entertain purposes, but it has done so through a long sequence of chance events. Thus in a natural process 'higher' forms of living came into being, life forms that need not only the language of physics but also the vocabularies of biology, the neurosciences, psychology and the social sciences.

The coexistence of multiple levels of organization and of description is one of the lessons of modern science. Physics and chemistry have more and more become differentiated but continuous wholes, while 'molecular biology' brings into this web of understanding all living beings as well. Sceptics might wonder whether science isn't reducing everything to atoms, described by physics, neglecting important aspects of our experience. To address this concern, let us briefly return to the issue of reductionism (see Chapter 2).

Multiple descriptions of reality

Tables and trees, humans and bees: we all consist of hydrogen, carbon, oxygen and other atoms. If one takes anything apart, one will find no other substances. That is part of nature's integrity: there is one type of substance, even when it comes to humans.

Such a 'materialist' view of humans might suggest to some a negative assessment of human worth. If we were to buy in the cheapest way the ingredients necessary for a human being, we would not need to spend much. Water, some rusty nails (for the iron in our blood), some matches for the phosphorus, some charcoal for the carbon: a human does not add up to much. However, if one follows through such an assessment of the worth of humans, one would have to include the costs of labour to put us together in the right way. Labour has been invested in us in many ways, by our parents, partners, friends and teachers. There also has been labour invested in the construction of human nature and culture during our whole evolutionary past, from the first replicating molecules to the present. One could reconstitute quite easily a simple chemical substance out of the constituent parts, such as water out of hydrogen and oxygen, but to reconstitute a human from matter requires this long biocultural history and is thus way beyond what is, or will become, feasible.

So what is this position I am trying to present? We are nothing but matter. As far as the entities involved, reductionism seems to hold true: everything is composed of substance as studied by physics. This substance is known quite well at various levels, as atoms and molecules, photons, quarks and gluons, even though we do not have the final answer as to the nature of matter 'deep down'. This unfinished quest within physics brings us to the issue of limit questions; we will return to that later. Here, however, we focus on reductionism and the reality of 'higher levels' of reality.

Higher levels are real and they do need their own concepts in order to be described adequately. Some fear that successful reduction eliminates the phenomena under consideration, but that fear is mistaken. Discerning the physiological basis for a trait rather affirms its reality. Genes are not less real for being understood as strands of DNA and pain is not less real if understood physiologically. More likely the opposite holds: if the doctor can locate the bodily process underlying my pain, my friends will take my complaints more seriously.

The astronomer Arthur Eddington described in the Introduction to his published Gifford Lectures, *The Nature of the Physical World* (1928), two tables in his study at home: the ordinary one is substantial as massive wood, coloured and permanent, while the scientific one is mostly emptiness; within that emptiness there are sparsely scattered electrical charges rushing about at great speed. The two tables are in fact a single table, described in different ways. The two descriptions support the same conclusions – I can place paper upon it and lean on it. Any scientific description of a table will have to incorporate the fact that I cannot put my hand through the table, unless with considerable force and with major consequences for the table and for my hand. There are two descriptions, different but not incompatible for all practical purposes. Though the scientific description does not eliminate the stability of the table it is nonetheless quite different, and at odds with some common-sense ideas about substance and the philosophical articulations of these ideas.

Though the precise relationship between the two descriptions is complex, and the revisionary effects of scientific descriptions on folk ideas sometimes significant, the picture is that complex entities are made out of more simple ones, and hence that there are underlying processes. In that sense, reductionism is true. So what! Such a form of reduction is not elimination; rather, it is integration of these phenomena into our multifaceted picture of the world. Such a reductionism is a form of holism as it reveals the pervasive coherence of reality.

Is science able to handle all phenomena and all experiences? Or is there a residue of phenomena and experiences that isn't handled well by science? As with many of the issues in this book, this is too big to handle in depth here, but let me offer some considerations on the issue.

Limitations of the sciences and the science of limitations

The novelist John Fowles wrote in the reflective essay *The Tree* (1979: 40–41):

> Ordinary experience, from waking second to second, is in fact highly synthetic (in the sense of combinative or constructive), and made of a complexity of strands, past memories and present perceptions, times and places, private and public history, hopelessly beyond science's powers to analyse. It is quintessentially 'wild', in the sense my father disliked so much: unphilosophical, irrational, uncontrollable, incalculable. In fact it corresponds very closely – despite our endless efforts to 'garden', to invent disciplining social and intellectual systems – with wild nature. Almost all the richness of our personal existence derives from this synthetic and eternally present 'confused' consciousness of both internal and external reality, and not least because we know it is beyond the analytical, or destructive, capacity of science.

Developing scientific images of the world should not be achieved by pruning lightly, that is by denying complex, 'wild' experiences for the sake of simplicity. Thus, we need to consider our inabilities, to show that these need not count against the integrity and intelligibility that naturalism ascribes to reality.

The inability to analyze our experiences in great depth may be due to the models of reality we use. Metaphors borrowed from technology are used to make sense of our experiences: 'letting off steam' and 'being under pressure' draw upon the language of nineteenth-century technology; 'tuning in' reflects the electromechanical technology of the early radio receivers, and the personal computer era has generated a whole new set of metaphors. This use of models derived from technology is fine as long as their metaphorical character is kept in mind. However, if the analogy between humans and technical artefacts such as clocks, steam engines or computers is made too tight it becomes ridiculous; 'wild nature', including human nature, is richer than such technological metaphors can express.

As I see it, the wildness of experiences is related by and large to various limitations that manifest themselves almost everywhere in nature. As humans we are unable to monitor our inner states, and the causal webs that shape our responses are the product of such a long, convoluted evolutionary history and embryological development as to be beyond detailed analysis. More generally, chaos theory has made clear what could have been obvious to students of historical evidence: we never have sufficient knowledge of all details to provide a full account of the course of events. Where we cannot trace all the underlying details we speak of chance, for instance when throwing dice. Even if a full account were possible, it would be so cumbersome as to be of little use; just as a map that provides as much detail as reality itself would have to be a map of a metre to a metre. We are limited with respect to detailed explanations of particular events.

The difference between scientific and manifest images developed over time. From the richness of our manifest images scientists restricted themselves at first to the study of gross simplifications, and then reconstructed from insights about these simplifications an understanding of more complex phenomena. We have gone through many cycles of simplification and building up again towards an understanding of complex phenomena. Because of the detour through the study of simpler systems, science now more fully understands 'wild' reality in its variety and at the same time grasps its own limitations in explanatory and predictive power.

The observation that science is unable to account for 'wild' nature is thus to some extent true: scientists are not able to predict events in full detail. However, science has over time become better and better at understanding complex phenomena. And, despite Fowles' claim, such an analytical understanding need not be destructive. To be fair to science, we should not dismiss science on the basis of straw men, that is models, simple theories and initial approximations. Nor, however, should a scientist dismiss phenomena lightly on the basis of overly simplistic models of reality.

In and through the sciences we have come up with all kinds of scientific images that differ significantly from the way we experience the world, our manifest images. In developing those scientific images we also have discovered some of our limitations. Not only those where in practice we lack enough information, as in chaos and self-understanding. There is an upper limit to the speed of light, about 300,000 kilometres per second. Knowledge of events that took place at such a distance that there has not been enough time for light to reach us yet is not available to us. In the world of the very small it has been discovered that certain pairs of properties, such as position and speed, cannot be measured at the same time with infinite precision. There are even limitations within pure mathematics; Kurt Gödel has shown that within any sufficiently rich system of assumptions there are theses that cannot be proved or disproved though some of these must be true.

None of these discoveries, however, counts against the scientific understanding of nature. Limitations on intelligibility are quite intelligible, and thus do not count against the idea that we live in an intelligible world with substantial integrity.

Science and naturalism

The main lesson of the scientific approach is that nature seems to have a multi-layered coherence and integrity, and that in this way nature is intelligible, despite our limitations to understanding everything. Once this reality exists, there are no signs of suspension of its regularities, no signs of any additional input of matter, energy or information, no signs of any tricks played upon us. The world could have been different, with an unruly dictator changing the laws at will, or with higher level phenomena not being in line with lower level processes. Naturalism is not logically necessary; here it is not assumed *a priori*. Rather, naturalism is an interpretation given to the success of science in making reality as a coherent web intelligible, success that is confirmed by the enormous powers that such an understanding has granted us in manipulating reality (technology). In the sciences we have come to recognize integrity across the rich diversity of phenomena and intelligibility despite the complexity of our world. Given this discovery of integrity and intelligibility, science seems to lead us towards a naturalistic understanding of reality.

With respect to our ideas about 'what there is' (*ontology*) this naturalism is the view that all objects around us, including ourselves, consist of the stuff described by chemists in the periodic table of the elements. This stuff is further understood by physicists to consist of elementary particles and forces, and beyond that is assumed to consist of quantum fields, superstrings or whatever. As I said before, our knowledge has not reached rock bottom yet. Hence, such a naturalism cannot be articulated on the basis of a fundamental ontology, a complete inventory of the world. Nor need such a naturalism imply that all phenomena can be described in terms of physics and chemistry, as we came to realize when we considered reductionism. A naturalist can hold that there are genuinely new objects with new properties, even though they have arisen out of other objects.

Ontologies may be revised over time, and vary with the level of description. Newton offered a theory of gravity in the late seventeenth century. Einstein came up with an improved understanding in 1915, with the General Theory of Relativity. When it comes to predictions of phenomena, there is substantial continuity from one theory to the other, so that one can see the later theory as an improved version of the earlier one, but these theories are radically different in their ideas of 'what gravity is'. For Newton gravity was a force working at a distance, whereas upon Einstein's approach there is no such force, as the consequences of gravity follow from the curvature of space-time. Qua ontology our view of reality has shifted, but for many situations the Newtonian description continues to be useful and its ontology of particles and forces has not disappeared from scientific discourse, though it has been shown to have limited validity.

So too when one considers matter. Fluids seem to fill their vessels; the dynamics of fluids is well described as if matter is divisible ad infinitum. In other contexts we have come to see matter as atoms, small building blocks. And these we have come to see as consisting of a nucleus, electrons and mostly empty space. Deeper down, scientists speak of quarks, and beyond that there are now theories about superstrings. Science does not offer a single story of 'what matter is'. There is no single, ultimate ontology, but there are multiple models and descriptions, each useful at a particular scale of phenomena.

With respect to *history*, naturalism understands living beings as the current stage in a bundle of evolutionary histories on our planet, which itself is seen as a transient phenomenon in a universe that has been expanding for some fourteen billion years. Naturalism considers social and mental life, including the capacities needed for science, as fruits of the long evolutionary process. We are no exceptions to reality though we may be rather remarkable manifestations of reality. These insights do not commit one to a particular view on ultimate origins; fundamental issues about the beginning of our universe are not settled. There is an irresolvable open end to our understanding, an openness which might allow one to believe in a Beyond which brings forth this world (theism) or to believe in a divinity which is intrinsic to nature (pantheism or religious naturalism), or to present oneself as an agnostic (we will never know). The science-inspired naturalistic view of reality presented here allows for more than one religious interpretation, as we will discuss later in this chapter.

Pan-experientialist naturalism?

There is a standard order from lower to higher among the major sciences, something like the following: physics – chemistry – biology – neurosciences – psychology. Atoms are configured in complex molecules typical of processes within living organisms; some of these organisms have developed in various degrees awareness of their environment and of themselves, an inner life. Atoms don't have sentience, but sentience has arisen in material beings. Most naturalists accept this order, acknowledging that physics offers in some sense the most basic view of reality, without thereby denying the reality and significance of phenomena such as sentience at higher levels.

Within the naturalist family (Flanagan 2006), however, a minority position reverses the order, and considers human *experience* to be typical of the fundamental ontology. According to process philosophy in the tradition of Whitehead all actual entities have some freedom, sentience and subjectivity. A vocal advocate of such a pan-experientialist naturalism is David R. Griffin (2000, 2006). Any naturalism that sticks to the usual order of disciplines he dismisses as materialist and atheistic. His more relaxed naturalism might make life easier for religious thought.

This is not the place for an extensive argument regarding the richer naturalism advocated by Griffin. However, this approach seems to mistrust the power of the process, as it denies the possibility that sentience and subjectivity have evolved. For such a pan-experientialist naturalist, subjectivity and sentience are among the basic ingredients at the most fundamental ontological level. Furthermore, the approach is substantially at odds with current science, where the disciplinary order indicated above does seem to express insights about the layered character of reality (see Peacocke 1993: 217; Drees 1996: 257–59). Thus, not considering it likely that understanding is improved by turning the multilayered scientific approach upside down, I will not consider such a modified naturalism in the remainder of this chapter.

Naturalism and normativity

Can a naturalist distinguish epistemology from psychology, truth from belief, mathematical triangles from human sketches and moral norms from evolved preferences? If practices such as science and considered moral judgement are considered to be human practices, and as such as fully natural phenomena rooted in our existence as primates, why should we take these practices as fundamentally different from folk wisdom, pseudo-science or prejudice? Naturalists deny that there is an absolute demarcation between science and non-scientific activities. However, at the same time they do prefer science over pseudo-science, and thus live by such a distinction. Is this not self-referentially incoherent? Naturalism faces a challenge when it comes to justifying the significance of its approach. That naturalism might be unable to articulate normative aspects of existence leads the philosopher Charles Taylor in his *Sources of the Self* (1989: 19–22) to the rejection of naturalism.

Naturalists will have to do without absolute norms and procedures, while maintaining these as ideals. The German philosopher Jürgen Habermas writes in his *Between Naturalism and Religion* (2008: 7) that 'it is indeed possible to deflate the Platonic ideas using the concept of idealizing presuppositions', without thereby falling into a scientistic form of naturalism he rejects. A more nuanced naturalism should allow for norms and other ideals of perfection. Public justification and individual reflection do strengthen the credibility of rules and norms; piecemeal improvement of morality and scientific methods and criteria makes a real difference (see for example Kitcher 1985, 1993). In a naturalistic approach, arguing for a normative position, whether in morality or in epistemology, will always be an unfinished project. It is a project in which naturalism can benefit from other philosophical styles, such as pragmatism (with its sensitivity to the way in which our norms are rooted in our practices) and Kantianism (with its reflection on the never fully accessible, always elusive, transcendent regulative ideals).

Are naturalists falling prey to scientism (Stenmark 2001)? That is, are they expecting too much from the natural sciences? Of course, some naturalists will have used methods and arguments from a particular domain elsewhere, where they turned out not to be adequate. As I indicated above, naturalists should allow for multiple domains or layers of reality, with a variety of methods and approaches. To further one's health, physical exercises may be more useful than exercises in physics. In social life the best solution may be the outcome not of calculation but of listening and looking for a consensus. Thus 'scientism' may be a valid criticism, if one makes a case as to why a certain approach is misplaced in a particular context.

However, the charge of 'scientism' can also become an easy excuse. 'Used inappropriately, accusations of scientism may not clarify debate but muddle it by serving a more general antiscientific agenda. Scientism thus becomes a way of "crying wolf," of creating alarm about a given scientific claim without adequately considering the merits of the methods and evidence in question' (Peterson 2003: 758). It can be a dismissive term for lazy people who do not make a well-focused argument. In the context of naturalism, the tendency is to push science as far as possible. Whether the use of science has been pushed too far will always need a specific argument, and it should be an argument that does justice to the multilayered understanding of reality that reasonable naturalists have come to acknowledge.

Four arguments for naturalism

We considered two areas of contention related to naturalism: the desire to have a richer form of naturalism that makes sentience foundational and the concern about the lack of absolute standards. Given these challenges, let me summarize four clusters of reasons in favour of naturalism, one epistemic, one pragmatic, one moral and one religious.

(1) The epistemic success of the natural sciences as they developed in the last century or two, resulting in corroborated theories that have a wide scope and great precision, unifying the understanding of phenomena in various contexts, is totally without equal in human history, compared to common sense, folk knowledge, religious myths, theological systems and philosophical speculations. This success makes it urgent to take these theories as our best available guides to the understanding of reality.

(2) The natural sciences, in conjunction with technology, have provided us with unprecedented means to act in reality. We not only have come to know

about electrons, but we have come to use them in electron microscopy and electronics. This practical power, which relies upon the intellectual unification achieved, supports the idea that the view thereby articulated is on a good track.

(3) Actions can be laudable or despicable; the ends of actions are a matter of moral judgment. However, regarding the means there is a major moral risk in playing down established scientific and medical knowledge. As an extreme example, we already mentioned the wilful irresponsibility of denying the relationship between AIDS and HIV, depriving people of valuable treatment. There are moral grounds for seeking to align oneself with the best available science (and historical, social and cultural knowledge) and thus with the larger view that modern science engenders.

(4) Any theist has good reasons to welcome the insight that nature has an impressive integrity and coherence. If this world is God's creation, any knowledge we have of this world is knowledge of God's creation. God is not to be found so much in the lacunae of our current knowledge, in the gaps, but rather in what we have uncovered. If our skills and powers are gifts of God, we should not look for God when we fail but rather appreciate God for all that has become possible. Nature, spoken of in such a perspective as creation, is not opposed to God but rather God's gift.

Divine action within nature's integrity?

The integrity and coherence of reality gives some urgency to the question of in what sense one might speak of divine involvement in the course of nature.

If one accepts some form of naturalism, one cannot at the same time argue for gaps in natural processes, such as gaps where God might have intervened or gone against the laws of nature to realize a result that would not have been possible by natural processes. Thus there seems to be a straightforward conflict between naturalism, with its emphasis on the integrity of nature, and the 'intelligent design' position, with its emphasis on the inability of natural processes to generate the complexity that we find. Some envisage along such lines a more general mutual exclusion of naturalism and theism (Goetz and Taliaferro 2008).

Not only would one have to consider such an anti-naturalistic position in relation to its coherence with scientific findings, but also in its religious consequences. Two considerations seem to me most important. First, if God is taken to be the creator of this world, why would God need to override the rules God has set? Upon the Newtonian understanding of gravity, nature was like an imperfect clock that needed manual correction from time to time, but if God is understood to be God, with all the perfections associated with God, is it appropriate to consider God as a maker of a deficient clockwork that from time to time needs interventions? Second, if one's worldview allows for specific, targeted interventions changing the course of nature, why does God not intervene where such an interruption might counter horrendous instances of evil? Thus not only God's creative powers but also God's morality seem questionable if one has a worldview that allows for interventions. Understanding divine actions as interventions in the course of natural processes need not exclude all religious options, however.

One alternative that has been discussed in 'religion and science' in recent decades is the idea of divine actions within the fabric of nature. Robert J. Russell (2008) of the Berkeley-based Center for Theology and the Natural Sciences argues that science shows that there is a flexibility and indeterminateness in natural processes, particularly at the level described by quantum physics, and that this flexibility allows for divine action *within* the processes of nature. Locating divine action in this intrinsic flexibility would not violate any laws of nature since the focus is on the choices left within the framework of those laws. The first of the objections articulated above, the fact that God would work against the order created by God, would not apply. Rather, God as creator of the framework of laws anticipated the divine interest in continuous involvement and therefore left the natural order to some extent incomplete, allowing for flexibility to manoeuvre. It resembles a 'God of the gaps' view, but this is not about gaps or failures in our understanding of reality. Rather, this approach seeks to base itself in discoveries made by science, especially the discovery of indeterminacy that is woven into the fabric of reality as understood scientifically.

I consider this a serious proposal, though it raises some questions of its own. Such a view of divine action within nature requires particular scientific theories, and particular interpretations of scientific theories, that allow for such flexibility. Whether quantum physics and the ontological interpretation of the uncertainty involved will remain a genuine option depends upon future developments of physics. Theologically speaking, this approach has divine actions deeply intertwined with natural ones, to some extent operating at the same level of causal factors that determine outcomes. Hence, God's actions appear to be a factor among other causal factors. Whether this is an advantage because it ascribes reality to them, or a disadvantage because it neglects categorical differences between divine and natural contributions, is a choice to be made in theological construction.

Furthermore, such an approach implies that God is temporal, acting at and thus living through successive moments. In such an approach God may be eternal in the sense of being everlasting, but it seems hard to reconcile this with the view that God is timeless in the sense that appealed to early theologians such as Augustine. And, again, the problem of evil is quite serious, as it might have been within God's ability to make minute changes, in human brains or elsewhere, that would have prevented various instances of horrendous evil. I consider this an option that faces some challenges of its own, but one that respects the sciences, though not within the naturalistic understanding that shapes the approaches considered in the remainder of this chapter.

In the context of a more robust naturalistic interpretation of nature, I see two genuine options, one dualistic and one monistic. It is possible to understand the divine role as providing nature with order and existence, and thus to argue for a form of *naturalistic theism*. Or else, one might abandon the dualism inherent in such ways of speaking of the divine, and speak of the divine as a qualification of the natural, *religious naturalism*. We will consider both in turn.

Naturalistic theism: seeing the world as creation

Naturalism, as considered above, is about intelligibility *in* nature. A subsequent question is: Is the framework of natural conditions and laws itself intelligible? Can one speak of the intelligibility *of* nature, a comprehensible and rational universe (Coyne and Heller 2008)? If so, should we think of a ground for this intelligibility, a ground which transcends nature? From the text of a book one may infer that there has been author, or perhaps multiple authors, or else some other process that generated the book. Can we conclude from the natural order to a creator? I will argue that a cosmological argument, from nature to its creator, cannot be based upon science. There is too much uncertainty in the scientific study of ultimate boundary issues, as well as too much argumentative weakness in the inference from the world to a divine maker.

The shift from intelligibility in nature to a more encompassing level, intelligibility of nature, has intellectual risks. This is well illustrated by the following remark, in the context of concerns about overpopulation: 'Every second a woman gives birth to a child. We must find that woman and stop her.' This is nonsense of course. While every human has a mother, there is not a person who is the mother of all. Questions about the whole are categorically different from questions about phenomena within that whole, just as the author of a novel is different from any person within the story – even if the story is autobiographical. Other argumentative problems with such reasoning were articulated in a lively way by David Hume in his *Dialogues Concerning Natural Religion*, posthumously published in 1779. An inference from the world to God, a cosmological proof for the existence of God, is asking too much.

The exclusion of a divine source does not follow from science either; a naturalistic view of reality may well be interpreted by embedding it in a more encompassing theistic view: naturalistic theism. In the following, we will continue our explorations from the scientific side, while moving gradually towards the existential and theological considerations.

Limit questions

When seeking to understand an event we can distinguish two aspects. Contingent features (features that could have been different) are explained in their particularity as consequences of *initial conditions* and *general rules and*

conditions. The weather today is the way it is because of the weather yesterday and the laws of atmospheric physics. Most explanations are about such
contingent facts. Once an explanation is offered, the particular event is no
longer contingent. Rather, it is now understood as the consequence of previous
conditions and laws. However, such an explanation relies upon initial conditions and laws that are contingent, and hence with any explanation further
questions for explanation – of the initial conditions and the laws – may arise.

The laws are explicable in a wider framework. For instance, Ohm's law on
electrical resistance can be explained on the basis of Maxwell's laws of electromagnetism and the properties of metals. One may envisage sequences of
explanations, as any question triggers further questions. The chemist refers to
the astrophysicist for an explanation of the origin of the various elements and
to the quantum physicist for an explanation of the bonds between atoms.
These explanatory sequences converge; that is part of the integrity and coherence of nature. In 1868 Thomas Huxley lectured 'on a piece of chalk',
explaining the whiteness of chalk as found in the cliffs of Dover, but also its
relative softness and its composition, by pursuing physical, chemical and geo-
logical lines of inquiry, showing how they all fitted together (Huxley 1868;
similarly Misner 1977; Weinberg 1992: 242).

The various questions about the structure of reality are passed on till they
end up on the desks of those engaged in fundamental physics, while questions
about origins end up on the desks of the cosmologists. Cosmology, the astrophysical study of the natural history of our universe, is nowadays largely a
regular discipline drawing on the repertoire of established physics, developing
hypotheses regarding the conditions in the early universe, tested against a
variety of increasingly precise observational data. This has resulted in the Big
Bang theory, a very successful scientific theory about the development of the
universe. In such astrophysical cosmology, the issue is to understand the universe as we observe it, applying rules and concepts of physics as we have them.
However, the Big Bang theory does not explain the Big Bang itself; we need a
new physics in order to push the explanatory quest in cosmology further. Such
a new physics brings one to the more speculative side of cosmology, where the
framework itself is in dispute.

At the end of the explanatory quests, the questions of physics and cosmology are intertwined. This was brought home forcefully by Steven Weinberg in
his book *The First Three Minutes* (1977): when we discuss the early universe
we need particle physics, and when we want to test particle physics we need to
study the early universe. The earlier a minuscule event in the history of the
universe takes place, the larger the scale of its effects in the later universe. To
understand the largest scale of the universe we need to go to the extreme end
of high-energy physics. Theories about the fundamental nature of matter are
explored for their cosmological consequences. In the quest for a most complete
understanding, cosmological research coincides with the quest for yet
unknown physics.

The physicist and the cosmologist have no scientific colleagues to whom they might shove off the remaining questions. This particular position of physicists and cosmologists in the quest for explanations may explain why they are drawn into philosophical and theological disputes foreign to geologists, biologists and chemists. Their work touches upon *limit questions* to the scientific enterprise, where the explanatory contingency of reality and its laws seems unavoidable. Or could science come up with complete theories?

Complete theories: no contingency left?

> The only way of explaining the creation is to show that the creator had absolutely no job at all to do, and so might as well not have existed.
>
> (Atkins 1981: 17)

The chemist Peter Atkins assumes that if there are no explanatory gaps to fill, there would be no need for a creator beyond the creative processes described by science. Atkins, an eloquent defender of the view that science leaves nothing to be explained, puts great weight on reduction to simplicity: beings such as elephants and humans arise through an evolutionary process given sufficient time and atoms. Atoms arise given even more simple constituents. Perhaps the ultimate unit to be explained is, as Atkins suggests, only space-time; particles being like knots of space-time. A major component in his argument is chance: through fluctuations, nothingness separates into +1 and −1. With such dualities, time and space come into existence. The +1 and −1 may merge again into nothingness. However, occasionally, still by chance, a stable configuration may come into existence, for instance our space-time with three spatial dimensions and one temporal dimension.

Atkins' idea is based on a speculative notion considered a few decades ago, 'pregeometry', promoted by John A. Wheeler. Though this idea has gone out of fashion, the fundamental issue has not changed significantly. For example, Hartle and Hawking (1983: 2961) wrote in their initial article on a 'no-boundary' cosmology that the wave function gives 'the probability for the universe to appear from Nothing'. Such claims face at least three kinds of problems:

Testability. Experimental tests and observations may well be insufficient to decide among the various research programmes in cosmology. Aesthetic judgments are, at least partly, decisive in opting for a specific scheme. However, what one considers elegant, another may reject (Stoeger 1988: 229; Barrow 1988: 373; Butterfield and Isham 2001).

Exhaustiveness. Could a single and relatively simple complete theory be fair to the complexity of the world? Or, as Mary Hesse (1988: 197) wrote, is it the case that for 'the explanation of *everything* there must in a sense be a conservation of complexity, in other words a trade-off between the simplicity and unity of the theory, and the multiplicity of interpretations of a few general theoretical concepts into many particular objects, properties and relations'? It seems that any simple unified theory will leave something unexplained, referred to as the product of chance and thus naturally contingent.

A vacuum is not nothing. The conceptual difference between a vacuum and nothing is fundamental, even though the notion of a vacuum comes quite close. According to modern cosmology, the conservation laws valid for the universe might conserve total quantities that are zero. Take, for example, electric charge. Negative charges of electrons are matched by positive charges of protons. Atoms are electrically neutral and so, it seems, is the observable universe. Similar arguments can be made about other properties: either they total up to zero or they are not conserved. Our universe may have arisen 'out of nothing', at least without input of any material. The universe might be equivalent to a vacuum (Tryon 1973). However, this equivalence of the universe with 'nothing' only holds with respect to totals. It is like someone borrowing a million Euros and buying stock for that amount. That person would be as wealthy, fiscally speaking, as someone else without any debt and without possessions. However, the first would be of far more significance to the financial market than the second. The first strategy also assumes more than the second: the financial system is taken for granted. Though as far as the conservation laws are concerned the universe might come from a 'vacuum', such a vacuum is not nothing. The vacuum considered here is a vacuum that behaves according to quantum laws which allow for the fluctuations to happen, just as the apparent millionaire can only get started once there are concepts of money and of borrowing.

Even successful scientific explanations do not explain without remainder, as any explanation has certain assumptions put into it. Many forms of apparent contingency may be explained and thus replaced by natural necessity, but such explanations introduce contingency at other levels, such as the contingency of the general laws and existence. Science answers many questions but there remain others which lead to such ultimate philosophical questions such as 'Why is there something rather than nothing?', 'Why is reality mathematically intelligible?' and 'Why are the laws or properties of reality as they are?'

Perhaps there will be new scientific answers beyond our current horizon, changing the specifics of our limit questions, but this only moves us further on in a continuing cat-and-mouse game of questions and answers. Science explains, but it does not explain the most encompassing questions. A theistic answer might be possible, but need not be the consequence. The theistic answer faces similar problems to the scientific answers, as any child can continue with 'why'questions. The theological tradition has resolved this by speaking of God as God's own cause (*causa sui*), or of God's necessary existence. Whatever the intellectual merits of such ideas, by then we have clearly left the domain of the natural sciences.

Human significance in a vast universe?

Aside from the open-ended quest for ultimate explanations, there is something else about cosmology in relation to human religion: our own significance, apparently lost in cosmology, though so dear to ourselves. In *The Restaurant at the End of the Universe*, Douglas Adams (1985: 71) describes the 'Total Perspective Vortex', a machine that destructs the soul by making one see the whole infinity of creation and oneself in relation to it. The effectiveness of this machine is evidence that life cannot afford to have a sense of proportion. The more we know of the vast universe, the more we become aware of the enormous incongruity of our own existence within the universe as a whole.

A major step in the rise of modern cosmology has been the adoption of 'Copernican' assumptions: the Earth is not the centre of it all, humans do not have a privileged position. Not only has the Earth been removed from the centre of the system of Sun, Moon and planets, but the Solar System is just one among many such systems, somewhere in one the spiral arms of the Galaxy, and our galaxy is just one of many galaxies. The earliest relativistic cosmological models assumed homogeneity and isotropy, the same conditions holding at all places, in all directions. Such strong assumptions have been relaxed somewhat, but the general tenor continues to be a denial of any privileged position for human observers.

A counter-movement in modern cosmology has been the appeal to 'anthropic principles' (Barrow and Tipler 1986). Rather than seeing human significance in terms of place, as occupying a central position (the geocentric universe), the argument has shifted to the properties of our universe relative to a wider class of possible universes. Perhaps the particular properties of the universe are not explicable in natural terms, but are what they are because that makes for a hospitable universe that allows for the emergence of humans.

Other things being equal, the age and size of the universe might be related to our existence, as the production of heavier elements in earlier generations of stars and biological evolution took some billions of years before the universe could produce complex, intelligent, observing and amiable beings, us. Turning this insight upside down, it is argued that intelligent observation by beings such as humans is only possible after about ten billion years. Thus biological beings can – so the argument goes – only observe a universe that is at least ten billion years old. Along this line of argument, the Weak Anthropic Principle (WAP) 'explains' the observed age of the universe. Our existence implies, and hence 'explains', that we observe a universe that is at least ten billion years old.

As I see it (see also Drees 1990, 2007a, 2008a), the Weak Anthropic Principle is true but devoid of relevance. Assume that we are certain that life depends on liquid water. We observe life, ourselves. WAP then predicts that our environment, our planet, will have a surface suitable for liquid water, and hence a temperature between zero and a hundred degrees centigrade. Our existence thus explains the temperature on our planet.

This is not an explanation but the common use of evidence: we observe A (life), we know that A and B go together (life needs liquid water), hence B exists (there must be liquid water). This does not explain why A and B are there, i.e. why there are living beings and planets with the right temperatures, nor does it explain why A and B go together. There is nothing wrong with the reasoning, but neither does the argument deliver significant insight.

The explanation of an event is in general something different from the explanation one offers when asked 'How do you know?' From the existence of this book you, as a reader, can infer the existence of its author. You can show the book, when challenged by someone else, to explain how you know about that person. However, the book does not explain the existence of the author. It only provides the grounds for your belief in his existence. Retrograde reasoning justifies beliefs, but it does not explain why the situation was that way.

There are also arguments about Strong Anthropic Principles (SAPs), which state that any possible universe *must* have the properties for life (or even for intelligent and observing life). This is a statement not only about the observable universe but about the class of all possible universes. This leads to an explanation of properties of the universe in terms of purpose: a property that is necessary for life is necessary for the universe.

Such teleological approaches, arguing for the purpose that everything must have, have a long history, but they are not accepted in contemporary science. As scientific proposals they fail, because they cannot rely on testable consequences about the class of possible universes as we cannot have empirical knowledge about universes that are merely possible. Furthermore, these arguments assume that we know what life and consciousness need in terms of the universe, whereas other forms of life might be possible under radically different conditions.

If applied on a small scale, say as 'planets must have the properties which allow for the development of life in some stage of their history', a Strong Anthropic Principle is surely false. It shows the nature of the SAP as a teleological argument: everything must have a purpose and therefore, for instance, the Moon must be populated. A teleological view of the universe is not something that follows from science. It is a metaphysical view, which fits well with belief in a Creator who likes living beings and therefore created a universe hospitable to life.

Teleology and plenitude, the idea that all possibilities must be actual, are metaphysical principles. Not that they therefore must be wrong, but they do not come from science. They diminish the residual contingency once science has explained what it is able to explain. Thus they do address our marginality but not on the basis of science. 'Contingency' can be used to speak of at least two different issues, namely *existential* contingency in the sense of being marginal and irrelevant (as with the Total Perspective Vortex machine) and *logical* and *natural* contingency, as the alternative to logical and natural necessity, that which is explained. The discussion on the 'anthropic principles' connects the two issues. Its advocates defend the claim that we are not marginal by arguing that our kind of existence is not logically contingent but rather to be expected.

Though design arguments in cosmology may at first sight resemble design arguments in biology, the situation is quite different. In biology, arguments for 'intelligent design' argue for gaps in the scientific account; explanations that claim some designer are in competition with an explanation by natural causes (e.g. Behe 1996, with his emphasis on the 'irreducible complexity' of states that purportedly could not have been reached along an evolutionary trajectory). In design arguments in cosmology, such as the anthropic principles to some extent are, there is no need for gaps in the scientific account – as it is the universe with its properties and generative processes that is considered to be admirable.

In my opinion, biological and cosmological design arguments are not to be combined (though this happens quite often). For if one wants to argue that the characteristics of the universe have been set up in such a way that the universe was to bring forth an interesting reality, which includes humans, one needs to assume that the processes are sufficient once their characteristics have been set, and need not be supplemented by interventions from an external agent. And vice versa, if one argues for interventions in the course of natural history, the original layout has not been so admirable. The early imagery of clocks that needed maintenance again and again is quite different from the image of a lawful universe that has no need of such a hypothesis to explain the phenomena observed.

Let me summarize the line of reasoning so far. Science leads to limit questions. These might be an incentive to move towards a theistic view: God created our reality, the universe with all its characteristics. However, the persistence of limit questions does not necessitate such a move. One cannot exclude further scientific explanations which in turn might raise further questions in an endless back and forth. And one might accept that reality in the end 'just is as it is', with those ultimate contingent features and all. For now, we will focus on the theistic option that accepts the naturalistic view of processes within reality while at the same time interpreting the universe as creation.

Creation: a view of God and of the world

Speaking of the universe as 'creation' expresses fundamental ideas about God and about the world. With respect to God, 'creation' is a way of articulating the categorical *difference* between God and the world – the one is creator, the other created – and of articulating that God is the sole source of reality. God and world are not only different but stand in an asymmetrical relation: God transcends (surpasses) the world and as the world's creator God is prior to the world.

The conviction that God is the *sole* source of reality stands in contrast to polytheistic views. In particular, it rejects the idea that the world is due to the interaction of good and evil divine principles. God as sole creator also excludes any need for raw material, in contrast to the Platonic tradition where a demiurge is supposed to form the world out of raw material, which limits the possibilities such a craftsman has (Plato's *Timaios*). This understanding of God's full freedom as creator is articulated in the doctrine of *creatio ex nihilo*, creation out of nothing, that is without any preconditions.

With respect to the world, the doctrine of creation implies that the world is *not autonomous and self-explicatory*. However, the notion that explanations ultimately reach beyond the world is not automatically at odds with the idea that phenomena within the world may be explicable on the basis of earlier conditions and general regularities. Seeing the world as creation does not imply that the world is totally unintelligible in natural terms, but it does indicate that religiously speaking the world is not ultimately intelligible without reference to God.

That the world is God's creation, with God understood as loving, also implies that the world is *valued positively*. The world is not an illusion but real. Neither is it a prison, with spiritually significant aspects of existence destined for some other reality. Rather, the material, created world is the place where humans and God are in relation. By describing the world as 'creation' the monotheistic traditions connect existence with value.

It has been argued that the rise of science has been possible because the world has been seen as God's creation. God was free to create the world differently; we cannot know what God did except through observation. Since God is believed to be trustworthy, one may also expect the world to be reliable and orderly rather than unruly. Hence, as creation the world is seen as a 'contingent order'. In studying such a contingent order, empirical explorations and mathematical analysis are needed. Along such lines, some have referred to the Christian understanding of the world to explain why modern science developed in Western Europe rather than in China or in Arab civilizations. However, technological and socioeconomic developments have played a role alongside religious ideas in creating conditions which made the rise of science possible; expecting a single decisive factor seems misguided (Cohen 1994; see also Drees 1996: 77–86). And even if the idea of creation has been essential to the rise of science, this does not imply anything about the truth of the idea itself (though it might counter the, equally naïve, criticism that Christianity has always obstructed the development of science).

Creation in biblical narratives

Though seeing the world as creation has some systematic aspects, it is important to note that the biblical creation narratives do not present a theory about origins. The Bible has no philosophical or cosmological treatises. Even the first book, Genesis, is mostly about the patriarchs of Israel, though it begins with a saga about the origins of the world, of humankind (Adam and Eve) and of the various peoples of the world (the sons of Noah). Modern people who open the Bible may thus assume that for the Hebrews the idea of God as the creator of the world came before thinking of God as the God of Israel. However, almost all scholars hold that in the religious history of Israel the emphasis was first on their particular experiences, narrated in terms of an exodus from Egypt and exile in Babylon. In the course of centuries they came to the remarkable claim that their God was not just one of the tribal gods but the Only One, the Maker of Heaven and Earth.

In the second century BCE, a period of Roman and Greek influences, we find the sole explicit Biblical reference to *creatio ex nihilo,* in 2 Maccabees 7:28, one of the deutero-canonical books, not part of the Hebrew canon but present in early Greek translations and accepted by the Roman Catholic Church as part of Scripture. An oppressive king seeks to suppress Jewish identity by forcing Jews to eat pork. Seven brothers refuse. They are tortured and killed. When the seventh son is about to be killed his mother encourages him by saying that God who has created heaven and earth out of nothing will also be able to restore him and his brothers on the day God chooses. *Creatio ex nihilo* is not introduced to explain the cosmos but serves to stress God's guarantee of the Jewish identity, undergirded by God's power as infinitely surpassing the power of an oppressive king.

The account of Genesis 1 is also about Jewish identity. The seventh day, the day God rests, refers to the Sabbath of the people. The story of the seven days ends with a reference to 'generations' (Genesis 2:4), a term elsewhere used in reference to the genealogy of Israel. In the Psalms, references to God's creative works and acts encourage believers to praise and find comfort in the Lord, without opting for a single cosmogonic tradition as to how God 'did it'. Images of making like a potter and commanding like a king occur side by side (Psalms 8, 19, 33, 148). In the later parts of the book of Isaiah, references to God as creator stress the universality of God's authority so as to make clear that the Persian king has a function in God's plans.

In the book of Job God's majesty, far beyond human understanding, is expressed partly by references to creation. In Proverbs a reference to God as creator expresses a moral consideration: 'Who oppresses the poor, insults his Maker' (14: 31). And in an earlier passage about wisdom being present at Creation (Proverbs 8: 22–31), the point is not to present a theory about processes in the beginning but rather to stress the importance of wisdom for living the life God intended.

The Bible does speak of God as creator but is not limited to a single model of how God has been creator. Speaking of God as creator is done for a variety of reasons, almost none of which is an explanation of origins. Putting science and the biblical understanding of creation in direct competition, as in creationism, neglects their different natures and functions. Seeing the universe as God's creation is not science; it is more about identity and value.

Creation in early Christianity

Seeing the universe as creation is a choice of worldview, in contrast to other views. 'New Age' is not a well-defined body of ideas, but it resembles in some respects Gnostic views of earlier times. In New Age books such as the *Course in Miracles* the material and messy world is not understood as having been created by God, and it is not valued positively. Rather, the world is a painful illusion which will lose its significance when we awake and come to spiritual insight. Also Gnostic is the tendency to understand good and evil in terms of knowledge and ignorance, symbolized as light and darkness. Thus suffering is our own failure and salvation our own responsibility (an attitude which increases our guilt when we fail to reach the blessed state). The Christian understanding of creation acquired its form in controversies with Gnostic ideas in the first two centuries of Christianity, for instance in Ireneus of Lyon's books 'against the heresies'. The symbol of creation affirms God's relation with us and our world and the world's reality and value.

Thus, seeing the universe as creation is not directly an issue that is or isn't in line with the scientific understanding of reality; it belongs at least as much on the other side of the scheme described in the previous chapter as it addresses matters of identity and values. However, seeing the world as creation does bring with it some intellectual issues that are more about worldview than about values, and we will turn now to some of these as they pertain to a naturalistic theism.

Naturalistic theism

Naturalistic theism avoids a confrontation with the natural sciences by emphasizing the uniqueness of God's mode of being and activity (e.g. Kaufman 1972; Wiles 1986; Stoeger 1995; Heller 2003; Knight 2007, 2009). This is articulated in the notion of *creatio ex nihilo*, which does not apply to any natural causality. God creates and sustains all things as their primary cause; all natural causes are real, just as are all entities and events, but they are so because they have been created by God. Such real natural causes are 'secondary causes'.

The distinction between primary and secondary causality was developed in the European Middle Ages – for instance by Thomas Aquinas – but its roots can be traced back at least to Augustine (Thomas 1983; McMullin 1985, 1988; Hebblethwaite and Henderson 1990; Burrell 1993). God creates everything – past, present and future events – and creates them not as an amorphous bag of events but with their temporal, spatial and causal relations.

The distinction between God and God's activity on the one hand and creatures and creaturely activity on the other is often articulated as a difference with respect to time: creatures are temporal whereas God, as conceived in this view, is not temporal. God's eternity is not everlastingness but timelessness. Accepting the whole natural world as the creation of a timeless, transcendent

God may be consistent with a naturalistic view of the world, since it accepts the temporal world as understood by the natural sciences as God's creation. There is no need for particular gaps within the world.

On such an understanding of God, theology and the natural sciences relate to each other with respect to the explanation of the natural world as a whole (rather than the explanation of phenomena in the natural world). Or at least the naturalistically minded theist would claim that the sciences are explanatory within the world, but not explanatory of the world as such; limit questions connect the scientific and the religious explanation. Those limit questions are not only questions about the beginning; they are also questions about existence and lawfulness. The question of why the universe is as it currently is is not answered merely by saying that this is so now since yesterday it was as it was yesterday. It is also necessary that the laws of nature are effective *at every moment*, that reality has existence at every moment. As long as we speak in terms of cause and effect we assume the ordinary notions of time and space. God can be thought of as the creator of the first moment; then and there the fuse was lit. However, since space and time are problematic concepts when we speak of the universe as a whole, we might distance ourselves from the notion of God as an engineer who started the whole business. In the theological tradition God has been referred to as the 'First Cause' which causes the 'secondary causes', that is the natural processes and natural laws.

Perhaps we should take even more license from our concepts of time, space and cause. Speaking of God as Ground of Being softens somewhat the dualistic scheme of God and creation but does not fundamentally undermine it. A major figure in the articulation of such a theological position has been Paul Tillich (Wildman 2006). In the religion and science dialogue, Arthur Peacocke (1993) might be the most prominent advocate of such a naturalistic theism. This view has come to be formulated often in panentheistic terms: understanding the world to be in God, even though God surpasses the world (Clayton and Peacocke 2004). I found a most inspiring poetic expression among aphorisms in *The Aristos* of John Fowles (1980: 27):

> The white paper that contains a drawing; the space that contains a building; the silence that contains a sonata; the passage of time that prevents a sensation or object continuing forever; all these are 'God'.

A creative development of such a position has been the suggestion of the theologian and scholar of the New Testament Gerd Theissen (1985) that we interpret religious history, including the contributions of Jesus, as a series of increasingly adequate adaptations to ultimate reality. Whatever the precise formulation, a Ground-of-Being position has more deeply ingrained naturalistic presuppositions, even though it maintains a concept of God as surpassing the world. Perhaps, when the immanence of God in the world is stressed, one might speak not of naturalistic theism, but of theistic naturalism.

Naturalistic theism has one major problem, as I see it. It is hard to give reasons, once one accepts a naturalist understanding of created reality, to explain why one would hold such a theological position; 'since there are no real "gaps" to fill, we may be left without an argument for God's existence of the kind that would convince a science-minded generation' (McMullin 1988: 74). Limit questions may exist but they do not point to one specific answer. There are other views that speak of our way of being at home in the universe – without the dualism implied in naturalistic theism. If religiously labelled, such a view would be *religious naturalism*.

Religious naturalism

Religious belief seems to be about the conviction that there is more than nature. Naturalism is perceived as the claim that there is nothing but nature. Is 'religious naturalism' a contradiction in terms, as naturalism is anti-religious? Some authors on 'religion and science' assume such a view of naturalism and invest their energy in arguing against naturalism, but others seek to explore religious options available once one accepts naturalism and a few of those self-identify as 'religious naturalists'.

The point of departure in this guide is that we ought to accept science, and with it naturalism as the position that is most respectful of the epistemic success of the natural sciences. It is preferable not only cognitively but also morally, as it incites us to work with our knowledge. The costs of rejecting naturalism are too high. The solution is to live with science and with naturalism. Among the religious and theological options in association with naturalism, one was discussed above: theistic naturalism, while here we concentrate on another one, religious naturalism.

Two motives driving religious naturalism

In arguments for naturalism, there are at least two different motives at work. Here I present naturalism as a response to the success of the sciences. The sciences provide an increasingly integrated and unified understanding of reality, resulting in precise predictions which correspond to empirical results. Inspired by the success of the sciences, naturalism is a 'low-level' metaphysics, seeking to follow as closely as is philosophically feasible the insights that the sciences offer (Drees 1996: 11).

The success of the natural sciences is, however, not the sole inspiration for naturalistic positions. For some, naturalism begins with the rejection of dualism. Some consider theism with its transcendent deity to be intellectually incoherent or religiously unacceptable. For those who dislike dualism, naturalism is attractive as a form of monism. Thus Jerome Stone (2003a: 89) defines naturalism as follows:

> Negatively, it asserts that there seems to be no ontologically distinct and superior realm (such as God, soul or heaven) to ground, explain, or give

meaning to this world. Positively, it affirms that attention should be focused on this world to provide whatever explanation and meaning are possible in life.

In this context, close cousins of religious naturalism would be monism and pantheism as *a priori* beliefs in the divinity, value or sacredness of natural reality, seen as in some sense a unity (analyzed in Levine 1994; advocated by Harrison 1999).

Answers to limit questions may be quite different for the two types of naturalists. If naturalism is defined as including the assumption 'that nature is necessary in the sense of requiring no sufficient reason beyond itself to account either for its origin or ontological ground' (Hardwick 1996: 5–6), a naturalist cannot accept the suggestion that limit questions might allow for a transcendent ground of reality. In my opinion, however, the science-inspired naturalist should not be too ideological with respect to limit questions, and thus should allow for the possibility of a naturalistic theism. Aside from this difference, however, both forms of naturalism might end up in a single larger tent, religious naturalism.

Religious naturalism

What might be *religious* naturalism? Does naturalism not exclude what is typical of religious life? The answer depends not only on one's understanding of naturalism but also on one's concept of religion. If one accepts naturalism, what might be left, and would that be enough to qualify as religious?

Jerome Stone describes religious naturalism as 'a variety of naturalism whose beliefs and attitudes assume there are religious aspects of this world that can be appreciated within a naturalistic framework. Occasions within our experience elicit responses that are analogous enough to the paradigm cases of religion that they can appropriately be called religious' (Stone 2003a: 89). Speaking of religious naturalism may thus be justified if the attitudes and responses are sufficiently analogous. For Stone there is no absolute transcendence, but he speaks of 'the sacred' in relation to 'situationally transcendent resources and continually challenging ideals in the universe' (1992: 17; 2003b: 798). Let me briefly introduce some further varieties of religious naturalism.

Gordon Kaufman interprets the Christian symbolism of God in the context of our existential concerns and our responsibility in a time of ecological and nuclear threats, but also as a figure of speech to speak of an overwhelmingly significant characteristic of processes in the universe: namely their 'serendipitous creativity' (Kaufman 1993, 2003). He connects such aspects with traditional understandings of God as Creator and the moral call and vision as understood in the Christian tradition.

Charley Hardwick gives up on ontology, speculations about the way the world is, while seeking to articulate theological content. 'Theological content can break free of ontology if this content is valuational rather than ontological. Such a valuational theism becomes possible when Rudolf Bultmann and Fritz Buri's method of existentialist interpretation is wedded to Henry Nelson Wieman's naturalistic conception of God' (Hardwick 2003: 111). He approvingly quotes Bultmann, who has said: 'the real meaning of myth does not present an objective world picture but instead expresses our understanding of ourselves in our world' (Hardwick 2003: 113). 'Although *God* does not refer (any more than rights, duties, values, or point masses need have ontological references), *God* or *God exists* can serve as a complex meta-expression for a form of life that is expressed as theistic seeing-as' (Hardwick 2003: 114).

In his book *Events of Grace* (1996), Hardwick reconstructs classical Christian conceptions such as sin and grace. This is not accidental, but part of his understanding of a religious naturalistic agenda. He does not seek a religious Esperanto without roots in a particular tradition. 'I am constantly reminded here of Santayana's dictum that "the attempt to speak without speaking any particular language is not more hopeless than the attempt to have a religion that shall be no religion in particular"' (Hardwick 2003: 115). Thus Hardwick articulates a Christian religious naturalism.

Other religious naturalists are less engaged with a particular tradition. Perhaps 'the evolutionary epic' might become *Everybody's Story* (Rue 2000). Some such more universal inspirations come from the side of scientists with a broader engagement with humanistic interests, such as Ursula Goodenough in *The Sacred Depths of Nature* (1998) and Stuart Kauffman's *Reinventing the Sacred* (2008).

There are also religious naturalists who dispense with all 'God language'. Donald Crosby speaks in this context of naturism (rather than naturalism) 'to distinguish it from conceptions of religious naturalism that make fundamental appeal to some idea of deity, deities, or the divine, however immanental, functional, nonontological, or purely valuational or existential such notions may be claimed to be. The focus of naturism is on nature itself as both metaphysically and religiously ultimate' (Crosby 2003: 117; 2008: ix).

A religious tradition?

Is religious naturalism a religious tradition, or is it an intellectual position, perhaps more philosophical than religious? There is no explicit institutionalization, as in some religions. There is no clear set of rituals that mark religious naturalists. However, 'religious naturalism' seems a subculture with an identity of its own (e.g. Cavanaugh 2000). This subculture has a history that, often unconsciously and occasionally consciously, might be a formative part of its identity (Stone 2008). One may refer to philosophers, scientists and theologians such as Henry Nelson Wieman, George Santayana, John Dewey, Charles Sanders Peirce, Mordecai Kaplan and Jack J. Cohen, and to some extent even Alfred N. Whitehead and William James, as forerunners. There is a major overlap between religious naturalism and American pragmatism.

One may go back further in time, beyond the last century and a half, and claim for religious naturalists that they are heirs of Spinoza and of his liberal

Christian and Unitarian friends and the subsequent Spinozists of various stripes, and of some of the German philosophers (Clayton 2000), as well as of the British scientists, such as Joseph Priestley, who became Unitarians. Of course, every figure is to be seen in the context of his time. Claiming them as ancestors is appropriation out of context, but that is precisely the intellectually ambivalent practice of tradition formation that strengthens identity. These exemplary figures are individuals who are perceived as somewhat heretical by the traditional religious community of their time, while standing in close contact with, if not being part of, the scientific community; precisely the mix that may fit contemporary religious naturalists.

There are Christian, Jewish and humanist dialects of religious naturalism, as well as biological, psychological and physicalist ones, reflecting upbringing, training and heritage as well as needs and situations. Some dialects are dialects of another tradition as well, just as a local dialect near the border of my country may be considered by some as a dialect of Dutch, whereas others might treat it as a dialect of German. Thus some essays may be read as liberal Christian essays as well as religious naturalistic ones. There is a wide range of styles, from the sober and minimalist (Stone, Hardwick) to the ecstatic and exuberant (Corrington 1997), from the analytical to the evocative (Goodenough 1998). Religious naturalism is an umbrella which covers a variety of dialects, of which some are revisionary articulations of existing traditions whereas others may be more purely naturalistic religions indebted almost exclusively to the sciences. There is family resemblance, with affinities and disagreements, not unity.

Religious naturalism also takes shape through stories. The evolutionary epic serves as a master narrative (e.g. Rue 2000), but there are also smaller stories that evoke attitudes and feelings alongside philosophical essays that convey intellectual claims. Ursula Goodenough's *The Sacred Depths of Nature* is an example. And it offers a setting for understanding the darker aspects of one's own existence: 'My somatic life is the wondrous gift wrought by my forthcoming death' (Goodenough 1998: 151). There is also plenty of work on more systematic theological elaborations (e.g. Stone 1992; Hefner 1993; Kaufman 1993, 2004; K.E. Peters 2002; Hardwick 1996).

In addition to reflection on the sciences and the philosophical clarification of various forms of religious naturalism, there is also work to be done by historians of religion and of culture by studying such more diffuse forms of religion, whether related to traditions or as 'something-ism', agnosticism and religious humanism. These could be studied historically and systematically, for motives and arguments as well as for dynamics.

Ultimate mystery: the serious agnostic

Am I a religious naturalist or a naturalistic theist? I don't know, and I don't consider this a problem. Labels constrain. I want to explore the various options, but in this attitude of exploring I fit the broader scientific and natur-alistic tradition considered in this chapter, or at least I hope I do. I am most interested in understanding what religious naturalism and naturalistic theism might mean, may become and will offer. I don't think that one should be a lazy agnostic, not seeking to explore and understand as much as possible. However, when one is serious, one might find more genuine options on the table than just one – and hence one can come to a situation where one doesn't know. Thus, rather than opting for a particular view, one might opt for epistemic modesty and become a serious agnostic.

Agnosticism is an attitude with appropriate antecedents and representatives in philosophical and theological thought (Joshi 2007; Kenny 2004); it may be an attitude present in theism as well as in religious naturalism in Kantian, empiricist and other varieties (Kaufman 1993; Keller 2008). What has been called 'negative theology' or the *apophatic* tradition stresses categorical differ-ences between God and creation, and thus the inadequacy of any analogy we construct. Such modesty with respect to our abilities may serve the reconcilia-tion of apparently different views, but it may also be part of a polemic against an orthodoxy that pretends to know it all. Nicholas of Cusa, theologian of the fifteenth century, titled a book *De docta ignorantia*, on learned ignorance, as opposed to ignorance due to a lack of learning. 'Learned ignorance' might be a motto for a serious agnostic.

There are risks to agnosticism, such as the risk of closing one's eyes to genuine knowledge, and also the risk that one pretends modesty while sug-gesting to know nonetheless. I once heard of a professor of theology who taught on the attributes of God, such as omnipotence, while also dedicating a session to the unknowable attributes. For the sake of consistency, and out of respect for the possible subject matter, restraint in speaking of that which is beyond our reach seems desirable. There is also a manipulative way of work-ing with the concept of mystery. This occurs when something is presented as a mystery but would be labelled more accurately a secret, with the answer being known to some who thus claim for themselves a privileged position of authority.

Honest agnosticism can be valuable; it might be an attitude that is combined with one of the more substantial positions, naturalistic theism or religious naturalism, preferred for whatever reasons. Religious views of the universe, its existence and laws need assumptions about a transcendent source or immanent values which are at least as problematic as the unexplained existence of the universe or its laws. Not being able to accept the finality of a scientific or a religious explanation, I personally think one does best in joining the physicist Charles Misner (1977: 95):

> To say that God created the Universe does not explain either God or the Universe, but it keeps our consciousness alive to mysteries of awesome majesty that we might otherwise ignore.

Chapter 6

Values in a world of facts

The integrity and coherence of the world may inspire one with awe and wonder as well as trigger a quest for an ultimate explanation, though ultimate explanations ask for more than what is delivered by science. Each of the two views considered above, naturalistic theism and religious naturalism, involves a similar value judgement: the world is good. If the world weren't good, why would it be appropriate to consider it the creation of a good God? Or, for the religious naturalist, if nature lacks moral and aesthetic quality, why associate nature with the sacred?

The world is not good. There is misery, illness, pain, decay, the death of beloved individuals and the disappearance of species. A religious view that does not acknowledge the waste in natural history and in human lives is unfair to important experiences. This also challenges 'religion and science', since quite a few argue that there is consonance between our scientific understanding and our religious appreciation of the world. I will argue that moral engagement with the world requires us to consider dissonance as well.

When we aspire to reduce misery, technology rather than theoretical science has primacy. We live in a technological culture, and are thereby engaged in transforming our world. Belief in the significance of such human actions challenges any naïve belief in harmony, and hence any straightforward argument from positive experiences to a religious understanding of reality.

Awareness of misery, or at least of the possibility that what is natural need not be good, underlies the distinction between facts and values, between the way the world is and the way the world is envisioned as it should be. In Chapter 4 we heard of a distinction between models *of* the world and models *for* the world, of cosmology and values, two elements that any theology holds together, even if in tension. However, values are expressed in human judgements, which are rooted in our biological nature, and thus they belong to the sphere of facts nonetheless. How to think of values in a world of facts? That will be the question towards the end of this chapter. But let us begin with consonance and dissonance, and the place of technology in 'religion and science'.

As indicated earlier with respect to other topics, all such issues are too big for the space allotted here, as well as being too big for my competence. The aim cannot be an exhaustive treatment but rather an introduction to some of the major issues at stake in 'religion and science'.

Creative dissonance

The absence of chemistry from natural theology

Order and design go together in arguments from nature to its Author, while many see disorder, diseases and imperfections as challenges to a religious view. Many writings on 'religion and science' argue that despite appearances to the contrary there is a good order underlying our world. In this context chemistry is often the odd man out. It isn't too important in the explanatory considerations, as the deepest explanations are supposed to be in the domain of physics and cosmology, while biology and neurology provide important windows on our own nature. Chemistry is just an intermediary between the physical and the biological.

Even worse, chemistry's ambition to purify elements and to create new materials seems to count against fundamental assumptions of natural theology. Chemistry presents us with the artificial, something new, in the midst of natural reality. Chemistry is archetypical for science in its transformative power, though in our days almost all the sciences have such an active, creative, world-changing side. Think of electronics that gave rise to the internet and of biotechnology with its consequences for food production and medicine.

In the seventeenth, eighteenth and nineteenth centuries many works of natural theology have been based on insights from biology, physics and astronomy, disciplines focused on describing and understanding reality. Such a view of science as uncovering the order present in reality fits well with the idea that there is a given order and a divine architect or ruler who set the laws that generated this order. Chemistry is almost completely absent from these natural theologies, as the historians of science John Brooke and Geoffrey Cantor observed in the final chapter of their *Reconstructing Nature*.

Interest in the artificial (and hence in chemistry) fits ill with any natural theology that argues from nature to its Author. Brooke and Cantor quote the political radical Richard Carlile who wrote in 1829 'With the doctrine of an intelligent deity it is presumption to attempt anything toward human improvement. Without the doctrine, it is not any presumption.' Brooke and Cantor (1998: 314), from whom this quotation has been taken, add: 'It is as if arguments for divine wisdom require this to be the best of all possible worlds, with the corollary that attempts at improvement would both be sacrilegious and ineffective.'

Not that chemistry had no religious associations at all, but it had different ones. Interest in chemistry aligned not with the legal and regal imagery of laws and the mechanical imagery of cathedrals and clocks but with a spiritualist view of nature, as argued convincingly by Eugene Klaaren in his *Religious*

Origins of Modern Science (1977). In chemistry one finds the theme of pur-
ification, material and spiritual, seeking to bring the divine out of the material.
Brooke and Cantor observe that emphasis on chemistry often correlated with
'a kind of process theology', not in the sense of Whitehead and Griffin but as a
view that sees in the further development of the world a role for humans
working with God.

If one speaks thus of humanity's role in creation, one distances oneself from
the idea that creation is in principle finished and complete and from the idea
that God bypasses humans in arranging everything. The history of humans is a
history in which humans have responsibility. If humans are seen as co-creators
with God, there is still something to be done: nature is not perfect but
ambivalent.

Christian theology and the ambivalence of reality

Awareness of the ambivalence of nature did not have to wait for the rise of
chemistry; this fact of life needed to be addressed in any religious perspective.
One interesting attempt in Christianity has been the approach taken by Marcion, in the second century CE. He held that God, the creator of this ambivalent world, the God for whom justice seems to be fairness, 'an eye for an eye',
could not be the same as God the Redeemer, the Loving Father of Jesus Christ,
in whom there is grace and abundant forgiveness. Marcion concluded that
there were two gods rather than one – the Creator being distinct from, and in
goodness less than, the Father of Jesus Christ.

The Christian churches have rejected Marcion's solution. In its creeds,
Christianity has affirmed that the same God is the Creator of heaven and earth
and the Father of Jesus Christ. In Roman Catholic thought this affirmation has
often been developed in terms of a continuity of nature and grace. In protestant
thought, the tension between nature and grace has been more in the forefront,
with grace being more important than any natural characteristic or achievement,
but even then creation and redemption are related to the same God.

In European history the tension between envisaging harmony and acknowledging tensions has also been a theme in novels. A famous example is Fyodor
Dostoyevsky's *The Brothers Karamazov* (1879–80), especially in the objections
of Ivan. 'If the sufferings of the children go to swell the sum of sufferings
which was necessary to pay for truth, then I protest that the truth was not
worth such a price.' One can also think of a short novel by the French philosopher Voltaire, *Candide ou l'Optimisme* (1759), written in the wake of the
earthquake of 1755 that destroyed Lisbon. In this novel the philosopher Pan-
gloss defends again and again the assertion that this is the best of all possible
worlds. The more he argues his case, the less convincing it becomes. The
earthquake of Lisbon, on All Souls Day of 1755, at a time of the day when
people were attending churches, has become an icon of natural evil, of disaster
wrought upon us by processes in nature (Breidert 1994), just as the horror of

the concentration camp at Auschwitz has become the typical example of moral evil, perpetrated by humans.

Theists face a complex situation. Among themselves, they do not agree how to handle the tension between the goodness of creation and the need for redemption. And they are challenged by others, some who argue that there are two ultimate realities (good and evil, or, like Marcion, one unjust but graceful and the other just but harsh), while others deny our world, with all its suffering, as an illusion or an imprisonment of divine sparks.

One area where the valuation of the world shows in relation to science is in the understanding of this vast universe, which in most places and at most times seems to be inhospitable to life. This applies also to the long-term future. When the Sun concludes its stage of hydrogen burning, some five billion years from now, the possibilities for earth-based life are grim. Science does not support a positive view of the world as assumed in the design arguments, and it does offer some pretty good reasons for a more pessimistic view. As the cosmologist Steven Weinberg wrote, at the end of his popular book *The First Three Minutes* (1977: 154):

> It is even harder to realize that this present universe has evolved from an unspeakably unfamiliar early condition, and faces future extinction of endless cold or intolerable heat. The more the universe seems incomprehensible, the more it also seems pointless.

This assessment is a direct challenge to those who rely upon a design argument which seeks to claim that our world is a good place to be, and thus a good job done well, indicating a good Creator. Weinberg's remark and similar considerations regarding the ambivalence of reality should be a stimulus to us to reconsider what we see as the nature of religious faith.

Religions are not just peculiar cosmologies, whether involving a Supreme Being or with demons, angels and other spiritual entities floating around. If one could make a convincing argument that there is 'a Maker' beyond the Big Bang that would be fascinating, but it would not be religiously relevant if there were not a moral dimension to it. In the New Testament we hear of two great commandments, to love God and to love one's neighbour, to be pursued with all the energy and knowledge one has. The commandment is not to believe in a certain explanation of the world or of phenomena in the world, but to live in a certain way, in a loving way. Similar calls can be found in the writings of the prophets and elsewhere.

Religion may be a response to encounters with *aspects of reality which we may not understand or control, but to which we feel positively related or for which we feel grateful*. This dimension of religion one might call *mystical*, since it has to do with a sense of being related to, or belonging to, something which surpasses us and our understanding. This is a dimension of religion many authors on the relationship between science and religion seem to identify with when they emphasise elements which correspond to, affectively speaking, a positive view of reality such as order, creativity, purposiveness, coherence, beauty or mystery. It is such a religiosity which stimulates the quest for design or an implicit order which is meaningful and good. This is the background of 'natural theology'.

The question arises whether by affirming reality, such a natural theology is not too conservative, too much affirming the status quo, and insufficiently critical, failing to do adequate justice to suffering and evil. Religions can also be seen as human responses to *aspects of reality we will not accept*. In this case, we might speak of a *prophetic* religion, since it relates to the experience of a *discontinuity* between values and facts, between our axiology and our cosmology. To articulate this dimension of religion, we seem to need a dualist element in religious language, articulating a contrast between what is and what should be. Such a dualism can be expressed in religious terms as the difference between earth and heaven, between the city of man and the city of God, between the present and the paradise, between the present and the Kingdom of God, between nature and grace, and in many other ways. Thus Gerd Theissen (1985: 4) wrote:

> Every faith contradicts reality in some way. That is inevitable, if faith is to be an unconditional 'Yes' to life. Think of all the horrors that could contradict this 'Yes'! Think of all the oppressive experiences against which it has to be affirmed: all the probabilities and certainties, including the certainty of one's own death!

The issue could perhaps also be argued in the context of the history of religions. John Hick (1989), following Karl Jaspers, distinguishes between the tribal religions which preceded the axial (transition) period around the middle of the last millennium BCE and the post-axial religions. The earlier religions located the individual within the social and cosmic order and thus are typical examples of religions which stress continuity between cosmological and axiological aspects, whereas the later religions emphasized transformation, salvation or redemption (and thus, in one way or another, relied upon a distinction between the social and cosmic order and the destiny of the individual).

The issue can perhaps also be formulated within the Hebrew and Christian tradition in terms of divine presence and absence. In his *The Elusive Presence* (1978) Samuel Terrien traces the role of hiddenness through the Bible. One example is the story of Jacob wrestling with a stranger during the night; the stranger cannot be seen in the light of the day nor is his name revealed (Genesis 32). 'Thick darkness' characterises the place of God, both at Mount Sinai and in the temple in Jerusalem (Exodus 20: 21; 1 Kings 8: 12; 2 Chronicles 6: 1). The Ten Commandments prohibit the carving of images. According to Isaiah (8: 17; 45: 15), God hides himself. Job is challenged to tell where he was when God laid the foundations of the earth. Job places his hand in front of his mouth and is silent (Job 38–40). Job does not so much acknowledge moral guilt as hubris. In Jesus God's presence is not obvious. Is this not the carpenter? Do we not know his parents, brothers and sisters? (e.g. Mark 6: 3). And he is not even able to save himself from the cross (Mark 15: 29–32)! But then the centurion recognises this man as the Son of God (Mark 15: 39). Through humiliation comes exaltation (Philippians 2: 5–11).

The life of Jewish and Christian communities is not structured around a holy place, a temple where God is present. Central to Jewish and Christian life are holy times of remembrance and expectation. The Sabbath recalls the creation and the exodus and is a foretaste of fulfilment. The Synagogue is a place of memory and hope, recalling God's great deeds in the past for the sake of the future. The hiddenness and absence can be seen mystically, in relation to God's holiness, but also in relation to prophetic engagement: this world is not as God intends the world to be.

Quite a few contemporary theologians, sometimes under the influence of Karl Barth, are very sensitive to such tensions within our world and within our faiths. This may explain to some extent why so many theologians, at least on the European continent, hesitate to follow old or new arguments of design that seek to establish that God shows through the processes of nature. They live, explicitly or implicitly, with a theology that incorporates also divine absence, not as atheism but as a way of being which is not in line with existence as experienced.

Concerns about the ambivalence of our world make debates on 'religion and science' complicated. Sometimes an appeal to the moral and theological inadequacy of scientific insights becomes a way of brushing difficult issues under the rug by abstaining from a genuine conversation with current scientific knowledge. But the reality of suffering and evil is a persistent challenge to arguments that seek to uncover consonance between scientific knowledge and theological convictions.

Consonance?

Natural theology with the intention of arguing from features of reality to the existence and nature of its Maker seems to focus too much on that which 'is' and thereby neglect the critical dimension, our longing for this world to be better. Besides, arguments in natural theology are often quite selective, focusing on nice features of reality but not addressing the darker sides of nature. But not only is 'natural theology' in this argumentative sense open to challenges. So too is an epistemically more modest argument about *consonance* between religious ideas and our understanding of reality. Consonance seems to assume that harmony is there to be discerned.

The term 'consonance' was used in passing by Ernan McMullin (1981: 52), in reflections on the similarity and dissimilarity of insights from Big Bang cosmology and the Christian idea of *creatio ex nihilo*.

The Christian cannot separate his science from his theology as though they were incapable of interrelation. On the other hand, he has learned to distrust the simpler pathways from one to the other. He has to aim at some sort of coherence of world-view, a coherence to which science and theology, and indeed many other sorts of human construction like history, politics, and literature, must contribute. He may, indeed, *must* strive to make his theology and his cosmology consonant in the contribution they make to this world-view. But this consonance (as history shows) is a tentative relation, constantly under scrutiny, in constant slight shift.

Whereas McMullin introduced the musical metaphor consonance mainly as a critical epistemic notion, arguing *against* simple pathways between science and theology, the term has acquired a more affirmative meaning in the writings of others. 'Consonance' has become a flag in 'religion and science', suggesting that there are two independent sources of insight which happen to be in harmony. Ted Peters, a Lutheran theologian associated with the Center for Theology and the Natural Sciences in Berkeley, gave a book he edited the title *Cosmos as Creation: Theology and Science in Consonance* (1989); a decade later, he titled another book *Science and Theology: The New Consonance* (1998).

Peters speaks of 'hypothetical consonance' on 'the domain of inquiry shared by science and theology' (1998: 1). Hypothetical in that 'It would be too much to say that the current state of the dialogue between science and theology consists of total accord or total agreement regarding the role that God plays as the world's creator and redeemer. (...) In its milder form consonance functions as an hypothesis: If there is only one reality and if both science and theology speak about the same reality, is it reasonable to expect that sooner or later shared understandings will develop?' (Peters 1998: 1).

Speaking of 'hypothetical consonance' adds epistemic nuance, but such caution does not address the more persistent value issue at stake. The assumption behind 'consonance' is that we are looking for *harmony* between theological and scientific ideas. However, many theologies articulate also a critical attitude towards reality, drawing on a dualism of the real and the ideal, of the way things are and the way they should be, between the present and God's reign. Arguing for 'consonance' risks becoming an argument that this is the best of all possible worlds, that evil is not genuine but only apparent or justified for a greater good.

In my opinion, the term 'consonance' assumes too much that harmony is something to be found. Rather, consonance is something that needs to be constructed – both in the intellectual sense that we need to change our ideas in order to make them 'fit' together and in the ethical sense that harmony needs to be constructed by changing this world, by changing our lives. Perhaps, as Geoffrey Cantor once suggested to me, rather than speaking of consonance we should speak of creative dissonance. Creative not only in the intellectual sense but also in the practical sense of technology, by which we seek to solve problems and thereby aspire to reduce the dissonance we experience.

Playing God? Religion and technology

Frederick Ferré tells the story of his father who in 1922 as a young boy in a farming community of Swedish immigrants in the USA heard the preacher fulminate against the 'shiny spikes of faithlessness'. 'Thunderbolts were God's to hurl, not man's to deflect. The fires of hell, deep under the earth on which the congregation now sat and quaked, were even then being stoked for those who insisted on rising in rebellion against God's will by installing newfangled lightning rods. Amen.' Even if one would have no doubts about hellfire, there seems to be something deeply confused about such a sermon.

> Could God's will truly be foiled by a steel rod and a grounding wire? Was it really wrong to protect family and livestock from the storms that swept in from the prairies with such seemingly undiscriminating force? [...] Should he believe that the God Jesus called 'our Father in heaven' really would punish farmers for taking whatever meager technological precautions might be available?
>
> (Ferré 1993: 27)

Religious objections to science-based technology surface again and again, and with them the warning that 'we should not play God'. However, we as modern humans cannot do without the technological side of science, restricting ourselves to the noble goal of understanding reality. Not only can we not do without technology, but doing without technology isn't desirable either. There is the mythical image of paradise, of an effortless pastoral life with fruit in abundance, but if one is more realistic, we need technology for morally lofty purposes: to feed the hungry, to clothe the naked, to care for the sick. Here we will focus on technology in relation to religion, as a particular aspect of the 'religion and science' debates.

Playing God?

Sometimes a concern is voiced that we go too far in our technological activities; we are 'playing God'. And even non-believers find 'playing God' a useful metaphor in criticizing new technologies. The American philosopher Ronald Dworkin suggested in 1999 that this metaphor arises because those new technologies do not merely raise ethical issues, but create insecurity by undermining a distinction that is vital to ethics. Underlying our moral experience is a distinction between what has been given and what is a matter of choice and responsibility. What is given is the stable background of our actions. We cannot change those elements. Traditionally this has been referred to in terms of fate, nature or creation: domains of the gods or of God. We assume a clear demarcation between who we are, whether the product of divine providence or of blind chance, and what we do in the situation we find ourselves in.

When new technologies expand the range of our abilities, and thus shift the boundary between what is given and what is open to our actions, we become insecure and concerned. It is especially in such circumstances that the phrase 'playing God' arises. The reference to 'God' signals that something that was experienced as a given becomes part of the domain of human considerations; something that was beyond our powers to change has been moved to our side of the boundary.

If so, the fear of 'playing God' is not the fear of doing what is wrong (which is an issue on our side of the boundary) but rather the fear of losing our grip on reality through the dissolution of the boundary. Dworkin argues that this fear is not necessary; humans have always played with fire and we ought to do so. The alternative is, according to Dworkin, an irresponsible cowardice for the unknown, a weak surrender to fate.

New technologies imply a different range of human powers and thus a changing experience of fate, nature, creation or God – if, and only if, God is associated with that which has been given, identified with creation. If God is seen thus, our technological activity will be seen as pushing God back to the margin. Antibiotics and contraceptives have contributed more to secularization in Western cultures than Darwin; practices are more important than ideas. This God who is pushed to the margin is a 'God of the gaps', not so much the gaps in our knowledge as the gaps in our skills. Upon a different theological view, transgressing such boundaries is called for.

Professional competence and the 'God of the gaps' in technology

A surgeon stands by my bed. She explains what they intend to do tomorrow. When she has left for the next room, the man in the bed besides me begins to talk. 'You know, my son was in medical school with her. When she had to do her exams, the professor said that she should have failed, but that he would let her pass so as to get rid of her.' I am down.

A pastor stands besides my bed. She reads Psalm 139, words of trust and consolation. 'If I take the wings of the morning and dwell in the uttermost parts of the sea, even there thy hand shall lead me, and thy right hand shall hold me.' I see my life in the light of eternity. My mood goes up again. When she has left for the next room, my neighbour begins again. 'You know, my daughter was in seminary with her. When this chaplain had to do her exams, the professor said that she should have failed, but that he would let her pass so as to get rid of her.' It does not bother me at all.

From surgeons, pilots and the engineers who design bridges we demand professional competence, and rightly so. (The example of the surgeon was made up; it is not fair to the responsible behaviour of those who train doctors.) With the pastor, and in ordinary contacts between one human and another, the issue is not so much particular knowledge and skills. I depend on the surgeon; when she has not slept well I am at risk. I no longer depend on the pastor; our conversation opened resources in myself (if adequate; sometimes pastors and friends close such resources and do more harm than good; read Job). The surgeon is, to speak religiously, a mediator who stands between me and my salvation; the chaplain isn't.

In daily life we do *not* put our trust in prayer and pious words. When something needs to be done, we want an engineer, a doctor, a pilot: a professional who is competent in the practice at hand. Only when the doctor is unable to offer a hopeful perspective does the temptation arise to spend money on aura-reading, pulverized shark cartilage (once popular on the Dutch pseudo-medical circuit as a 'cure' for cancer), prayer-healing, or whatever. When life becomes difficult we look for something to hold on to, but we prefer to begin with strategies that play by regular professional standards.

In conversations on 'religion and science', there is the critical expression 'God of the gaps'. This refers to the tendency to focus on gaps in our knowledge, on limitations in our current understanding, and to assume that such gaps are where God's actions might be. Far more satisfactory, in my opinion, would be to see reality as we understand it as God at work. Emphasizing gaps is a risky strategy, like building upon ice; whenever we become blessed with greater understanding, the role of any 'God of the gaps' will be diminished. But that is not the point here; there is not only a 'God of the gaps' in our dealings with science.

In our dealings with technology we are also tempted to fall back upon a 'God of the gaps'. Occasionally with gratitude, but often without paying much attention, we use the fruits of science and technology – antibiotics, electric lights, water drainage, computers, the contraceptive pill, etc. When the doctor fails, when there is no cure yet, we fall back upon God, or upon other elements from the rich treasury of (pseudo-) religious offerings. The expression 'God of the gaps' may have its home in conversations on the theoretical side of science, where too many believers are anxiously looking for that which science is unable to explain. However, a similar danger arises in the context of the practical side of science – looking for God when our human skills fall short of what we wish we could do. Praying to God when technology fails results in an instrumental type of religiosity – God is supposed to help us when we need help, but to keep out of our way as long as we do well.

Against the tendency to assume that the religious dimension comes into play when the engineers and doctors are finished, it seems preferable to appreciate the efforts of the professionals, and not only to appreciate them commercially but also religiously. When the computer in the plane or the equipment in the intensive care unit of the hospital fails, I hope that the staff of the maintenance department will not pray 'that thou wouldst slay the wicked, O God' (Psalm 139: 19). We look to the engineers for our salvation. This is not to be seen as an anti-religious move, as we may appreciate their knowledge and skills as gifts of God, as the potential to serve their neighbours 'with all your heart, and with all your soul, and with all your strength, and with all your mind' (Luke 10: 27).

Creative creatures

Various notions are used in religious circles to describe the human role, both in relation to environmental concerns and in relation to modern biotechnology. Are we to be seen as stewards, or rather as co-creators?

Let me begin with a summary of the Bible, in a single sentence. The Bible begins on high, with paradise, which is followed by a long journey through history, with the expectation of final salvation. The liturgy is one of memory and hope. The Sabbath recalls the creation and the exodus and is a foretaste of fulfilment. This U-profile (Frye 1982: 169) implies that images of the good are present in two varieties, as images of a past paradise and as images of a City of God, a new heaven and a new earth, God's coming reign. If humans are considered stewards, one looks back to a good situation which has to be kept and preserved. If humans are seen as co-creators then one's eyes are mainly on the future, on that which is to come.

In relation to the use of human knowledge and power, some of the stories may be illuminating. In the synagogue Jesus meets someone with a withered hand. Will he heal on the Sabbath? Jesus asks: 'Is it lawful on the Sabbath to do good or to do harm, to save life or to kill?' The priority is clear. In this story of healing, from Mark 3, and in many other stories, a human is freed of the burdens of his past. A tax collector and a prostitute are again set on the way of life, the possessed relax and deaf people hear. Those who have been less well-off get new chances and are seen in a new light. Though often neglected, discipleship as serving the poor and needy has resurfaced again and again in the history of Christianity. This resulted in particular in the care for orphans, widows and people who were seriously ill.

There is one parable which is explicitly about stewardship (Matthew 25: 14–30). A landlord entrusts his property to three servants. One receives five talents (a talent being a monetary unit of that time), one two talents and the third only one talent, 'to each according to his ability'. The parable of the talents may be familiar. The one with five talents made another five, the servant with two talents made two, while the one with only one talent buried it and returned it to his master. In the end the landlord commands that the worthless servant be cast into the outer darkness; there men will weep and gnash their teeth.

From this brief tour of biblical texts and images I conclude that in biblical language the good is not only in the past but also in the future, that humans – even when considered as stewards – can be active and even ought to be active although the initiative is with God, and that this activity is normatively determined as care for those who need it.

If one speaks of human action as *co-creation*, one distances oneself from the idea that creation is in principle finished and complete and from the idea that God will bypass humans in arranging everything. The history of humans is a history in which humans have responsibility. However, if the difference between God and humans is emphasized, the notion of co-creation doesn't fit too well. If God's mode of action is totally different from ours, we are not creators with God. Being creator, giving existence as Ground of Being, is something that can be said only of God. A similar problem applies to the notion of stewardship, which rests upon the idea that the steward takes on certain tasks of his lord, tasks that his lord could have executed himself.

Emphasizing the difference grants room for human responsibility, for human creative activity. Upon such a view, God has created the world with all its regularities and all its freedom. God is not delegating power in some half-hearted way, intervening whenever things are different from God's intentions. God does not shift to manual control to correct the consequences of free human actions. In this perspective, humans are not co-creators in the sense in which God is a creator, but they are *creative creatures*, beings who creatively act in creation. My preference is for thinking through terms in which God's mode of action is fundamentally not in competition with human actions and natural processes; either these processes are God at work or God is the ground of these processes and of existence, but God is not an additional factor among other factors.

Stewardship has become prominent in reflection upon the ecological damage that we have done. In that context, stewardship has the connotation of conservation. It fits reticence better than actively changing nature. But human activity is not only a threat to God's good creation. It has also been seen as taking up the work God entrusted to us to work for the good, under the guidance of the Holy Spirit – whether this work is primarily social or ecological. Human creativity does not diminish God. On the contrary, the more someone develops their creativity, the more they surpass current limitations, the more God becomes God. We cannot shift the burden of responsibility to God; we are responsible. Our task is to make the world conform better to God's intentions, or, as Isabel Carter Heyward (1982) puts it with a remarkable verb, our task is 'to god the world'. In such theological projects we aren't doing theology on the basis of positive experiences of beauty and goodness, but rather out of engagement with justice, with love. This makes us focus on transformation as a central theological theme.

With respect to our cosmology, the worldview component of a theology in the terms introduced in Chapter 4, technology requires us to envisage not only the real but also the possible, not just the order and laws of nature but also the flexibility within nature. Technology uses the flexibility within nature without transgressing any laws; we fly not by suspending gravity (that would be magic), but by using gravity for our purposes. With respect to values, technology requires us to be alert to the expansion of the domain of choices, but which choices we make will not come from the scientific or technical side by itself. Focusing on technology might make us sensitive to elements neglected when we focus on science mainly as source of understanding rather than as a source of transformative power.

Technology's place in 'religion and science'

The standard view of technology's place in relation to 'religion and science' is illustrated in the titles of two books by Ian Barbour: *Religion in an Age of Science* and *Ethics in an Age of Technology*. This may seem an obvious pair of titles but it is nonetheless a particular and consequential way of dividing the field, as was pointed out to me by Ronald Cole-Turner in a discussion some decades ago. Why not also *Religion in an Age of Technology*? And does the absence of *Ethics in an Age of Science*, the fourth combination of the pairs (science, technology) and (religion, ethics), imply that there is no moral issue in relation to scientific knowledge, but only in relation to its use in technology?

The underlying issue is in part the understanding of 'science'. The case for including technologies in our understanding of the sciences has become far more convincing over time, with a fundamental transition taking place in the eighteenth and nineteenth centuries with the rise of chemistry and the control of electromagnetism. Modern technology is interwoven with science; the computer would not be possible without the understanding provided by quantum physics and genetic engineering depends on understanding the double helix of DNA. And vice versa, progress in understanding depends upon progress in construction.

The underlying issue is also the understanding of 'religion'. If 'religion and science' is pursued for an apologetic interest then the prime interest in science is the understanding of reality it aspires to offer. But religious traditions have not only this 'explanatory' function but often also an evocative function and a transformative interest, calling on people to work better for this world, seeking to liberate humans from bondage. Such liberationist theologies should certainly have an interest in the way we humans transform reality, for better or for worse.

Back to the story of the surgeon and the chaplain. If we appreciate the competence of the surgeon, what is left for the chaplain? If our health is a technical problem that needs to be fixed, why would we be interested in, and even moved by, Psalm 139? In the next chapter I will return to the quest for words and images that articulate meaning in a world of matter.

Technology changes our self-understanding. Who has never been 'under stress', feeling 'huge pressure'? Do you occasionally need 'to let off steam'? We may consider ourselves as made in God's image, but we speak of ourselves as if we are in the image of machines. Technology and humanity aren't that far apart; the artificial is integral to our nature. Perhaps values aren't strange to our existence as natural beings either; what would they be if not natural?

Are values natural?

Awareness of misery, or at least of the possibility that what is natural need not be good, underlies the distinction between facts and values, between the way the world is and the way the world is envisioned as it should be. When discussing the definition of religion of Clifford Geertz in Chapter 4 we learned of a distinction between models *of* the world and models *for* the world, between cosmology and values, two elements that any theology holds together, even if in tension. Though we thus distinguish values and facts, our values are expressed in human judgements, which are rooted in our biological nature and our material brains – and thus in some way the values belong to the sphere of facts. Can 'religion and science' help us to think of values in a world of facts?

The evolution of moral culture

Humans have come into being through an evolutionary process. Most of us do not mind when this is applied to the almost complete loss of fur, but we might find it a more sensitive issue when we consider moral and mental matters. There is an explanatory interest in whether morality could come to be through evolution, since evolution seems to favour self-interest whereas moral behaviour is to the benefit of others. And there is a categorical question as to whether a morality that evolved would really be moral? We begin with the question of whether evolution could bring forth something like morality, perhaps more cautiously described as pro-social behaviour.

Let us begin with close kin. Social behaviour towards children, nephews and nieces is evolutionary intelligible as a form of genetic 'self-interest', perhaps not too much deserving of the epithet 'moral'. Genes that promote social behaviour within the family promote the spread of copies of themselves in the next generation. Support of one's partner is also evolutionary intelligible, since the shared investment in children results in common interests. And for beings with a reasonable memory, helping one's neighbour is evolutionary intelligible as well. After all, at another time I may request help from my neighbour.

Helping a stranger may perhaps be understood as an example of 'indirect reciprocity'. By displaying social behaviour I may raise my status among my friends and neighbours, and indirectly this may pay off. There may also be explanations in terms of the collective interest of my tribe, village or nation. By doing something for my group this group may thrive in comparison with competing groups. Hence by serving the group I will benefit my children as well.

We may benefit even more when we invest less in the common cause than we appear to, so that we profit from the benefits that befall our group without sharing the burden as much as the others do. The evolution of deception is, upon this view, intertwined with the evolution of social behaviour; free-riding is a recurrent concern.

To be explained is not only the behaviour but also our own make-up; sociobiology has to some extent been succeeded by evolutionary psychology. There may not be an all-encompassing evolutionary explanation of the rise of pro-social behaviour and of the habit of evaluating the behaviour of others in moral terms, but various ideas along such lines as are indicated here may do the job quite well (e.g. Alexander 1987, 1993; Irons 1991; Kitcher 1985; Midgley 1994; Nitecki and Nitecki 1993; Ruse 1993; Sober & Wilson 1999).

Is moral behaviour less valuable when it is evolutionary intelligible? Is it dishonest, not genuine? We withdraw our hand from a flame. Those who did not do so became handicapped or died from infections. Hence they produced fewer children or were less able to protect and support them. Nonetheless, to the question 'Why do you withdraw your hand?' the answer is not 'In order to have more children' but 'Because it hurts.' That the sensibility to pain and the reflex to withdraw have evolutionary explanations does not make the pain less real or the verbal explanation offered less real. So too for morality: the existence of an evolutionary explanation for pro-social behaviour does not imply that we are not driven by genuine moral considerations and sentiments. Rather, moral sentiments are the means by which a fruitful social life has become possible. There is no reason to deny human culture in the name of an evolutionary explanation. The genetic background is not necessarily at odds with altruistic cultural codes. On the contrary, evolution has made us into beings who may have altruistic motives.

> Kin-selection (...) can make it extremely adaptive to be nice to others. (...) Because these tendencies do *not* spring from calculation, but from inherited dispositions, they cannot be regularly switched off when someone less closely related heaves in sight. They are not strictly proportioned to blood relationship, but respond to many other cues, such as familiarity, admiration, liking, and the special needs of others. And in human beings, the complexities of culture can give them a much wider range of channels than is possible for other species. (...) Virtue is as real a fact in the world as vice is, and the variety of genuine human motives is also real.
>
> (Midgley 1985: 127)

Explanation and justification

One concern might be that a biological approach undermines the possibility of any *objective* values with respect to which we can evaluate moral behaviour. It is indeed at odds with an evolutionary perspective to consider human values as revealed or as entities residing in some timeless realm. Thus we seem to be left with a subjectivist view of values as rooted in the emotions of the individual, or with an evolutionary view which grants the presence of values shared by various organisms in so far as these organisms share a common evolutionary past or have similar interests in similar situations. The sociobiologist E. O. Wilson claims that values are rooted in deeper structures of the brain: 'ethical philosophers intuit the deontological canons of morality by consulting the emotive centers of their own hypothalamic-limbic system' (Wilson 1975: 563; see also Wilson 1975: 3; 1978: 6). A sociobiological understanding of those emotive centres would, in his view, not so much undermine ethics as offer an explanation *and* foundation for the values we need. Wilson believes that we can thus understand that we need to support human rights and protect biodiversity (Wilson 1978: 198–99; Wilson 1992).

There is something odd about the emphasis on the limbic system. Why would an evolutionary biologist consider the higher structures of the brain, including the capacity to reason about consequences and about principles on the basis of which certain behaviour could be defended, to be superfluous, not modifying the functioning of the limbic system, nor affecting canons of morality? The 'oversight' of the role of higher structures in the explanation of moral behaviour is, as I will argue here, even more problematic when it comes to the justification of moral behaviour.

The claim that scientific insights, and especially insights from biology, deliver the values we need, has been disputed by various philosophers, including philosophers who do not reject sociobiological explanations of human behaviour (e.g. Singer 1981; Kitcher 1985). To take an example, Singer considers a sociobiological explanation for double standards with respect to extramarital sexual activity of humans. The greater proclivity towards sexual promiscuity among males and towards restraint among females is explained in a straightforward way: males may gain considerably in terms of number of offspring by inseminating multiple females, whereas females gain from male support with parenting, and thus from luring males into more lasting relationships. However, Singer points out that even if we accept a sociobiological explanation of these differences in behaviour and of traditional moral attitudes with respect to such differences, we still may consider such a double standard an example of sexism which is morally unacceptable.

Even when there is an explanation, there is room for a considered moral judgement which differs from conventional moral sentiments. The more so, according to Singer (1984: 154), since sociobiological explanations actually allow us to distance ourselves from any innate tendencies:

> by explaining the widespread acceptance of the double standard, we also remove any lingering idea that this standard is some sort of self-evident moral truth. Instead it can be seen as the result of the blind evolutionary process and, as such, something about which we should make a more deliberate decision, now that we have understood it.

I agree with this argument: a biological explanation does not offer a justification but rather an opportunity to reconsider the behaviour. But then the question arises as to what standards we use to evaluate our 'natural' moral sentiments.

The committed biologist might say that we do not escape our biology here; we only bring into play further values which are also part of our biology, and we strive for coherence – a coherence which may imply that we have to give up on the double standard referred to above. In this process of evaluating our moral sentiments, we may reach agreement with humans from different cultural backgrounds, since we share a common biological history and structure; rape may be wrong for all humans, and judged to be so by all reasonable ones, and human rights may be universal for humans. However, so the argument might be continued, rape would not necessarily be wrong on a planet in the Andromeda galaxy, for a species with a different biology (Ruse 1989). We cannot go beyond the resources we have: the values which are handed down to us by cultural traditions (which, upon a sociobiological view, are themselves fruits of a selective process) and the capacities we owe to our constitution.

The view that all moral judgements are forged upon us by our past and that they are in a fundamental way species-dependent (as in the example about Andromeda) seems to me to be insufficient for morality; it still identifies the moral justification with an explanation of how we came to have the preferences which we turn out to have; there is no room for a contrast between 'what is' and 'what ought to be', and no role for justification but only for explanation.

Justification

In naturalist terms there is no room for the justification of ethical decisions in relation to entities in some Platonic realm, as if we come to hold moral principles by intuiting an absolute moral order. However, there are proposals for ethical justification other than an appeal to moral absolutes or to biologically based sentiments.

A *procedural* view of moral justification such as that offered by John Rawls (1971) may be compatible with an evolutionary view (Alexander 1993: 180ff). It does not justify claims about categorical objective moral truth, but such an absolute, 'rational intuitionist notion of objectivity is unnecessary for objectivity' and can be replaced by a social one (Rawls 1980: 570). This is, in my view, a valuable complement to and corrective of our ethical intuitions as rooted in our biology. Ethical objectivity need not be linked to a realm of ethereal entities such as abstract values. Rather, it 'involves the existence of a standard beyond personal wishes, a standard in which the wishes of others are given their place' (Kitcher 1985: 432). A procedural form of ethical justification may offer us ways to cope with the conflicting interests of individuals.

This emphasis on procedures is not a separate way to morality, as if ethical values could be deduced by thinking alone. The biological dimensions come into play in at least two ways: we owe our moral intuitions (such as conceptions of persons, of suffering and of a well-ordered society) our capacity for reflection to our evolutionary past. We do not start as blank minds, developing moral notions out of nothing. Rather, we reflect upon our moral intuitions and thus consider whether they have certain general features which we consider desirable. For instance, the 'golden rule' which states that one should not do to someone else what one would not want to happen to oneself is a general ethical principle which could be brought to bear upon many moral intuitions.

In our reflection we may test our moral judgements by criteria such as generality and disinterestedness, coherence, contribution to happiness and to the reduction of suffering, etc. We owe our intuitions to the evolutionary past, but they can be considered and corrected since we have the ability to evaluate our primary responses and to act upon such evaluations, though we do not easily act upon them, as the apostle Paul observed (Romans 7:19). Such difficulties underline that genuine ethical behaviour does not come to us 'by nature', but rather requires moral effort; ethics does not predict what is most likely to happen.

The ability to engage in abstract forms of reflection, which allow us to distance ourselves from our 'natural' inclinations, is itself a natural capacity. It may have served other functions in our evolutionary past; thinking allows for flexible responses to changing circumstances and thinking ahead may considerably diminish risks. Whatever the origin of the human capacity for reflection on one's own behaviour and the behaviour of others, we now have this capacity and can use it for new purposes, such as a reconsideration of our moralities. This human capacity for reasoning, and the patterns of reasoning which we are able to pursue, is subject to development as well.

The criteria which we use in moral evaluations, such as disinterestedness, may also be seen as the product of our evolutionary past. At some moment in the past one of our hominid ancestors asked a fellow hominid the equivalent of the question 'Why did you do that?' in the presence of a third party, and the answer was couched not in terms of emotions (I like to do that) or in terms of self-interest (that works out best for me) but in terms which were sufficiently general to be recognizable and acceptable to all bystanders, and thus, perhaps, brought the others to similar behaviour (Singer 1981: 92ff). We have developed the habit of evaluating and justifying behaviour in terms which are sufficiently general to be acceptable to the whole group.

Formal analysis, the application of criteria such as disinterestedness and coherence, and the moral deliberation of many people together are important for the credibility of morality, precisely because they surpass and may correct the conclusions of our ordinary biological and psychological mechanisms. One might include all these elements in a sociobiological description, but then ethical considerations would not have been eliminated, but rather would have been included in a modified sociobiology which includes consideration of the mechanisms by which we override the psychological processes explained by more traditional sociobiology. Or one could say that our moral intuitions are explained by sociobiology, but that these intuitions need not be our best ethical conclusions since we can reconsider them.

More has been delivered than needed

Just as for morality, one can make the same argument with respect to the acquisition of knowledge, epistemology: Is that nothing but psychology? Well, either we expand psychology by including scientific procedures such as double blind-experiments by which we correct our ordinary belief-forming processes, or we acknowledge the difference between psychology and epistemology. There is no need at all to say that epistemology, or, in the present context, morality, is eliminated in a naturalist view.

One could make a similar case about mathematics. The basics of counting and measuring are clearly to be found in social life, as counting is useful when sharing food and keeping track of enemies, and in more recent contexts in trade and agriculture. In that context, one of the simplest instances of Pythagoras' formula, namely $3^2 + 4^2 = 5^2$, was employed early in human history as a way to create approximately straight corners. The general form that we ascribe to Pythagoras came about later, through abstraction and reflection. One need not assume that humans can somehow intuit a realm of mathematical entities (such as perfect triangles) to assume that humans can come up with genuine mathematical truths, as these might be developed by abstraction, generalization and idealization from the natural. Well, the philosophy of mathematics is another world in itself, but the analogy functions as an indication that one might envisage a limiting case of moral principles that go far beyond any real-life human inclination, and in that sense is not factual but ideal – without introducing anything but the factual qua ontology.

To put it another way, evolution has delivered more than was ordered. Means can be used for new purposes. The fingers did not evolve to play a piano, but they can be used to play the piano. In evolutionary history new uses of old organs can be found again and again. Intelligence and communication, brains and language will have been useful for the four essential F's: feeding, fighting, fleeing and [reproducing], but once intelligence and language evolved, they have been used in other tasks as well.

The 'more' that was delivered allows morality to be genuinely moral, for our intelligence allows us to reconsider our own behaviour. As indicated above, we may discover that we are 'naturally' inclined to treat men and women differently. However, by becoming aware of this we can also act against the apparently self-evident 'natural'. Communication may also contribute. Imagine that once an offended hominid asked a fellow hominid: 'Why do you behave thus?' The one who is challenged could not just appeal to self-interest or emotions. In the presence of others he or she was challenged to justify the behaviour in question with arguments that would be recognizable and acceptable to the others, and thus to formulate general principles justifying his or her behaviour. In many incidents of this kind, natural behaviour guided by enlightened self-interest may have become reconsidered, intentional behaviour. The social context of our lives may have pushed towards universality and accountability, hallmarks of morality.

We are occasionally open to reasons, to argument. Since ideas spread faster than genes (transferred only to offspring), culture may develop enormously. There is no reason to assume that the biological basis would always overrule the effects of culture. Thanks to the emergence of culture as a second kind of heritage, alongside the genetic one, and thanks to the capacity for reflection and to the impulse to public justification, we are not victims of our evolutionary heritage. We are biological beings, but as these particular biological beings we have a moderate amount of freedom with respect to our genetic drives. We therefore also have responsibility.

Material thinking

Evolutionary approaches challenge our self-image in many ways. We are biological beings. We are nothing but material beings. According to the scientific understanding that informs our culture, including our medical practices, there is no immaterial ghost in the machine, no soul that departs at death. We are psychosomatic unities, bodies that display mental behaviour. Chemicals in coffee, wine and Prozac influence our moods. And the reverse is also true: ideas, beliefs and desires influence our bodies.

Regarding humans as material beings challenges our self-image. Material processes go their way; they are not 'about' anything. But the sounds we utter and the markings we scribble on paper are 'about something' – we write about love, we do arithmetic, we put down on paper how to prepare an apple pie.

If thinking is just a complex chemical and electrical process going on in our bloody brains, why would it be different from the digestion which goes on in our bowels? What would be left of the content of thinking, the truth and significance of words, ideas and symbols? If the conclusion of the scientific view of the world was that bloody brains are merely complex chemical machines that produce noises mistaken for meaningful words, we would be caught in a paradoxical situation – since science itself is one of the activities which assumes that we are engaging ideas, not merely generating noise.

The sceptical attitude seems to follow from the idea that all the work in brains is done by chemical processes. It may be that the current state of the brain corresponds to a particular state of mind, but the next state of mind is merely the by-product of the way the brain will be in a second from now, and that is a matter of circuits and neurotransmitters, not of ideas. Thus if you are thinking about '23 + 47' and say '70', you do not say 70 because of the mathematics, but because of the way the brain is wired. The picture seems to be as follows:

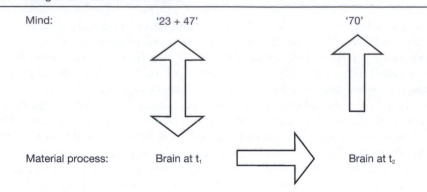

Figure 6.1

All the work seems to be done at the lower level, by the physical processes, with no real contribution from the meaning of the ideas, in this case the numbers and the instruction to add those two numbers. However, in me writing this book and you reading it, we are engaged in an exchange of ideas. At least, that is what we aspire to do. Thus an extremely reductionist view of human personhood seems insufficient; ideas are more than an irrelevant by-product of the material processes. We seem to need a ghost in the machine. Is the scientific picture essentially incomplete, unable to account for human thinking?

This pessimistic conclusion rests upon a false dichotomy, the assumption that the outcome is either due to a materially mediated process, with no regard for the meaning of the operations involved, or that it is driven by the meaning of the notions, in this case the mathematical rules of addition, and that that somehow operates independently of the material process. The confusion arises if one neglects the specifics of the horizontal arrow, which indicates the complex physiological process between hearing '23 + 47' and answering '70'. This process is a material process, but it is not just any process. We give the answer we give because we have been trained (and thus the process has been prepared) to make precisely those connections, from the time we started to learn words and numbers. There is a lot of content involved in the horizontal arrow, the nature of our thinking – many years of training and a huge volume of memories.

One could make a similar analysis of computers. According to one description, there is nothing but a physical process going on. Seen thus, there is no reason to believe that a computer gives the correct answer to the question '23 + 47'. If it were to answer '69' there would also have been a complex process going on in the chips of the computer. Physics would still hold. However, we expect the computer to reply '70' because that is the right answer. With computers we have started to use a second level of description, describing them as machines that deal with numbers (and, beyond that, with texts and ideas). The crux is that engineers have designed the computer in such a way that our expectations regarding the way numbers and ideas are managed correspond to the physical processes executed.

This parallel of content and process need not be there. Some years ago there was a problem with a Pentium chip; certain calculations went astray. There was nothing wrong with mathematics, the world of ideas. There was nothing wrong with physics – the electrons behaved according to the laws of nature. The correspondence between the world of material processes and the meaning we ascribed to the symbols involved was not constructed as it should have been (Jongeling 1997).

Back from the computer to humans: thanks to all the learning that has gone on, embodied in cultural concepts and in actual training, we as material beings can make adequate associations and hence think adequately. This is not downgrading humans; rather, it is upgrading our view of matter. We humans are biological beings with brains, and it is precisely because we are constituted thus that we can deal with content without paying attention to the underlying material processes. But we remain fallible. If we make mistakes, we will start to consider the underlying process. Have I heard you correctly? Or, if it is a more persistent problem, do I really know the meaning of those words? Or, if the problem is more severe, we sometimes have to conclude that the organization is damaged by a tumour or a stroke, incapacitating the processes we rely upon.

Much more is involved in reflection upon the relationship between the content and the processes that go on in our brains; this is the domain of the philosophy of mind, the neurosciences and related disciplines. There is no consensus, no grand theory that is widely accepted. Though there are deep problems, given the categorical differences between the mental and the material, the dualism of mind and matter advocated by Descartes seems to have been abandoned by almost all, as such a dualism makes any interaction between thoughts and actions totally mysterious. Instead, material processes can correspond to content, and in that sense to meaning.

Let us return to the main issue of this chapter, values in a world of facts, in the context of 'religion and science'. Facts and values are categorically different, though the practice of judging and valuing has arisen in this world of facts. Effective judgements do not only appeal to sentiments and interests but seek to draw others into the judgement – and thus have to appeal to more general considerations. Along a trajectory of abstraction, generalization and universalization, core elements of our judgements may be articulated that transcend the immediate situation and persons involved, and such core elements could be considered values, or at least a human approximation to values, if these are taken in a more absolute, Platonic way.

Again, the philosophical analysis requires much more than such a brief sketch, but this is an indication of one way in which values as well as other 'Platonic' realities such as those of mathematics might be incorporated in a worldview that is nourished by the sciences, without degrading values to nothing but interests or other empirical facts. Such a view of values might also allow us to articulate dissonance between ideals and realities, and thus to value our engagement with reality when that engagement draws upon science and technology. The next chapter further explores our engagement with reality, as we seek meaning in a material world.

Chapter 7

Meaning in a material world

We know, collectively, a great deal about our world, though our knowledge is also limited. Certain phenomena are intractable, even though they fit well in our general understanding of reality. Limit questions regarding science and reality will not find a definite answer, at least not with the tools provided by science. In a book of aphorisms, *The Aristos* (1980: 20), the novelist John Fowles gave a positive appreciation of such limitations to our knowledge.

> We are in the best possible situation because everywhere, below the surface, we do not know; we shall never know why; we shall never know tomorrow; we shall never know a god or if there is a god; we shall never even know ourselves. This mysterious wall round our world and our perception of it is not there to frustrate us but to train us back to the now, to life, to our time being.

Fowles knows why we do not know why: to train us back to life! 'To train us back to life': from the perspective of science the claim that this must be the purpose of our limitations is inadequate; as far as we can know, it has simply happened that we are endowed with our capacities and our limitations. However, the emphasis on the wider context of knowledge, our lives, fits well with the situated character of all our exploring, including the situated character of 'religion and science'. Our knowledge and our capacity for knowledge have arisen in the midst of life, and if we are to use them anywhere at all, it will have to be there.

In Chapter 4 I proposed to understand religious and non-religious views as ways of holding together a vision of the way the world is and of the way the world should be. There are multiple possible proposals for this 'holding together'. For instance, value can be invested in reality (a religious naturalistic position, see Chapter 5), or value can be considered to be transcendent (naturalistic theism, *ibid.*). Or value might be dismissed as nothing but a figure of speech serving interests, as a hard-nosed empiricist might see it. The theistic view of values as transcendent articulates more easily the dissonance between ideals and reality, whereas the naturalistic emphasis on immanence, value as a qualification of reality, does justice more easily to the fact that value judgements are made by natural beings, humans (see Chapter 6). This guide to the debates in 'religion and science' is not a place to cut such knots, but rather an attempt to explore some of the fundamental issues and options in the field.

Knowledge, values and their integration in a religious or non-religious vision arise in a creative process of exploration that has its roots in human practices, in daily life. In the development of an integrated vision there is substantial under-determination as higher levels of integration are not logically derivable from the more immediate observations and experiences to which they relate, but are rather imaginative construals of the way the world might be and the values we might consider universally valid.

In any such construal, personal preferences play a role, and thus the way we have been brought up, the culture of arts, letters, games and television we have encountered and the religious traditions that have come down to us from ages past. One might see both reality and values as guaranteed by a God who is the grounds of both goodness and reality. Or one might envisage nature as a creative reality that brings forth novelty and goodness, and there are other options. These cultural and personal influences can be represented by an upward arrow in the scheme first introduced in Chapter 4, an arrow that bypasses the sciences and their interpretation as well as ethical reflection.

There is also a downward movement. The way we conceive our values and worldview, connected or disconnected, can have its impact downwards, on the way we live and the way we appreciate our lives, on our preferences and feelings, our fears and hopes. Or, as the definition of religion by Clifford Geertz (see Chapter 4) has it, on our moods and motivations.

In this concluding chapter the focus will be on the role of human imagination in relating our lives to our visions, providing us with orientation and a sense of belonging in this universe. As this is a book about 'religion and science', we will begin by considering the role of stories in relation to a scientific understanding of our existence; towards the end we will turn to scientific images and stories for illumination of our existence in this world.

Stories with an aura of facticity

Around campfires and in courts, and in temples, huts and houses, humans have told each other stories about the origin of their world, of the hunting grounds of their tribe, of women and men, of the discovery of wheat and of fire, of the sun and the moon. Creation stories expressed how humans understood themselves in relation to their environment.

Such ancient myths are sometimes compared to science, as if the issue were factual correctness, say about a worldwide flood or about creation in seven days. When creation stories are judged by this standard, they fail. When treated as factual claims, these narratives of a distant past are ready for the

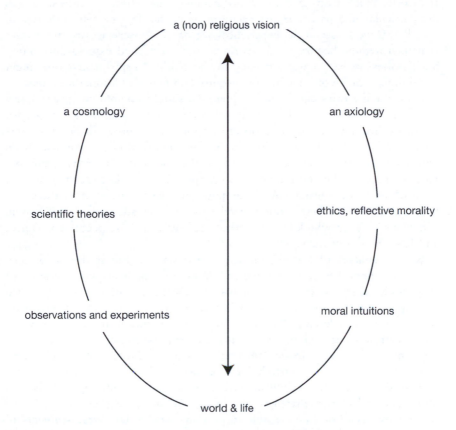

Figure 7.1

dustbin, or, more respectfully, for a museum of cultural history. 'That is how people in the past thought about these things, but now we know better.'

However, creation stories can be appreciated as expressions of what moved people, what excited them, what frightened them, what made them feel grateful. In that sense they go beyond the limitations of their own worldview. We can recognize to some extent their feelings and concerns, since we face similar challenges. Wonder about existence, awareness of dependence upon forces that are beyond our control, a sense of responsibility: such themes from past narratives can and should be articulated as well in the language of our time. How can we hold on to a humane sense of meaning, how can we articulate religious convictions in the context of what we know about our world?

In the central axis of the scheme, one might look for a justified creation story. This would be a reflection on our place and task in the light of the sciences. The natural sciences approach as objective as possible a perspective on the world, as if operating from a 'third person' perspective. In contrast, stories are particular and partisan; they relate to us in the 'first person', in terms of the choices we face and the experiences we have. We seek words and images that interpret the history of the world as *our* world and express our values. Such stories nourish a way of being in the world, 'a spirituality' one might say – though this word has by now acquired so many additional meanings.

Images and stories can be misleading. We should attempt to speak clearly and correctly. As I see it, the critical attitude of modern culture is a great gift. Thus, explication and justification are important. In order to be taken seriously, and to nourish the desired moods and motivations, a story needs an appropriate 'aura of facticity', to recall another element of Geertz's definition. Facticity need not be understood in too simplistic a way. Even for the story of Cain who killed his brother Abel the question need not be whether these two people existed but whether this is a relevant and plausible account of human behaviour – a man who kills his brother. At least in that respect this narrative still has 'an aura of facticity'.

Not all spheres of life provide a role for science, but if the larger narrative is to appeal to well-educated people in our time, some consideration of its possible adequacy relative to what we have come to know about the world may well be asked for. In such a justification one can relate to mainstream science as it has developed over the last few centuries. It is, in my view, far less attractive to seek to save a religious vision by constructing a science of one's own, as is done in fundamentalism (e.g. 'creationism') as well as by spiritual seekers (e.g. parapsychology, astrology). Nor is it a good strategy to play down science too much; science is not merely offering models that allow us to calculate the strength of a bridge. With the theories and models of the last two centuries we are able to describe and explain large segments of reality very successfully. If one holds a high view of science as uncovering the way the world is, the scientific input into our understanding of the world we live in should be major. But even if science is taken more modestly, there still may be a good reason to engage in stories that integrate current scientific understanding with our existential concerns.

The English philosopher of science Mary Hesse emphasizes the limited scope of theories: 'no truths about the substance of nature which are relevant to metaphysics or theology can be logically derived from physics' (1988: 189). This is not only because she has a fairly modest understanding of science as her understanding of religion is relevant as well, an understanding of religion that is on the side of life as lived rather than on the side of theology as explanatory theory.

> In any case, it is unprofitable in an antimetaphysical age to seek to make the world safe for religion by metaphysics. Such a procedure is anachronistic and intellectually barren for believers and unbelievers alike. But there is no need for it. In relation to the Christian religion, at least, there

are no intellectual foundations for belief except in the continuing tradition of practice, theology, and changing historical experience, which are all rooted in the Great Schema itself.

(Arbib and Hesse 1986: 243)

Rather than looking for scientific contributions to a metaphysical theology of nature in the traditional sense, it may be more fruitful to regard 'religion and science' as 'debates about an appropriate *language* for theology, and a source of appropriate *models*', as the issue is how theological concepts 'may be expressed in a language accessible to those nurtured in the scientific framework' (Hesse 1981: 287).

Maybe the issue is merely about communication 'to those nurtured in the scientific framework', as Hesse has it. Qua ambition I prefer to be somewhat more realist in intention, treating our visions not just as useful for communication but also as explorations that aim to provide a *possible* interpretation of the way things are. According to the definition by Geertz, stories and images are essential as they are manifest forms of symbols that influence moods and motivations, but they can only do so persistently if they are understood to reflect to some extent the way the world really is.

Demanding too much facticity may actually undermine the effectiveness of symbols and of a story. We can be moved by the Harry Potter stories and other fiction. And while we accept their non-reality (and thus the many ways in which they should not be taken too seriously), we can also acknowledge their realism about human friendships, and about good and evil. Thereby, though fiction, they may convey something of 'the way things really are'. Whatever the form of realism, stories need to connect to life as lived; that is where they have meaning. We are creative creatures with substantial powers; we can modify our world.

Old traditions and new visions

'Give me that old-time religion, it's good enough for me' is an appealing line in one of the spirituals. However, the 'old-time religion' is challenged by new insights as well as by the recognition of so many other respectable religions on this planet of ours. Should we not opt for a global system of ethical norms and factual beliefs, a 'naturalist religion' that could be 'everybody's story' (Rue 2000)? Should we replace the variety of religious traditions with the scientific understanding of reality?

Religions are particular, and so are cultures, languages and individuals. Nobody speaks language; we always speak *a* language. This analogy makes me wonder whether the ideal of a global, science-inspired religion is possible and desirable. If one were to replace the historic languages with a single global language, whether Esperanto or English, much of the richness of human cultural history would become inaccessible. Each language allows for a slightly different perspective on reality. Not that there is no change. Languages are not fixed, nor are they isolated from each other. Translations are possible even if they never completely catch the nuances of the original. Languages are influenced by each other and exchange words and phrases. We cannot coexist without interacting.

Not only is there a plurality of languages, but also of religious traditions. Different traditions offer different symbols, examples and ideals of a good life. One always lives within a tradition and is at best familiar with a few; human life is too short and the diversity too rich to become at home in all. Thus even when one assumes that other traditions may promote rich experiences and respectable moral behaviour, one can still make a good case for raising one's children primarily within the scope of a more limited set of stories, parables and commandments. To abandon the richness that is in the details of particular historical traditions for a science-based 'evolutionary epic' seems to be more than is needed. Something would be lost if the various religions were replaced by a single one, whether through dominance of one particular tradition or by a 'scientific religion' invented for the purpose.

In this context, biology offers a better analogy than physics or chemistry. Diversity has arisen as the result of a long historical process with various contingencies. Biodiversity is a treasure; it is to be valued. Even if one knew evolutionary theory and the conditions on Earth three billion years ago, one could not have predicted all life forms that were to emerge. From a biological point of view, our understanding is encompassing; there is no reason to assume that any of the life forms that have emerged were not the results of evolutionary processes. However, our knowledge is also limited. Not only is it impossible to predict the actual variety, but there are always more details than we will ever be able to explain explicitly. There is implicit wisdom in all organisms.

The variety of religious traditions, with their narratives and symbols, their rituals and exhortations, is equally impressive. Here, too, much can be understood as having served biological or social functions. Here, too, there may be more in the tradition than can be made explicit. The same argument applies to human nature and to human upbringing: there is more going on within us than we can make explicit or manage intentionally. If we tried to replace all stories, poetry, gestures, examples and songs with explicit and univocal statements, we would lose much. Given the opaque nature of human nature, religious narratives may be considered to be valuable communicators of wisdom.

Thus, 'old-time religion' may be a valuable resource of 'well-winnowed wisdom', wisdom that has shown its value over the course of millennia of human communal life. However, we have to live with those religions in a new world, or rather in a world understood and functioning differently due to science and technology. Thus we also need to understand our heritage in ways appropriate to our circumstances and challenges.

Change and continuity in theories

What might be the best way to proceed with images and concepts offered by religious traditions as part of our heritage? I think that the development of physics offers a helpful analogy.

When we consider major transitions, such as those from Newton's ideas about space and time to Einstein's views, or from classical to quantum conceptions of matter, we may be struck by the newness of the concepts involved. There seems to be no continuity in the way reality is seen, that is in ontology. However, there is continuity at less abstract levels of knowing, for instance with respect to predictions of the orbits of planets. The way from the older to the newer view is not via a translation at the level of theories. Rather, new theories are proposed, creatively. However, new theories have to do justice to well-established experiences and experiments coded and covered in the old theories.

Similarly in religion. Continuity with the insights of earlier humans, including those found in the Bible and the writings of the early theologians, should be sought at the level of life as lived. The more abstract levels, including notions such as the Trinity, the virgin birth, heaven and even God, are constructions, comparable to the scientific theories just considered, and such constructions or interpretations may change drastically even though one seeks to be fair to the underlying experiences. In many cases, fundamentalists, as well as those who reject Christianity because they think it has to be fundamentalist, make the error of conflating different levels. They take the original expressions to be as important as the underlying experiences and concerns themselves, and seek to stick to those higher-level interpretations.

If the analogy with the development of physics is adequate, the way to renew religious language and models is to consider how those images functioned for humans in earlier periods, and to find out as much as is possible what the underlying concerns and experiences were. In so far as we recognize those experiences and concerns and see them as our own, we can attempt to develop new images and models, new ways of dealing with them in images which are credible in our time, in the context of all else that we take seriously, including science. Rather than focusing on the truth claims embodied in metaphors and models, we can give primacy to the relevance these images had and may have in and for human lives.

At home in the universe?

If we cannot prove the universe to be a cosmos, a world in which we are at home, can we at least imagine it to be one? The myths of the Stone Age and their embodiment in Stonehenge and the like may be attractive to some modern-day pagans, who appropriate such myths while cutely misunderstanding them. However, are there more contemporary myths which may be adequate to scientific knowledge while at the same time generating for us a sense of 'being at home in the universe'? Let us briefly consider two versions inspired by science, as well as the religious symbol of 'creation'.

Place – Powers of Ten

There is an educational video titled 'Powers of Ten', developed in 1977 by the designers Ray and Charles Eames, narrated by the scientists Philip Morrison, after a 1957 book by the Dutch Christian pacifist and educationalist Kees Boeke. This video has been used to introduce people to the universe, at various scales.

The initial scene is a homely one – a couple picnicking in Chicago, near Lake Michigan. The camera zooms out, as if moving out our point of observation – a factor of ten in ten seconds. And again a factor of ten. And so on. We recognize at some point Chicago, and just a few steps later 'planet Earth' as a whole, a planet that with the advent of space travel has come to be perceived as 'our home'. A few steps later we see the many millions of stars that together form 'our Galaxy'.

Though this sequence of images may be interpreted as relativizing our significance, showing us that we are nothing but a speck of dust in a huge universe, it may also be interpreted as showing the opposite: even though we may not always notice it, due to the scale of observation, we are there in the centre of the picture. We are at home in the universe. At any scale, this is where we are – even though the vast expanse is some steps removed from reality as we experience it. As the website www.powersof10.com quotes Charles Eames, its message is 'Everything is connected'. A similar sense of 'home' may be evoked by the pictures of Earth rising above the horizon of the moon: a 'pale blue dot' (Carl Sagan) that is our home.

Our Stone-Age minds are not well suited to handling logarithmic (or exponential) scales. We may understand the mathematical trick, but we may not be as familiar with the images thus presented as we are in distances understood along linear scales. Thus it may be an interesting challenge to educationalists and artists to convey this sense of distance and of our place, and thereby to induce a sense of awe and reverence for the majestic universe we are part of, as well as responsibility for the tiny part that is our more immediate home.

The artist Thomas Rockwell has explored various other proposals for envisioning our cosmos and nurturing a sense of place in the universe, arguing that this is what has been done through the ages – the cathedrals and Dante's *Divina Comedia* also provided us with such visions. 'Cosmographies not only offer a map of the cosmos but also label and give visual form through icons and symbols to cosmic entities and values that define a religion' (Rockwell 2002: 608). By the way, when in previous chapters I wrote about the multi-layered character of our descriptions of reality, I was using spatial imagery too. Whether as a help in theoretical exploration, or as a more artistic conveying of our place and meaning, visual metaphors are often helpful to us humans.

Time – the evolutionary epic

Traditional myths not only locate us in space but also in time, by relating us and our fellow humans to previous generations, to history. Here too there are attempts to re-imagine our existence in relation to our scientific understanding. Quite a few authors have come to speak of 'the epic of evolution'. In her *Sin and Selfish Genes* (2009), Marie V. Nielsen offers a comparative analysis of Christian and biological narratives; here we consider the 'evolutionary epic' by itself.

In terms of such an epic, natural history becomes more than just a sequence of events: there is a drama that unfolds, there are a few central characters, there may be episodes and transitions, as in Eric Chaisson's *Epic of Evolution: Seven Ages of the Cosmos* (2006), which begins with the epoch of particles, followed by those of galaxies, stars, planets and chemistry, with biology and culture, including technology, as the two final stages. Though Chaisson's book is connected to a course that is supposed to convey an overview of the sciences, it also has an explicit moral message: 'we have an obligation, a moral responsibility to survive, especially if we are alone in the Universe. The great experiment that intelligent life represents must not end in failure' (Chaisson 2006: 436). In recent years the focus has often been on ecology and environmental concerns, as in Loyal Rue's *Everybody's Story*, which sees the epic of evolution as about 'constructing a new wisdom tradition that couples an evolutionary cosmology to an ecocentric morality' (Rue 2000: xii).

Using the image of weaving with loom and fabric, Philip Hefner (1998: 543; 2003: 69) and Loyal Rue see the evolutionary epic as the basic framework for understanding reality and value, and upon this framework 'many tapestries of meaning may be woven', including modified versions of the major religious traditions that have come down to us from ages past (Rue 2000: 137). Such epic presentations of our world may well serve to induce in us a sense of reverence and wonder, awareness of our dependence on what has gone before us and who has preceded us, and responsibility for the web of life, just as traditional creation myths were to support moral and religious attitudes (Lovin and Reynolds 1985).

The grand visions and epics need not induce such responses. They may be too big to align well with our intuitions and experiences. Science does not need narrative integration. On the contrary, the practice of science is at its best when we seek to free it from unwarranted anthropomorphisms in attitudes and explanations. Not only are we not psychologically prepared for such cosmic stories, but philosophically the mix of elements in myths is problematic as well. Any transition from facts to values, from 'is' to 'ought', has been deemed a naturalistic fallacy, and rightly so. The idea that there is a moral obligation to survive and thus to continue the history of intelligent life in the universe does not come from science but is a *value* articulated in the context of current scientific understanding.

The stories don't deliver scientific insight (though they communicate current knowledge), nor do they justify values (though they may ground them psychologically); they integrate the knowledge and values in a way that may be grasped by us as humans. Unifying scientific and existential concerns – seeing our universe as a cosmos – is not warranted in scientific or logical terms. However, as a human imaginative project it may well be of value to us, shaping our self-understanding in a helpful way.

Let me conclude, then, with an attempt to articulate core ideas in a poetic narrative. Not that the poetry is particularly good, but the limitation imposed by the form may help focus on essential elements. A more extensive version of the following 'creation story' was published in my *Creation: From Nothing until Now* (Drees 2002a), where it provided the narrative framework for an interpretative exposition of faith in the context of our natural and cultural history. In brief, it seeks to address the persistence of mystery, our dependence on processes long before even the Earth was formed, the emergence of life with all its complexities, the rise of intelligence, religion and morality, the rise of science and critical thinking, and our current situation – to use this multi-faceted heritage wisely in new circumstances. The present book can be seen as an academic reflection on the nature of such a project in 'religion and science'.

A creation story

> There was a time
>   when there was no time,
>   when time was not yet.
> The time
>   when there was no time
>   is a horizon of not knowing
>   a mist where our questions fade
>   and no echo returns.
> Then,
>   in the beginning,
>   perhaps not the beginning,
>   in the first fraction of a second,
>   perhaps not the first fraction
>   of the first second,
>   our universe began
>   without us.
> In billions of galaxies
>   the universe made itself
>   from dust stars
>   from stars dust.

Much later,
    from dust from stars
    from dust
    from stars from dust
    swirled our Sun
    and from leftovers
    the Earth, our home.
Thus,
    after ten billion years,
    there was evening
    and there was morning:
    the first day.
Life
    a modest beginning,
    undirected,
    a history of failing
    and occasionally
    a small success.
A molecule
    carried information
    from generation to generation,
    history bred purpose,
    by chance.
Billions of years later
    cells merge,
    sex and ageing,
    death and deception.
A rare slow lungfish
    slithered through the grass;
    thus came amphibians to pass.
Yesterday
    a few million years ago
    the East Side Story:
    groups of apes groom,
    hunt and call.
Sticks, stones, fire
    eating from the tree of knowledge
    the tree of good and evil,
    power, freedom,
    responsibility:
Beasts became us
    more was delivered than ordered,
    more than we can bear?

Religion
   cement of the tribe
   response to power
   of mountains,
   the storm, the sea,
   birth and death,
   power as large as gods.
A new age,
   a prophet warns
   king and people,
   a carpenter tells
   'a man
   who fell among robbers,
   was cared for
   by an enemy'.
Look, measure and count,
   challenge knowledge
   and authority!
Enlightenment
   way out of immaturity.
In us
   our heritage,
   matter,
   information,
   and a box
   full of stories.
Between
   hope and fear
   our neighbours
   life
   here on Earth,
   between
   hope and fear
   the great project
   of thought
   and compassion
   on a road of freedom.

Engaging in 'religion and science'

An epilogue

Science plays a role in the way we live, whether religiously or non-religiously. Religion plays a role in the way we live with science. In the previous chapters we have reflected upon contemporary debates in 'religion and science'. Many such debates are non-debates, as participants differ not only in the answers given but pose different questions, or have a different understanding of what religion is about. In this Epilogue, I'll consider once more contemporary 'religion and science' discussions, present the analytical emphasis I would like to encourage, and discuss some of the substantial issues that arise.

The state of the art in 'religion and science'

The Oxford Handbook of Religion and Science (Clayton and Simpson 2006) is a thousand-page exposition of religion in its relation to the sciences. It covers various religions (including indigenous ways of life, religious naturalism and atheism); it covers a variety of scientific disciplines; it addresses contemporary controversies. Its fifty-five contributions represent well the state of the art for this field.

The *Oxford Handbook* is also exemplary for that which it does not do. Most authors are advocates of the perspectives they discuss; a Christian contributes on Christianity and science, an ID advocate on intelligent design and an atheist on atheism and science. By having advocates write on these positions, the contributions tend to rationalize and legitimize the religious (or non-religious) positions presented, rather than analyze their problems. Diversity and disagreements *within* traditions are played down; the author's position is the position of the tradition. Someone speaks for Christianity, but his Christianity is Anglican. Another writes on Buddhism and science, but speaks for a particular version of Tibetan Buddhism. The focus is mainly on theological content and metaphysical issues. Hardly is there any consideration of other dimensions of religious traditions such as institutions, communities, ethos and rituals, or of the social setting, issues of education, law, minorities and political power.

Also absent is engagement with cultural conditions and social studies of science. The material engages the theoretical side of science, neglecting technology except for one chapter on biotechnology, one on feminist perspectives on medicine and a section on Islam and technology. There is nothing on chemistry, which in its history was less involved in natural theologies that supported a monotheistic view of God as creator and giver of the laws of nature; chemistry was more affiliated with spiritualist approaches.

As is fairly characteristic of the modern 'religion and science' conversation, the authors are mostly from North America and the UK; a few are from elsewhere in Western Europe, one is from South Africa and one from India. Though it is not necessarily a consequence of this, the book is also focused on discussions as they developed in the English-speaking world. The European Protestant reticence with respect to natural theology, often associated with the theologian Karl Barth, isn't represented. Perhaps it is difficult to include such contributions; once a theologian opts for less engagement with the sciences, there is also less reason for them to contribute to 'religion and science'.

Implicitly, 'secularization' is the driving anxiety, and re-establishing the plausibility of religious beliefs is treated as the remedy. This makes secularization an intellectual development, rather than, for instance, a consequence of the rise of European states that provide services such as social welfare that make religious communities superfluous.

I think these characteristics by and large explain why 'religion and science' seems to be of little interest to fully fledged theologians, but also to scholars in religious studies and others in the humanities and the social sciences. In reflecting upon 'religion and science' we should seek to be more attentive to a richer and hence more complex understanding of religion in its relation to the sciences in contemporary societies. Focussing on social, cultural and disciplinary contexts might enrich the significance of such studies, as the engagement with 'science and religion' becomes a window on the way humans in their societies deal with scientific research and science-based technology, as well as a window on their identities, values and traditions.

Historians of science and of 'religion and science' are the exception to the weaknesses listed above. In various recent studies they stress the contextual character of discourses on religion and science and the changing conceptions of 'science' (or natural philosophy) and of 'religion' (e.g. Brooke 1991; Brooke and Cantor 1998; Harrison 1990; Livingstone 2003; Numbers 2006). I already referred to Livingstone (2003: 112–23), who showed that Calvinist responses to Darwinism in the late nineteenth century differed from place to place, reflecting local interest, whether polemical, colonial or otherwise.

Such historical research incites attentiveness to contexts and interests. Though in their self-understanding and ambitions science and religion are universal, they are set in a particular disciplinary and confessional frame, at a particular place and time. But neither are science and religion just local, as local processes appropriate and adapt discussions going elsewhere. Engaging with science and religion in a globalizing world, we can see that processes are 'glocal', that is they are local in the context of the global. This interaction between the specific and the general might provide a good framework for considering debates on religion and science.

Local purposes and glocal dynamics

Different purposes shape reflections on 'religion and science' in different contexts, as considered in more detail in Chapter 2: apologetics, intra-religious controversy and humanistic concerns.

In books by scientists for a wider audience, information on science is sometimes packaged with a touch of religion. When this concerns cosmology and physics the message may be one of awe and wonder. In expositions on evolution the message often is that believers shouldn't worry, as science doesn't undermine important elements of morality or faith. Such an apologetics for science among religiously minded people may be more prominent in the American context than in the European one, where secularization has worked out differently, with more regard for science and more apologetic needs on the religious side. Apologetics for religion is a useful purpose for 'religion and science' in a science-appreciating environment, arguing for the plausibility or possibility of a particular religious view. Or for its social and moral relevance, as in engagements on biomedical issues and environmental concerns (e.g. Deane-Drummond and Szerszynski 2003; Drees 2009).

'Religion versus religion' might be another context, with science providing ammunition to promote the interests of a particular group within a religious tradition. American controversies over evolution are above all religious controversies over the proper Christian response to modern culture and the authority to speak on behalf of Christianity. The Dalai Lama draws on science in presenting Buddhism in the Western world, but thereby also promotes one of the four major sects of Tibetan Buddhism and transforms Tibetan Buddhism (Lopez 1998, 2008). In our time, the interpretation and representation of Islam is contested among Muslims, between moderates and Islamists (using, for the sake of convenience, such general labels). All draw upon science to argue that they best represent the true faith.

A third context, alongside apologetics and intra-religious controversy, is concern about the scientific image of ourselves and our world, where the purpose of 'religion and science' may be to appease perceived challenges to our psychological identity and our moral life. There is not only a 'defensive' side to this, arguing against 'reductionism'. The sciences are often claimed in the service of particular 'spiritual' or religious practices and visions. As is evident in bookshops with extensive sections on 'mind and spirit', science (or pseudo-science) has a major role in the context of spirituality and esoteric religiosity, by and large independent from mainstream religious institutions (Hanegraaff 1996). Though in those circles there is much sentiment against mainstream science and medicine (e.g. against vaccinations), there is also a desire to have alternative points of view supported by the natural sciences, and a substantial part of such 'New Age' vocabularies draw upon the sciences.

While context is important, contexts are not isolated from each other. Rather, the situation is *glocal*: local developments in a context of globalization are influenced by processes elsewhere. American controversies over evolution have been exported, making anti-evolutionism a symbolic identity issue for modern conservative religious groups elsewhere. However, in the transfer from one context to another, transformation takes place. Leading American creationists such as Duane Gish have shown up in Turkey, as evident from publications of the Turkish creationist Harun Yahya, but Yahya's writings are to be understood in the context of the struggle for the secular and Islamic identity of Turkey rather than in the American context of public schools and Christianity. And when Yahya's *Atlas of Creation* showed up in Western Europe among young Muslims, again the context was different, as there it played a role in politics of identity, assimilation and integration as young Muslims of Turkish descent negotiated their identities as Muslims in such European countries.

Too often, the 'religion and science' discussion is taken to be universal, as if the issues are the same everywhere. Insights into the transfer and transformation of ideas and practices are illuminating as windows onto cultural specifics and on cultural dynamics in a globalizing world.

Objectives in 'religion and science': study and engagement

The aim of studying 'religion and science' may be to understand human culture and society, especially the ways in which we humans handle religious identities and scientific knowledge. How do religious attitudes, beliefs, practices and vocabularies shape responses to science? And how do science and technology reshape modern culture; what is their role in the dynamics of religious change? By engaging in contextual and comparative approaches, we may clarify the glocal nature of such processes, that is the transfer of particular ideas from one context to another in conjunction with the transformation of such ideas in the local setting.

However, 'religion and science' is not an object of study like the activity of a strange tribe out there. Whether we participate in debates on 'religion and science' or not, we all live with our values and convictions in the modern world, and science is the prime way of understanding that world. Thus there is not only a need for serious study *of* 'religion and science', as an object to be studied, but also for serious reflection *in* 'religion and science'. It is like politics: to understand what is going on it is important to be attentive to the processes involved, coalitions formed, feuds fought, games played. But politics is also about ideas for a good society. We need to study interests and ideas.

In terms of religious and non-religious visions as presented here (Chapter 4), science informs our views of the way the world is. By and large this is the domain of the scientists, who have to teach others about their results, but philosophy of nature and philosophy of science are also involved. Because of religious interests, there may be specific areas of science that are followed attentively. For those who are interested in 'mystery in an intelligible universe' that would mean following cosmology and theoretical physics. These disciplines present science in its most encompassing form. They might inform metaphysical considerations on issues such as time, causality and reality, as well as on the rational intelligibility of the universe; they may generate epistemological reflections on the reaches of our understanding and the persistence of limit questions.

For others, the prime areas of interest might be the coherence and integrity of reality, but also its 'layered' character and its creative potential. Phenomena emerge out of lower-level processes, but have their own characteristics, understood through a descriptive and explanatory vocabulary that is appropriate to their level of reality. In terms of substance, this involves consideration of reductionism, emergence and supervenience, for instance in philosophy of mind. But this is also an issue of epistemology, of reflection upon our ways of getting to know reality and the multiple languages we use to describe phenomena. Most importantly, it is the area in which we need to distinguish between explanation and justification – not everything that happens is thereby to be endorsed.

A third cluster of interests centre on the articulation of worldviews, the integration of scientific knowledge in a fairly encompassing vision of the way things are. As argued above (Chapter 4), there is underdetermination, as the science does not uniquely determine our worldview. Can we clarify the freedom in our conceptual constructions at this most encompassing level, drawing upon the analysis of underdetermination within the sciences?

Religion is not only about a worldview; Clifford Geertz spoke also of an ethos. In religious reflection we also address morality, our most comprehensive view of values, a vision for the way the world should be. This is less directly the domain of the sciences, but there are many facets of this reflection in which science might be involved to understand 'values in a world of facts'.

At the level of human life as lived there is the study of human emotions, human moral intuitions and institutions, pro-social behaviour and deceit. Psychology and social sciences may well be involved, and more recently the physiological dimensions of brain processes and hormones have become amenable to research as well.

More reflectively, there is the issue of how our empirical and theoretical understanding of human nature coheres with a meaningful understanding of human moral judgements as genuinely moral, rather than something else. There is a major role for philosophies of biology and of psychology to reflect upon an evolutionary understanding of humans and its consequences for human morality. In Chapter 6 the analogy with mathematics was made in terms of the practice of counting and measuring and the 'Platonic' world of mathematical truths. Such analogies for understanding values in a world of facts might deserve further scrutiny, thus engaging philosophies of mathematics.

Substantial moral issues might also engage our attention. What do we think of biotechnology and of ecological threats? Should we value nature as it would be without human interference, or does that notion rest upon an artificial distinction between the natural and the artificial? Religious leaders have spoken out on various moral issues related to modern technology – asserting moral leadership in debates that require critical consideration of the values involved and of the consequences that may follow.

Last but not least, there is the philosophical question of whether we can move beyond casuistic approaches or a pragmatic approach to morality and articulate values in an encompassing way. This would hardly be a project that involves science, in so far as the engagement with science has been handled in the discussions just mentioned, but would consider the nature of values in a world of facts, and the nature of morality in a world of biological beings.

Characteristic of religious visions is that they integrate a worldview and values, for instance in a concept of creation that affirms that the world has its grounds in God, but also that the world is to be valued. Thus the religious core is at stake in the integrative effort to hold together visions of the way things are and the way they should be, our worldview and our values. Reaching out to the valuational side makes a worldview religious; reaching out to the understanding of reality makes values religious.

What is the work to be done in this area? A major task is to clarify how this integration works – an integration that may have a built-in tension, as values need not align with the way things are. Religious or non-religious visions that have those two dimensions of values and worldviews are constructed by humans, not out of the blue but drawing imaginatively on traditions and personal preferences – major issues that deserve further clarification.

Human identity brings out another dimension of this integration – its descent from the Olympus of speculative thought into the realities of human lives, where it might inspire people. It is a challenge for academics in 'religion and science' to engage in a translation of academic reflections into accessible forms such as stories and poetry, to convey them but also to test them against the real world in which humans live and act. It matters that we articulate 'meaning in a material world'.

In the preceding pages I have presented two different perspectives, both important. The first could be characterized as an *outsider* perspective on 'religion and science', studying religion, science and their interactions in modern societies. The other is an *insider* perspective, participating in the effort to articulate viable visions, whether religious or non-religious. The combination of these two approaches is itself the deepest challenge, and it is one that fits squarely in 'religion and science', though it is a challenge that is not exclusive to 'religion and science'.

We can discuss ideas (thinking) and we can study brain processes (physics, chemistry), but how do the two fit together? We can engage in science and we can engage in science studies, but aren't social studies of science undermining the standing of science? We can engage in moral discourse and we can explain in evolutionary terms how humans have come to be such judgemental animals – but doesn't the explanatory approach undermine the moral character of the moral judgements? We can engage in the articulation of religious visions but at the same time we can study the evolution of religions in anthropological, evolutionary, psychological and sociological terms. What does our understanding of the evolution of human religions do for a humane evolution of religions? My hope is that this guide may contribute to a well considered approach to 'religion and science in context'.

Bibliography

Abrecht, P. 1989. 'Foreword.' In *The New Faith-Science Debate: Probing Cosmology, Technology, and Theology*, ed. J. M. Mangum. Minneapolis: Fortress and Geneva: World Council of Churches.

Adams, D. 1985. [orig. 1980] *The Restaurant at the End of the Universe*. New York: Pocket Books.

Alexander, R. D. 1987. *The Biology of Moral Systems*. New York: De Gruyter.

—— 1993. 'Biological considerations in the analysis of morality.' In *Evolutionary Ethics*, eds M. H. Nitecki & D. V. Nitecki. Albany: SUNY Press.

Alexander, S. 1920. *Space, Time, and Deity: The Gifford Lectures at Glasgow, 1916–1918*. London: Macmillan.

Almond, G. A., R. Scott Appleby & Emanuel Sivas. 2003. *Strong Religion: The Rise of Fundamentalisms Around the World*. Chicago: University of Chicago Press.

Altschuler, G. C. 1979. *Andrew D. White – Educator, Historian, Diplomat*. Ithaca: Cornell University Press.

Arbib, M. A. & M. B. Hesse. 1986. *The Construction of Reality*. Cambridge: Cambridge University Press.

Atkins, P. W. 1981. *The Creation*. Oxford and San Francisco: Freeman.

Barbour, I. G. 1966. *Issues in Science and Religion*. Englewood Cliffs, NJ: Prentice-Hall.

—— 1990. *Religion in an Age of Science*. San Francisco: Harper & Row.

—— 1993. *Ethics in an Age of Technology*. San Francisco: HarperSanFrancisco.

—— 1997. *Religion and Science: Historical and Contemporary Issues*. New York: HarperSanFrancisco.

Barrow, J. D. 1988. *The World Within the World*. Oxford: Clarendon Press.

Barrow, J. D. & F. J. Tipler. 1986. *The Anthropic Cosmological Principle*. Oxford: Clarendon Press.

Behe, M. J. 1996. *Darwin's Black Box: The Biochemical Challenge to Evolution*. New York: Free Press.

Boeke, K. 1957. *Cosmic View: The Universe in Forty Jumps*. New York: John Day.

Brauer, M. J., B. Forrest & S. G. Gey. 2005. 'Is It Science Yet? Intelligent Design Creationism and the Constitution.' *Washington University Law Quarterly* 83 (1), 1–149.

Breidert, W., Hrsg. 1994. *Die Erschütterung der vollkommenen Welt: Die Wirkung des Erdbebens von Lissabon im Spiegel europäischer Zeitgenössen*. Darmstadt: Wissenschaftliche Buchgesellschaft.

Brooke, J. H. 1991. *Science and Religion: Some Historical Perspectives*. Cambridge: Cambridge University Press.

Brooke, J. H. & G. Cantor. 1998. *Reconstructing Nature: The Engagement of Science and Religion*. Edinburgh: T & T Clark.

Burrell, D. B. 1993. *Freedom and Creation in Three Traditions*. Notre Dame, IN: University of Notre Dame Press.

Butterfield, J. & C. J. Isham. 2001. 'Spacetime and the philosophical challenge of quantum gravity.' Pp. 33–89 in C. Callender & N. Huggett, eds, *Physics Meets Philosophy at the Planck Scale: Contemporary Theories in Quantum Gravity*. Cambridge: Cambridge University Press.

Capra, F. 1975. *The Tao of Physics: An Exploration of the Parallels Between Modern Physics and Eastern Mysticism*. Berkeley: Shambala.

Carroll, Lewis. 1939. *The Complete Works of Lewis Carroll*, illustrations by J. Tenniel, introduction by A. Wollcott. New York: Modern Library.

Cavanaugh, M. 2000. 'What is Religious Naturalism? A Preliminary Report on an Ongoing Conversation.' *Zygon: Journal of Religion and Science* 35, 241–52.

Chaisson, E. 2006. *Epic of Evolution: Seven Ages of the Cosmos*. New York: Columbia University Press.

Clayton, P. 2000. *The Problem of God in Modern Thought*. Grand Rapids, MI: Eerdmans.

—— 2004. *Mind and Emergence: From Quantum to Consciousness*. Oxford: Oxford University Press.

Clayton, P. & P. Davies, eds. 2006. *The Re-Emergence of Emergence: The Emergentist Hypothesis from Science to Religion*. Oxford: Oxford University Press.

Clayton, P. & A. Peacocke, eds. 2004. *In Whom We Live and Move and Have Our Being: Panentheistic Reflections on God's Presence in a Scientific World*. Grand Rapids: Eerdmans.

Clayton, P. & Z. Simpson, eds. 2006. *The Oxford Handbook of Religion and Science*. Oxford: Oxford University Press.

Clifford, W. K. 1879. 'The Ethics of Belief.' In W. K. Clifford, *Lectures and Essays*, eds L. Stephen & F. Pollock, Volume II. London: Macmillan, 177–211.

Cohen, H. F. 1994. *The Scientific Revolution: A Historiographical Inquiry*. Chicago: University of Chicago Press.

Cornwell, J. 2007. *Darwin's Angel: A Seraphic Response to 'The God Delusion'*. London: Profile books.

Corrington, R. S. 1997. *Nature's Religion*. Lanham, MD: Rowman & Littlefield.

Coyne S.J., G.V. 1998. 'Evolution and the human person: The pope in dialogue.' In *Evolutionary and Molecular Biology: Scientific Perspectives on Divine Action*, eds R. J. Russell, W. R. Stoeger & F. Ayala. Vatican City State: Vatican Observatory Publications and Berkeley: Center for Theology and the Natural Sciences, 11–17.

Coyne, G. V. & M. Heller. 2008. *A Comprehensible Universe: The Interplay of Science and Theology*. New York: Springer-Verlag.

Crean, T. 2007. *God is No Delusion: A Refutation of Richard Dawkins*. San Francisco: Ignatius Press.

Crick, F. 1994. *The Astonishing Hypothesis: The Scientific Search for the Soul*. New York: Touchstone, Simon & Schuster.

Crosby, D. A. 2003. 'Naturism as a Form of Religious Naturalism.' *Zygon: Journal of Religion and Science* 38, 117–20.

—— 2008. *Living with Ambiguity: Religious Naturalism and the Menace of Evil*. Albany: State University of New York Press.

Dalai Lama (XIVth). 2005. *The Universe in a Single Atom: The Convergence of Science and Spirituality*. New York: Morgan Road Books.

Dawkins, R. 1986. *The Blind Watchmaker*. London: Norton.

—— 2006. *The God Delusion*. London: Bantam.

De Vries, H., ed. 2008. *Religion: Beyond a Concept*. (The Future of the Religious Past, Vol.1.) New York: Fordham University Press.

Deane-Drummond, C. & B. Szerszynski. 2003. *Re-ordering Nature: Theology, Society, and the New Genetics*. London: T & T Clark.

DeLay, T. 1999. Contribution to the debate on the 'Consequences for Juvenile Offenders Act, of 1999'. *Congressional Record – House*, June 16 1999, H4366; accessed at http://thomas.loc.gov on 21 October 2008.

Dennett, D. C. 1995. *Darwin's Dangerous Idea: Evolution and the Meanings of Life*. New York: Simon & Schuster.

—— 2006. *Breaking the Spell: Religion as a Natural Phenomenon*. New York: Viking (Penguin).

Denton, M. 1985. *Evolution: A Theory in Crisis*. London: Burnett Books.

Dieks, D. 1992. 'Doomsday – or: the dangers of statistics.' *The Philosophical Quarterly* 42 (166, January), 78–84.

Dippel, C. J. & J. M. de Jong. 1965. *Geloof en Natuurwetenschap I: Scheppingsgeloof, natuur, en natuurwetenschap*. 's-Gravenhage: Boekencentrum.

Drayer, E. 2004. 'Gods Woord heeft steeds minder lezers.' *Trouw*, section *de Verdieping* (21 oktober), 11.

Drees, W. B. 1990. *Beyond the Big Bang: Quantum Cosmologies and God*. La Salle: Open Court.

—— 1996. *Religion, Science, and Naturalism*. Cambridge: Cambridge University Press.

—— 2002a. *Creation: From Nothing until Now*. London: Routledge.

—— 2002b. '"Playing God? Yes!" Religion in the Light of Technology.' *Zygon: Journal of Religion and Science* 37 (3 Sept 2002), 643–54.

—— 2003. '"Religion and Science" Without Symmetry, Plausibility, and Harmony.' *Theology and Science* 1 (1 April 2003), 113–28.

—— 2004. 'Where to Look for Guidance? On the Nature of "Religion and Science".' *Zygon: Journal of Religion and Science* 39 (2 June 2004), 367–78.

—— 2005. '"Religion and Science" as Advocacy of Science and as Religion versus Religion.' *Zygon: Journal of Religion and Science* 40 (3 September 2005), 545–53.

—— 2006. 'Religious Naturalism and Science.' In *The Oxford Handbook of Religion and Science*, eds P. Clayton & Z. Simpson. Oxford: Oxford University Press, 108–23.

—— 2007a. 'Is Cosmology Religiously Significant?' In *Science, Religion and Society: An Encyclopedia of History, Culture, and Controversy, Volume 1*. Eds A. Eisen & G. Lederman. Armonk, NY: M. E. Sharpe, 406–14.

—— 2007b. 'Should we "teach the controversy"? Intelligent Design, science and religion.' In *Knowledge in Ferment: Dilemmas in Science, Scholarship and Society*, eds A. in 't Groen et al., Amsterdam: Leiden University Press, 155–69.

—— 2008a. 'Our Universe – A Contingent Cosmos?' In *Religions Challenged by Contingency*, eds D. M. Grube & P. Jonkers. Leiden: Brill, 221–43.

—— 2008b. '"Religion" in Public Debates: Who Defines, For What Purposes?' In *Religion: Beyond A Concept*, ed. H. de Vries. New York: Fordham University Press, 464–72.

—— 2008c. 'Academic and Religious Freedom: An Introduction.' In *The Study of Religion and the Training of Muslim Clergy in Europe: Academic and Religious Freedom in the 21st Century*, eds W. B. Drees & P. S. van Koningsveld. Amsterdam: Leiden University Press, 13–28.

—— 2009. ed. *Technology, Trust, and Religion: Roles of Religions in Controversies on Ecology and the Modification of Life*. Leiden: Leiden University Press.

Dworkin, R. 1999. 'Playing God.' *Prospect Magazine* 41 (May). Available at www. prospect-magazine.co.uk/article_details.php?id=3934, last accessed 4 March 2009.

Eaves, L. B. 1989. 'Spirit, method, and content in science and religion: The theological perspective of a geneticist.' *Zygon: Journal of Religion and Science* 24: 185–215.

—— 1997a. 'Spirit, Method, and Content in Science and Religion.' In *Beginning with the End: God, Science, and Wolfhart Pannenberg*, eds Carol Rausch Albright & Joel Haugen. Chicago: Open Court, 308–40.

—— 1997b. 'Behavioral genetics, or What's missing from theological anthropology?' In *Beginning with the End: God, Science, and Wolfhart Pannenberg*, eds Carol Rausch Albright & Joel Haugen. Chicago: Open Court, 341–47.

Eddington, A. 1928. *The Nature of the Physical World*. New York: Macmillan.

Edis, T. 2007. *An Illusion of Harmony: Science and Religion in Islam*. Buffalo: Prometheus Books.

Ferré, F. 1993. *Hellfire and Lightning Rods: Liberating Science, Technology and Religion*. Maryknoll, NY: Orbis Books.

Feynman, R. P., R. B. Leighton & M. Sands. 1963. *The Feynman Lectures on Physics*, Volume 1. Reading, MA: Addison-Wesley.

Finocchiaro, M. A. 1989. *The Galileo Affair: A Documentary History*. Berkeley: University of California Press.

Flanagan, O. 2006. 'Varieties of Naturalism.' In *The Oxford Handbook of Religion and Science*, eds P. Clayton & Z. Simpson. Oxford: Oxford University Press, 430–52.

Fowles, J. 1979. *The Tree*. St Alban's: Sumach Press. (Text only; also in John Fowles & Frank Horvat, *The Tree*, Boston: Little, Brown and Company, 1979; no page numbers.)

—— 1980. *The Aristos*. Revised edition. Falmouth: Triad/Granada.

Frankenberry, N. K. & H. H. Penner. 1999. 'Cifford Geertz's Long-Lasting Moods, Motivations, and Metaphysical Conceptions.' *The Journal of Religion* 79 (4), 617–40.

Frye, Northrop. 1982. *The Great Code: The Bible and Literature*. New York: Harcourt Brace Jovanovich.

Geertz, C. 1966. 'Religion as a Cultural System.' In *Anthropological Approaches to the Study of Religion*, ed. M. Banton. London: Tavistock, 1–46. Reprinted in C. Geertz, *The Interpretation of Cultures*. New York: Basic Books, 1973.

Giberson, K. W. 2008. *Saving Darwin: How to Be a Christian and Believe in Evolution*. New York: HarperCollins.

Goetz, S. & C. Taliaferro. 2008. *Naturalism*. Grand Rapids: Eerdmans.

Goodenough, U. 1998. *The Sacred Depths of Nature*. New York: Oxford University Press.

Goodenough, U. & T. W. Deacon. 2006. 'The Sacred Emergence of Nature.' In *The Oxford Handbook of Religion and Science*, eds P. Clayton & Z. Simpson. Oxford: Oxford University Press, 853–71.

Gould, S. J. 1999. *Rocks of Ages: Science and Religion in the Fullness of Life*. New York: Ballantine.

Gregersen, N. H., ed. 2003. *From Complexity to Life: On the Emergence of Life and Meaning*. New York: Oxford University Press.

Gregersen, N. H. 2006. 'Emergence and Complexity.' In *The Oxford Handbook of Religion and Science*, eds P. Clayton & Z. Simpson. Oxford: Oxford University Press, 767–83.

Griffin, D. R., ed. 1988. *The Reenchantment of Science: Postmodern Proposals*. Albany: SUNY Press.

—— 2000. *Religion and Scientific Naturalism: Overcoming the Conflicts*. Albany, SUNY Press.

—— 2006. 'Interpreting Science from the Standpoint of Whiteheadian Process Philosophy.' In *The Oxford Handbook of Religion and Science*, eds P. Clayton & Z. Simpson. Oxford: Oxford University Press, 453–71.

Guessom, N. 2008. 'The Qur'an, Science, and the (Related) Contemporary Muslim Discourse.' *Zygon: Journal of Religion and Science* 43, 411–31.

Habermas, J. 2008. *Between Naturalism and Religion: Philosophical Essays*. Cambridge: Polity.

Hanegraaff, W. J. 1996. *New Age Religion and Western Culture*. Leiden: Brill.

Hardwick, C. D. 1996. *Events of Grace: Naturalism, Existentialism, and Theology*. Cambridge: Cambridge University Press.

—— 2003. 'Religious Naturalism Today.' *Zygon: Journal of Religion and Science* 38, 111–16.

Harris, S. 2004. *The End of Faith: Religion, Terror, and the Future of Reason*. New York: Norton.

Harrison, P. [Paul]. 1999. *The Elements of Pantheism: Understanding the Divinity in Nature and the Universe*. Shaftesbury, Dorset: Element Books.

Harrison, P. [Peter]. 1990. *'Religion' and the Religions in the English Enlightenment*. Cambridge: Cambridge University Press.

—— 2008. 'Religion, the Royal Society, and the Rise of Science.' *Theology and Science* 6 (3): 255–71.

Hartle, J. B. & S.W. Hawking. 1983. 'Wavefunction of the Universe.' *Physical Review* D 28: 2960–75.

Haught, J. F. 2008a. *God after Darwin: A Theology of Evolution*. Second Edition. Boulder, CO: Westview Press.

—— 2008b. *God and the New Atheism: A Critical Response to Dawkins, Harris, and Hitchins*. Louisville: Westminster.

Hebblethwaite, B. & E. Henderson, eds. 1990. *Divine Action: Studies Inspired by the Philosophical Theology of Austin Farrer*. Edinburgh: T & T Clark.

Hefner, P. J. 1993. *The Human Factor: Evolution, Culture, and Religion*. Minneapolis: Fortress.

—— 1998. 'The Spiritual Task of Religion in Culture: An Evolutionary Perspective.' *Zygon: Journal of Religion and Science* 33, 535–44.

—— 2003. *Technology and Human Becoming*. Minneapolis: Fortress.

—— 2008. 'Religion-and-Science: Never Alone, Always in a Crowd.' *Zygon: Journal of Religion and Science* 43, 291–96.

Heller, M. 2003. *Creative Tension: Essays on Science and Religion*. Philadelphia: Templeton University Press.

Hesse, M. 1981. 'Retrospect.' In *The Sciences and Theology in the Twentieth Century*, ed. A. R. Peacocke. Stocksfield: Oriel Press.

—— 1988. 'Physics, Philosophy, and Myth.' In *Physics, Philosophy and Theology*, eds R. J. Russell, W. R. Stoeger & G. V. Coyne. Vatican: Vatican Observatory, 185–202.

Heyward, I. Carter. 1982. *The Redemption of God*. Lanham, MD: University Press of America.

Hick, J. 1989. *An Interpretation of Religion: Human Responses to the Transcendent*. Houndmills, Basingstoke: Macmillan.

Hitchins, C. 2007. *God is Not Great: How Religion Poisons Everything*. New York: Warner Books.

Hoodbhoy, P. 1991. *Islam and Science: Religious Orthodoxy and the Battle for Rationality*. London: Zed Books.

Hooykaas, R. 1972. *Religion and the Rise of Modern Science*. Edinburgh: Scottish Academic Press.

Horwich, P., ed. 1992. *World Changes: Thomas Kuhn and the Nature of Science*. Cambridge, MA: MIT Press.

Hubbeling, H. G. 1987. *Principles of the Philosophy of Religion*. Assen, NL: Van Gorcum.

Hübner, J. 1990. 'Science and Religion Coming Across.' In J. Fennema & I. Paul, eds, *Science and Religion: One World – Changing Perspectives on Reality*. Dordrecht: Kluwer, 173–81.

Humes, E. 2007. *Monkey Girl: Evolution, Education, Religion, and the Battle for America's Soul*. New York: HarperCollins.

Huxley, T. H. 1868. 'On a Piece of Chalk.' *Macmillan's Magazine*. Reprinted in T. H. Huxley, *Collected Essays*, Volume VIII. New York: Appleton, 1894, 1–36.

IAP. 2006. *IAP Statement on the Teaching of Evolution*. Trieste: Interacademy Panel on International Issues, June 21, 2006. Available at www.interacademies.net/Object.File/ Master/6/150/Evolution%20statement.pdf, accessed 21 Oct 2008.

Iqbal, M. 2002a. *Islam and Science*. Aldershot: Ashgate.

—— 2002b. 'Islam and Modern Science: Questions at the Interface.' In *God, Life, and the Cosmos: Christian and Islamic Perspectives*, eds T. Peters, M. Iqbal & S. N. Haq. Aldershot: Ashgate, 3–41.

Irons, W. 1991. 'Where did morality come from?' *Zygon: Journal of Religion and Science* 26, 49–90.

James, W. 1902. *The Varieties of Religious Experience*. New York: Modern Library.

John Paul II. 1998. 'Message to the Pontifical Academy of Sciences, 22 October 1996.' In *Evolutionary and Molecular Biology: Scientific Perspectives on Divine Action*, eds R.J. Russell, W. R. Stoeger & F. Ayala. Vatican City State: Vatican Observatory Publications and Berkeley: Center for Theology and the Natural Sciences, 2–9 [the French original and an English translation].

Johnson, P. E. 1991. *Darwin on Trial*. Washington, DC: Regnery Gateway.

—— 1997. *Defeating Darwinism by Opening Minds*. Downers Grove, IL: InterVarsity Press.

—— 1998. 'Afterword: How to Sink a Battleship. A Call to Separate Materialist Philosophy from Empirical Science.' In *Mere Creation: Science, Faith and Intelligent Design*, ed. W. A. Dembski. Downers Grove, IL.: InterVarsity Press, 446–53.

Jones, J. E. 2005. *Kitzmiller et al. versus Dover Area School District, et al., Memorandum Opinion by Justice John E. Jones III*, at http://www.pamd.uscourts.gov/kitzmiller/ kitzmiller_342.pdf, last accessed on 13 October 2008.

Jones, R. H. 1986. *Science and Mysticism: A Comparative Study of Western Science, Theravāda Buddhism and Advaita Vedānta*. Lewisburg: Bucknell.

Jongeling, B. 1997. 'Wat is reductionisme?' In *De mens: meer dan materie? Religie en reductionisme*, ed. W. B. Drees. Kampen: Kok, 38–54.

Joshi, S. T., ed. 2007. *The Agnostic Reader*. Amherst: Prometheus.

Kauffman, S. A. 2008. *Reinventing the Sacred: A New View of Science, Reason and Religion*. New York: Basic Books.

Kaufman, G. D. 1972. *God the Problem*. Cambridge, MA: Harvard University Press.

—— 1993. *In Face of Mystery: A Constructive Theology*. Cambridge, MA: Harvard University Press.

—— 2003. 'Biohistorical Naturalism and the Symbol of "God".' *Zygon: Journal of Religion and Science* 38, 95–100.

—— 2004. *In the Beginning … : Creativity*. Minneapolis: Fortress.

Keller, C. 2008. *On the Mystery: Discerning Divinity in Process*. Minneapolis: Fortress.

Kenny, A. 2004. *The Unknown God: Agnostic Essays*. London: Continuum.

Kitcher, P. 1982. *Abusing Science: The Case Against Creationism*. Cambridge, MA: MIT Press.

—— 1985. *Vaulting Ambition: Sociobiology and the Quest for Human Nature*. Cambridge, MA: MIT Press.

—— 1993. *The Advancement of Science. Science without Legend, Objectivity without Illusions*. New York: Oxford University Press.

Klaaren, E. M. 1977. *Religious Origins of Modern Science: Belief in Creation in Seventeenth-Century Thought*. Grand Rapids: Eerdmans.

Knight, C. C. 2007. *The God of Nature: Incarnation and Contemporary Science*. Minneapolis: Fortress.

—— 2009. 'Theistic Naturalism and "Special" Divine Providence.' *Zygon: Journal of Religion and Science* 44(3), 533–542.

Kronjee, G. & M. Lampert. 2006. 'Leefstijlen in zingeving.' In *Geloven in het publieke domein: Verkenningen van een dubbele transformatie*, eds W. B. J. H. van den Donk et al. Amsterdam: Amsterdam University Press, 171–208.

Kuhn, T. 1962. *The Structure of Scientific Revolutions*. Chicago: University of Chicago Press.

Lakatos, I. 1970. 'Falsification and the Methodology of Scientific Research Programmes.' In *Criticism and the Growth of Knowledge*, eds I. Lakatos and A. Musgrave. Cambridge: Cambridge University Press.

Leslie, J. 1996. *The End of the World: The Science and Ethics of Human Extinction*. London: Routledge.

Levine, M. P. 1994. *Pantheism: A non-theistic Concept of Deity*. London: Routledge.

Lindbeck, G. A. 1984. *The Nature of Doctrine*. Philadelphia: Westminster.

Lindberg, D. C. & R. L. Numbers. 1986. 'Beyond war and peace: A reappraisal of the encounter between Christianity and science.' *Church History* 55: 338–54.

Lindberg, D. C. & R. L. Numbers, eds. 1986. *God and Nature: Historical Essays on the Encounter between Christianity and Science*. Berkeley and Los Angeles: University of California Press.

Livingstone, D. N. 2003. *Putting Science in its Place: Geographies of Scientific Knowledge*. Chicago: University of Chicago Press.

Lopez Jr., D. S. 1998. *Prisoners of Shangri-La: Tibetan Buddhism and the West*. Chicago: University of Chicago Press.

—— 2008. *Buddhism and Science: A Guide for the Perplexed*. Chicago: University of Chicago Press.

Lovin, R. W. & F. E. Reynolds. 1985. 'In the beginning.' In *Cosmogony and Ethical Order: Studies in Comparative Ethics*, eds R. W. Lovin, F. E. Reynolds. Chicago: University of Chicago Press.

McCutcheon, R. T., ed. 1999. *The Insider/Outsider Problem in the Study of Religion: A Reader*. London: Cassell.

McCutcheon, R. T. 2007. *Studying Religion: An Introduction*. London: Equinox.

Mackie, J. L. 1967. 'Fallacies.' *The Encyclopedia of Philosophy*, Volume 3, ed. P. Edwards. New York: Macmillan, 169–79.

McMullin, E. 1967. 'Introduction: Galileo, man of science.' In *Galileo, Man of Science*, ed. E. McMullin. New York: Basic Books.

—— 1981. 'How should cosmology relate to theology?' In *The Sciences and Theology in the Twentieth Century*, ed. A. R. Peacocke. Stocksfield: Oriel Press and Notre Dame: University of Notre Dame Press.

—— 1984. 'A case for scientific realism.' In *Scientific Realism*, ed. J. Leplin. Berkeley: University of California Press.

—— 1985. 'Introduction: Evolution and Creation.' In *Evolution and Creation*, ed. E. McMullin. Notre Dame, IN: University of Notre Dame Press, 1–56.

—— 1988. 'Natural Science and Belief in a Creator: Historical Notes.' In *Physics, Philosophy, and Theology: A Common Quest for Understanding*, eds R. J. Russell et al. Vatican City State: Vatican Observatory Press, 49–79.

—— 1992. *The Inference that Makes Science*. Milwaukee: Marquette University Press.

—— 1994. 'Enlarging the known world.' In *Physics and Our View of the World*, ed. J. Hilgevoord. Cambridge: Cambridge University Press.

—— 2008. 'Academic Freedom and Competing Authorities: Historical Reflections.' In *The Study of Religion and the Training of Muslim Clergy in Europe: Academic and Religious Freedom in the 21st Century*, eds W. B. Drees & P. S. van Koningsveld. Amsterdam: Leiden University Press, 31–46.

Midgley, M. 1985. *Evolution as a Religion: Strange Hopes and Stranger Fears*. London: Methuen.

—— 1992. *Science as Salvation: A Modern Myth and its Meaning*. London: Routledge.

—— 1994. *The Ethical Primate: Humans, Freedom, and Morality*. London: Routledge.

Miller, J. D., E. C. Scott & S. Okamoto. 2006. 'Public Acceptance of Evolution.' *Science* 313 (11 August), 765–66, with online supporting material at www.sciencemag.org/cgi/content/full/313/5788/765/DC1 (last accessed 11 Nov 2008).

Miller, K. R. 1999. *Finding Darwin's God: A Scientist's Search for Common Ground Between God and Evolution*. New York: HarperCollins.

Misner, C. W. 1977. 'Cosmology and Theology.' In *Cosmology, History, and Theology*, eds W. Yourgrau & A. D. Breck. New York: Plenum Press.

Morowitz, H. J. 2002. *The Emergence of Everything: How the World Became Complex*. Oxford: Oxford University Press.

Morris, H. M. 1989. *The Long War Against God: The History and Impact of the Creation/Evolution Conflict*. Grand Rapids: Baker House.

Murphy, N. 1990. *Theology in the Age of Scientific Reasoning*. Ithaca: Cornell University Press.

Murphy, N. & G. F. R. Ellis. 1966. *On the Moral Nature of the Universe: Theology, Cosmology, and Ethics*. Minneapolis: Fortress.

Murphy, N. & W. R. Stoeger. 2007. *Evolution and Emergence: Systems, Organisms, Persons*. Oxford: Oxford University Press.

Nagel, T. 1986. *The View from Nowhere*. New York: Oxford University Press.

NAS. 2008. *Science, Evolution, and Creationism*. Washington, DC: National Academy of Sciences and Institute of Medicine. Available at http://cart.nap.edu/cart/deliver.cgi?&record_id=11876, accessed 21 Oct 2008.

Nielsen, M. V. 2009. *Sin and Selfish Genes: Christian and Biological Narratives*. Leuven: Peeters.

Nitecki, M. H. & D. V. Nitecki, eds. 1993. *Evolutionary Ethics*. Albany: SUNY Press.

Numbers, R. 2006. *The Creationists: From Scientific Creationism to Intelligent Design*. Cambridge, MA: Harvard University Press.

Otto, R. 1950. *The Idea of the Holy: An Inquiry into the Non-rational Factor in the Idea of the Divine and its Relation to the Rational*. London: Oxford University Press. [Orig. German, 1917.]

Overton, W.R. [1982] 1988. 'McLean v. Arkansas, United States District Court Opinion (Jan.5, 1982).' In *But Is It Science? The Philosophical Question in the Creation/Evolution Controversy*, ed. M. Ruse. Buffalo: Prometheus, 307–31.

Peacocke, A. 1993. *Theology for a Scientific Age: Being and Becoming – Natural, Divine, and Human*, Enlarged edition. London: SCM.

Pedersen, O. 1983. 'Galileo and the Council of Trent.' *Journal for the History of Astronomy* 14: 1–29.

—— 1991. *Galileo and the Council of Trent*. Vatican City State: Vatican Observatory. (Revised reprint of Pedersen 1983.)

Peters, K. E. 2002. *Dancing with the Sacred: Evolution, Ecology, and God*. Harrisburg: Trinity Press International.

Peters, T., ed. 1989. *Cosmos as Creation: Theology and Science in Consonance*. Nashville: Abingdon Press.

—— 1998. *Science and Theology: The New Consonance*. Boulder, CO: Westview.

Peters, T. & M. Hewlett. 2006. *Can You Believe in God and Evolution? A Guide for the Perplexed*. Nashville: Abingdon.

Petersen, A. C. 2006. *Simulating Nature: A Philosophical Study of Computer Simulation Uncertainties and Their Role in Climate Science and Policy Advice*. Apeldoorn: Spinhuis.

Peterson, G. R. 2003. 'Demarcation and the Scientistic Fallacy.' *Zygon: Journal of Religion and Science* 38, 751–61.

Platvoet, J. G. & A. L. Molendijk, eds. 1999. *The Pragmatics of Defining Religion: Contexts, Concepts and Contests*. (Numen Studies in the History of Religions, Vol. 84.) Leiden: Brill.

Popper, K. S. 1959. *The Logic of Scientific Discovery*. London: Hutchinson. [Orig. *Logik der Forschung*, 1935.]

Quine, W. V. O. & J. S. Ullian. 1978. *The Web of Belief*, 2nd edition. New York: Random House.

Rawls, J. 1971. *A Theory of Justice*. Cambridge, MA: Harvard University Press.

—— 1980. 'Kantian constructivism in moral theory.' *Journal of Philosophy* 77: 515 – 572.

Ricoeur, P. 1967. *The Symbolism of Evil*. New York: Harper & Row.

Rockwell, T. 2002. 'Visual Technologies, Cosmographies, and Our Sense of Place in the Universe.' *Zygon: Journal of Religion and Science* 37 (3), 605–21.

Rorty, R. 1994. 'Religion as a Conversation-Stopper.' *Common Knowledge* 3 (1), 1–6.

—— 2003. 'Religion in the Public Square: A Reconsideration.' *Journal of Religious Ethics* 31 (21), 141–49.

Roszak, T. 1969. *The Making of a Counter Culture: Reflections on the Technocratic Society and Its Youthful Opposition*. Garden City, NY: Doubleday.

Rue, L. R. 2000. *Everybody's Story: Wising Up the Epic of Evolution*. Albany, NY: SUNY Press.

Ruse, M. 1989. 'Is rape wrong on Andromeda?' In *The Darwinian Paradigm: Essays on the History, Philosophy, and Religious Implications*, ed. M. Ruse. London: Routledge.

—— 1993. 'The new evolutionary ethics.' In *Evolutionary Ethics*, eds M. H. Nitecki & D. V. Nitecki. Albany: SUNY Press.

—— 2001. *Can a Darwinian Be a Christian? The Relationship between Science and Religion*. Cambridge: Cambridge University Press.

Ruse, M., ed. 1988. *But Is It Science? The Philosophical Question in the Creation/Evolution Controversy*. Buffalo: Prometheus.

Russell, R. J. 2008. *Cosmology from Alpha to Omega: The Creative Mutual Interaction of Theology and Science*. Minneapolis: Fortress.

Russell, R. J., W. R. Stoeger & F. Ayala, eds. 1998. *Evolutionary and Molecular Biology: Scientific Perspectives on Divine Action*. Vatican City State: Vatican Observatory Publications and Berkeley: Center for Theology and the Natural Sciences.

Sagan, C. 1995. *The Demon-Haunted World: Science as a Candle in the Dark*. New York: Random House.

Schleiermacher, F. 1996. *On Religion: Speeches to its Cultured Despisers*, transl. Richard Crouter. Cambridge: Cambridge University Press. Translation of *& Über die Religion: Reden an die Gebildeten unter ihren Verächtern* (1799).

Segal, R. A., ed. 1998. *The Myth and Ritual Theory: An Anthology*. Malden, MA: Blackwell.

Sellars, W. 1963. *Science, Perception and Reality*. London: Routledge & Kegan Paul.

Sharpe, E. J. 1983. *Understanding Religion*. New York: St Martin's Press.

Silberstein, M. 2006. 'Emergence, Theology, and the Manifest Image.' In *The Oxford Handbook of Religion and Science*, eds P. Clayton & Z. Simpson. Oxford: Oxford University Press, 784–800.

Singer, P. 1981. *The Expanding Circle: Ethics and Sociobiology*. Oxford: Clarendon Press.

—— 1984. 'Ethics and sociobiology.' *Zygon: Journal of Religion and Science* 19, 141–158.

Smith, J. Z. 1998. 'Religion, Religions, Religious.' In *Critical Terms for Religious Studies*, ed. M. C. Taylor. Chicago: University of Chicago Press, 269–84.

Sober, E. & D. S. Wilson. 1999. *Unto Others: The Evolution and Psychology of Unselfish Behavior*. Cambridge, MA: Harvard University Press.

Söling, C. 2002. *Der Gottesinstinkt: Bausteine für eine evolutionäre Religionstheorie*. Dissertation, defended at the Justus Liebig Universität, Giessen, Germany; available at http://bibd.uni-giessen.de/ghtm/2002/uni/d020116.htm (last accessed 11 Dec 2008).

Stahl, W. A., R. A. Campbell, Y. Petry & G. Driver. 2002. *Webs of Reality: Social Perspectives on Science and Religion*. New Brunswick, NJ: Rutgers University Press.

Stenmark, M. 2001. *Scientism: Science, Ethics, and Religion*. Aldershot: Ashgate.

Stoeger, W. R. 1988. 'Contemporary Cosmology and its Implications for the Science-Religion Dialogue.' In *Physics, Philosophy and Theology*, eds R. J. Russell, W. R. Stoeger & G. V. Coyne. Vatican City State: Vatican Observatory and Berkeley: Center for Theology and the Natural Sciences, 219–47.

—— 1995. 'Describing God's Action in the World in the Light of Scientific Knowledge of Reality.' In *Chaos and Complexity: Scientific Perspectives on Divine Action*, eds R. J. Russell et al. Vatican City State: Vatican Observatory and Berkeley: Center for Theology and the Natural Sciences, 239–61.

Stone, J. A. 1992. *The Minimalist Vision of Transcendence: A Naturalist Philosophy of Religion*. Albany, NY: SUNY Press.

—— 2003a. 'Varieties of Religious Naturalism.' *Zygon: Journal of Religion and Science* 38, 89–93.

—— 2003b. 'Is Nature Enough? Yes.' *Zygon: Journal of Religion and Science* 38, 783–800.

—— 2008. *Religious Naturalism Today: The Rebirth of a Forgotten Alternative*. Albany, NY: SUNY Press.

Stout, J. 2004. *Democracy and Tradition*. Princeton: Princeton University Press.

't Hooft, G. 1997. *In Search of the Ultimate Building Blocks*. Cambridge: Cambridge University Press.

Taji-Farouki, S. 2004. *Modern Muslim Intellectuals and the Qur'an*. Oxford: Oxford University Press.

Taylor, C. 1989. *Sources of the Self: The Making of Modern Identity*. Cambridge, MA: Harvard University Press.

Terrien, S. 1978. *The Elusive Presence: Toward a New Biblical Theology*. San Francisco: Harper & Row.

Theissen, G. 1985. *Biblical Faith: An Evolutionary Approach*. Philadelphia: Fortress.

Thomas, O. C., ed. 1983. *God's Activity in the World: The Contemporary Problem*. Chicago, CA: Scholars Press.

Torrance, T. F. 1981. *Divine and Contingent Order*. Oxford: Oxford University Press.

Tryon, E. P. 1973. 'Is the Universe a Vacuum Fluctuation?' *Nature* 246 (1973): 396f.; reprinted in *Physical Cosmology and Philosophy*, ed. J. Leslie. New York: Macmillan, 1990, 216–19.

Van Fraassen, B. C. 1980. *The Scientific Image*. Oxford: Oxford University Press.

—— 1984. 'The problem of indistinguishable particles.' In J. T. Cushing, C. F. Delaney & G. M. Gutting, eds, *Science and Reality*. Notre Dame: University of Notre Dame Press.

—— 1994. 'The world of empiricism.' In J. Hilgevoord, ed., *Physics and Our View of the World*. Cambridge: Cambridge University Press.

Wallace, A. B. 2003. *Buddhism and Science: Breaking New Ground*. New York: Columbia University Press.

Watling, T. 2009. *Ecological Imaginations in the World Religions: An Ethnographic Analysis*. London: Continuum.

Weinberg, S. 1977. *The First Three Minutes*. New York: Basic Books.

—— 1992. *Dreams of a Final Theory*. New York: Pantheon Books.

Welch, C. 1972, 1985. *Protestant Thought in the Nineteenth Century*. (2 vols.) New Haven: Yale University Press.

White, A. D. 1896. *A History of the Warfare of Science with Theology in Christendom*. (2 vols.) New York: Appleton & Co.

Whitehead, A. N. 1929. *Process and Reality*. New York: Macmillan.

Wildman, W. J. 2006. 'Ground-of-Being Theologies.' In *The Oxford Handbook of Religion and Science*, eds P. Clayton & Z. Simpson. Oxford: Oxford University Press, 612–32.

Wiles, M. 1986. *God's Action in the World*. London: SCM Press.

Wilkes, K. V. 1988. *Real People: Personal Identity without Thought Experiments*. Oxford: Clarendon Press.

Wilson, D. S. 2002. *Darwin's Cathedral: Evolution, Religion, and the Nature of Society*. Chicago: University of Chicago Press.

Wilson, E. O. 1975. *Sociobiology: The New Synthesis*. Cambridge, MA: Harvard University Press.

—— 1978. *On Human Nature*. Cambridge, MA: Harvard University Press.

—— 1992. *The Diversity of Life*. New York: Norton.

Wolterstorff, N. 1997. 'Why We Should Reject What Liberalism Tells Us about Speaking and Acting for Religious Reasons.' In P. J. Weithman, ed., *Religion and Contemporary Liberalism*. Notre Dame: University of Notre Dame Press, 162–81.

—— 2001. *Thomas Reid and the Story of Epistemology*. Cambrdige: Cambridge University Press.

Yahya, Harun. 1999. *The Evolution Deceit: The Scientific Collapse of Darwinism and Its Ideological Background*. Istanbul: Okur Publications.

—— 2006. *Atlas of Creation*. (Volume 1.) Istanbul: Global Publishing.

Yinger, J. M. 1970. *The Scientific Study of Religion*. London: Macmillan.

Index